"PAUL GALLICO is the author of a thriller likely to chill you to the marrow. The title of the novel is

TRIAL BY TERROR" *

It's the story of a correspondent who crashes the Iron Curtain . . . and learns first hand how tyrants extract confessions from innocent men.

"An amazing story of love, jealousy and determination . . . excitement and suspense."

Cincinnati Enquirer

"Grim and exciting."

New York Herald Tribune

"Authentic and chilling."

San Antonio Express

"An expert tale of horror and suspense."

San Francisco Chronicle

"Power-packed."

Miami Herald

"Hair-raising."

Los Angeles Herald-Express

Quoted from *The Cleveland Press

Trial by Terror

PAUL GALLICO

Author of:

THE ABANDONED
THE LONELY
CONFESSIONS OF A
STORY WRITER
THE SNOW GOOSE
ETC.

A DELL BOOK

Published by
DELL PUBLISHING COMPANY, INC.
261 Fifth Avenue
New York 16, New York

Reprinted by arrangement with
Alfred A. Knopf, Inc.
New York, N. Y.

Designed and produced by
Western Printing & Lithographing Company

Cover painting by Walter Brooks

Printed in U. S. A.

This book is a novel — a work of fiction. It describes no actual persons or events. It is "real," however, in its portrayal of the thinking and the tactics of government behind the iron curtain and the means by which "public confessions" are elicited in the iron-curtain countries.

1

WARNING

Andreas Ordy, Minister of Affairs in the Cabinet of the Communist Government of Hungary, sat in his office in the Barascy Palace in Budapest, facing a battery of still and newsreel cameramen and microphones, prepared to make an important speech. He was a short, stocky man, partly bald, in a rumpled shirt and tie, and a shapeless, ill-fitting coat of the type affected by Moscow-trained government officials who want to give the impression of belonging to the proletariat. He had a good forehead and crafty, intelligent eyes and might have been good-looking once, but there was an overlaid expression of cynicism in the mouth and the lines about it as though he had lived too long exposed to the inner and outer atmosphere of brutality. The fingers that gripped the sheet on which his speech was written were thick, peasant fingers. But for the rest he had country lawyer, politician-come-to-power, written all over him.

The broadcast director consulted his stop watch, then coughed, cleared his throat, made a wigwag signal with his hand, and said discreetly, "Excellency—"

A hush then fell upon the room except for the whispering whirring of the motor-driven cameras. The Minister adjusted his distance to the microphone, looked up at the broadcast director, and at the final signal that the moment had arrived began to read his speech, which was a short one and therefore, by its very brevity, gained in impressiveness.

"We have just," he began, "through the alertness of the police and other servants of the People's Democratic Government of Hungary, exposed a dangerous conspiracy against the State planned and executed by spies and saboteurs instigated by the United States of America and the Western imperialist Fascist nations.

"As you are all aware, the American spy, Frobisher, was arrested before he could carry out his treacherous design. He has received a fair trial. He has made a full confession of his criminal designs upon the Hungarian people. He has, therefore, been found guilty and has been sentenced to a term of twenty years' imprisonment.

"But others will come again, the spies, snoops, lackeys, and saboteurs of the Western warmongering capitalist nations. They will not learn from the just and merciful lesson administered today by the incorruptible judge-presidents of the People's Court. Their criminal determination to undermine Hungarian democratic principle with Hitlerite Fascism will outweigh their judgment.

"Well, we shall be ready for them, as we were ready for the convicted spy, Frobisher. We will apprehend them. We will try them. They will confess. We will find them guilty. But with this one difference—the next American we convict of spying or sabotage against the Hungarian State we shall hang out of hand."

2

THE NEW BOY

THERE WAS A MOMENTARY LULL in the argument raging in and about the editorial room of the Paris Edition of the *Chicago Sentinel* as Mme. Visson, secretary to Nick Strang, the editor-in-chief, poked her head inside the door, looked about, and asked, "M'sieur Strang—he is not here?"

Cass McGuire, the night-club columnist, who was nearest the door, said, "Not here."

Mitchell Connell, head of the copy desk, added, "Haven't seen him."

Mark Mosher, the tall, lean, nervous young city editor, a New York boy from N.Y.U., was just answering his telephone in his atrocious college French, *"Wee-wee. Ici le* Chicago Sentinel. *Kesky voo voolay?"* But he also took in the secretary's query. Into the telephone he shouted, *"Attenday oon moment. Ne kitty pas.* Get it? Hang on a moment." He called over to Mme. Visson, "I think Nick went upstairs to Transoceanic Press for a minute."

The secretary said, "Thank you. If he returns here, will you tell him, please, there is coming in a very important call from Belgrade for him."

Mark said, "Okay," and went back to his telephone.

In the slot, Mitchell Connell, the copy chief, a professorial-looking man with a sardonic eye and a fine Navy-type beard he affected both as a hang-over from service in the Pacific and as a tribute to the fact that he had once published a literary magazine on the Left Bank, sailed a story across the desk to one of the two copyreaders and said, "Stick a B head on that. Bring up into the lead the fact that Garry Davis is returning home under a French immigration quota."

He glanced at his spike, which was reasonably clear, produced a French Gaulois cigarette from a paper packet, lit it, leaned back in his chair, and grinned mischievously in the direction of Jimmy Race, the new man from Chicago, who had momentarily returned to overwhelming his typewriter at his desk, situated at the far end of the L-shaped city room, between the two telephone booths and the travel department.

He said, "So you think we're all sitting back on our fat fannies, lapping up *vin rouge* instead of working, Nick is a lousy editor, and the paper's blowing a hot story. Well, maybe so, new boy, maybe so, but after you've been around here for a while—"

Jimmy Race rose to the bait. The typewriter stopped its immediate clacking, and his chair creaked and protested under his weight as he slewed around, for he was a huge man, close to six feet four in height, with a massive head topped by reddish hair, cut stand-up fashion, that added to his height, and heavy limbs that seemed to fill his clothes to bursting. He turned his intense gaze, marked by the unusual darkness of the pupils of his greenish eyes, on Mitchell Connell.

"It wasn't what I said," he replied, and his voice had the compelling quality and deep resonance of a barrel chest backed by enormous lung power, "but if that's how it looks to you—"

Cass McGuire, who had been interviewing one of the *types,* also known as characters, who occupied the long mourners' bench at the far end of the city room, pushed his chair back with a pleased grin and said, "Yipee! Here we go again!" To his *type,* a Belgian who was proposing to leap from the second *étage* of the Eiffel Tower without a parachute to test a foam-rubber shock suit he claimed to have invented, he said, "Beat it, I'm busy. Okay, so jump. I'll give you a note in the column."

A reporter, delighted to abandon his strike story, which he was finding dull, said, "I don't think that's what Jim meant, Mitch. Everybody knows we don't milk a story here the way we do back home, and I guess the Frobisher case isn't any exception."

"Oh, I don't know," put in Joe Short, the stocky, aggressive little news editor who had been a tank driver under Patton. He glanced over his schedule and read off, " 'Frobisher sentencing, Budapest, Transoceanic—Washington reaction and statement by Acheson—Washington Bureau, statement head of Frobisher's firm in New York. Mrs. Frobisher to make personal appeal—Transoceanic Vienna—' I think we've got pretty good coverage. The *Herald Tribune* won't have any more. After all, Transoceanic has been the only one able to keep a man in Budapest. We might have had a better story on Frobisher's wife in Vienna if our man Klaussen there hadn't reported sick."

"Uhuh!" Jimmy Race boomed. "Wonderful! And not a line on how they got Frobisher to stand up in a Hungarian court and confess to something he didn't do. You call that reporting?"

They were all listening now, the rest of the reporters, copyreaders, and feature writers in the room as well as the heterogeneous collection of characters on the mourners' bench, which included the usual out-at-elbow individual, peddling selections on the races, a man selling boxer puppies, of which he had two in his coat, a Frenchman with a nude head and an awesome black beard who was nothing more formidable than the press agent for the Tour de France bicycle race, and a small Chaplinesque man with a narrow face, little mustache, and sad eyes who was distinguished chiefly for the hideous color and pattern of the muffler he wore around his neck and inside his jacket in the inevitable manner of Central Europeans, a scarf of snakeskin design in green, ocher, and red.

Everybody was interested in the Frobisher case, for it had been a bitter challenge to the prestige of the United States from behind the iron curtain. It had been a typical Communist trial. Photographs showed Frobisher, apparently unharmed, standing before the microphone in court. Everyone suspected or knew he had been tortured or somehow coerced into making his confession as had Cardinal Mindszenty and many others, but nobody could prove it.

Cass McGuire, a wiry, beady-eyed little Irishman who tried to pattern both himself and his Paris night-club column after Walter Winchell, said, "I was talking to one of my contacts in the Dinazarde the other night. He's a White Russian who hangs out there. He says they give them some sort of a drug."

Joe Short suggested, "He didn't look beat up from the pictures. I hear it's some kind of an operation. They cut a nerve or something leading to the brain."

Jimmy's snort of disgust shook the desk and caused Janet Goodpenny, the plain-looking librarian, to turn from a steel file cabinet where she was trying to find something for Mark Mosher and stare at him through the lenses of her dark horn-rimmed glasses, but what was going on in her mind no one could have imagined.

"I hear—I hear—somebody said—" Jimmy mimicked. "And nobody knows and nobody tries to find out. Hell, there's been the Mindszenty case to start it off, then those Bulgarians, and a half a dozen chumps in Prague, all confessing themselves into jail or to the executioner, and now an American. One of our own guys. Frobisher isn't any more a spy than I am. If he had been an agent, or working in counterintelligence, he would have been the last to admit it. Those guys always clam up."

Another reporter, named Felix Victor, said quietly, "Maybe he confessed to what he did in order to protect someone else."

Jimmy Race looked at him with distaste. Victor was the type of young American intellectual most likely to bother him since he was lazy and easygoing, and his meanings were frequently concealed like booby traps beneath what he said, and it was always more difficult to bustle aside a time bomb of an idea than merely a physical presence. Besides, Victor was unkempt, given to soiled shirts and torn socks and a general air of having gone happily and dirtily Left Bank. Jimmy himself was a two-shower-a-day man and exuded health and energy.

"Yeah. Maybe! You're another one of the 'maybe' boys. Are there any 'find-out' guys around here? Here's the hottest story of the year and we haven't got anybody digging in Hungary, or anywhere else!"

This was a big, tough guy, this new man from Chicago, Mitchell Connell decided. He had impressed the staff because he had written and published a war novel and sold stories to the slick magazines. He was a livewire, hot-shot reporter with a big-city reputation and a lot of ability tucked away inside his heft. Nevertheless, for the cause of amity in the city room and his own position as copy chief, arbiter, and leader of office rhubarbs Connell decided that Race wanted a little slapping down.

"Looked at your passport recently, bub?" he asked. "It's stamped 'Not Valid for Travel in Hungary.' And a lot of other places, too."

Jimmy gave vent to an explosive laugh. "Hah! Don't tell me you chaps would let a little thing like that stop you."

Connell continued in milder vein. "Nick isn't a ball of fire on an all-out story but he gets out a good newspaper full of what's going on for a cockeyed kind of circulation, keeps his nose clean and his staff out of trouble. Believe me, that's an achievement over here. You don't operate on this side of the water the way you do back in the States."

Ferdie Hoffman, the special-features writer who also doubled in sports, came out from behind the French racing-sheet he had been studying. He said to Jimmy Race, "If you don't like it over here why don't you go back to the country you came from?"

A quick grin spread over Jimmy Race's big features and made him look suddenly boyish. He said, "You lousy bunch of foreigners. I'll wake you up yet."

Now the expression on the face of the little librarian, Janet Goodpenny, who from the safe vantage of her file cabinets was still staring at the huge newcomer to the staff, was less difficult to interpret. It was compounded of one hundred parts pure worship.

3

COMPLAINT FROM BELGRADE

MME. VISSON, THE SECRETARY, had contacted the editor up on the fifth floor with Stokes, the Transoceanic Press Chief, and advised him of the expected call. He came down immediately.

Nick Strang said, "Belgrade, eh?" as he entered his office. "I wonder who?" He looked in on his wife, who was working on her editorial page in the small inside office that adjoined his. "Suzy, have you put in a call for Belgrade?"

Suzy replied, "I didn't know one could. Let me listen in. I'm dying to know."

Suzy Strang followed her husband into his office. Although she spoke perfect English, she was a Frenchwoman born and bred of the dark-haired southern race with the ivory skin and strongly marked features. Her hair, almost crow's-wing blue in its blackness, neatly gathered at the back of her head, breathed vitality and care. The dark line of her brows above liquid, expressive eyes, the somewhat overlong, thin nose and full fresh mouth, marked the divisions of her countenance, so regular that Nick sometimes compared her face to a well-kept garden. All of these features—the eyes, the mouth, the translucent skin, the whole shapely head—appeared, however, to shine with illumination that came from within, the combination of quick intelligence and that extra aura which was peculiar to all Frenchwomen who had worked in the Resistance movement, as Suzy had, and lived in the imminent presence of torture and death.

The phone rang. Nick and Suzy both picked up their receivers. The operator said, "*'Allo?* Chicago Sentinel? *Monsieur le rédacteur Strang? Ne quittez pas. Monsieur le Ministre des Services Borvitch vous demande de Belgrade. C'est un appel de priorité."*

Nick whispered, "Vaclav Borvitch. I met him during the war, with Tito and later when he was in the Yugoslav Embassy in London. My pal—when he wants something."

The instrument gave forth a series of clicks and buzzes and then finally contained a voice, thin as a string, calling apparently from another planet.

Two minutes later Suzy was shouting with laughter, her instrument covered, while Nick was trying to stifle his own chuckles. The noise attracted Dad Lapham, the managing editor, who was passing in the corridor, and he paused, sticking his head inside the door, a wiry, kindly, alert, graying little man. "Who's on the other end," he asked, "Danny Kaye?"

Nick muffled his mouthpiece while the voice from Belgrade continued to rattle away. He replied to Dad, "This is one for the book. Indignant subscriber! It's Tito's Minister of Services calling from Belgrade. He wants to know why he hasn't been getting his *Sentinel*. Breakfast doesn't taste the same without the Paris Edition. He says he's following the Frobisher case in Budapest and ours is the only sheet he can understand."

Suzy's expressive face was alight with unholy joy, and her eyes were fairly dancing. She said, "He doesn't know that we've been banned in Yugoslavia by his own Press Minister since last week."

Dad Lapham twinkled at her happily from the doorway. "And what *you* don't know is that it was those Rosenberg articles on Yugoslavia you printed on your editorial page that *got* us banned." The old man, forty years a veteran on the *Sentinel* since he came out of Kansas in the old days, loved to catch Suzy out. He adored her and Nick and fathered them both as he did everyone else on the staff. He said to Nick, "Hey, while you got him on, ask him if it's true about Tito and that there opera singer."

Nick said equably, "Oh, shut up." He returned to the telephone. "Hello, Vaclav. . . . You'd better speak to your Minister of Press and Censorship and get straightened out. We've been shut out of Belgrade for a week. . . . No. . . . How would I know who gave the order? You get it rescinded and I'll see that you get back copies. The Frobisher case? You know he's been sentenced to twenty years. . . ." He scrabbled among the papers on his desk and turned up a short piece of Transoceanic Press printer copy. "The latest thing is a story out of Budapest in which Minister of Affairs Ordy says that the next American caught spying in Hungary he will hang, but don't let that give you ideas. . . . Oh, you know Ordy—well, that's only what he says. Okay, Vaclav, tell your Press Minister not to be an ass and you'll get your copies regularly. Nice to talk to you."

He hung up the receiver, grinning. Suzy wore an enchanted expression. "One of those golden moments," she said. "I would give my new hat to be present when they have their little conference."

Another idea crossed Nick's mind, and the smile faded from his face. He said, "Maybe I shouldn't have printed those pieces that got us kicked out of Yugoslavia."

Dad said, "I didn't think they were so tough."

"Tough enough to get the market closed to us. It's a double rap. We don't get to peddle our papers and they don't get to read the things we think might be good for them. It's better to get into countries like that with something than be kept out altogether. It was my fault."

It was like him, Suzy thought, to accept the blame, just as it was his temperament to accept the compromise of presenting a half measure, a watered-down version, in the broader interest of getting his paper sold, circulated, and read. She knew that he had become infected with her enthusiasm for the articles. She was not sorry she had influenced him, for sometimes she felt his cool and unswerving objectivity as a kind of abrasive restraint. But she was also well aware that it was this that made him capable of editing and publishing a free and independent American newspaper in Western Europe, one of two mirrors on the Continent capable of shedding light upon the mystery called the United States of America, its people, their beliefs and ways of thinking.

Dad said, "Long as I'm here, I figure you'll want to lead with the sentencing of Frobisher in Budapest. A fairly good picture came through." Dad reflected a moment and then added, "Jimmy Race is pretty steamed up over the case. I mean he's really burning. They've been having a hell of an argument out in the editorial room. He wants to write a think piece about it. Would you have any objection?"

Nick replied, "It all depends how well he can think."

Suzy said quickly, "He spoke to me about it. He said I ought to– I mean I have a place for it on my page I'm holding for it, if it turns out–"

Nick looked at her curiously for a moment and seemed about to speak, but he said nothing. It was Suzy who then filled in the silence. "In a way I can understand how he feels. There is something deeply shocking in a country failing to lift a finger to help one of its nationals who is being made a victim of–"

"Always provided he is innocent," Nick remarked curtly.

Dad looked surprised. He said, "Well, you don't believe the confession, do you?"

Nick replied dryly, "I don't believe *any* confession wholly. On the other hand I cannot credit them with being such fools as not to pick a customer on whom they can hang something. After all, Frobisher was G2 during the war." Nick paused and then added, "Sometimes those habits are hard to shake. What's Jimmy's angle?"

Suzy wrinkled her brow and thought. It had seemed

so clear when Jimmy was explaining it to her, and right and necessary, but then everything had a way of assuming importance when expounded by Jimmy. The vehemence, the physical vitality and sense of youthful power and enthusiasm behind his gestures, but, above all, his physical bulk, the size and weight of his limbs, the way he towered when he stood up, or filled a chair when he sat down, had a numbing effect on opposition. But now when she tried to recall what the piece was to be about, she found that nothing very concrete remained with her.

"He thinks that something ought to be done about it," she said, and found herself looking a little helplessly and ruefully at her husband, who was grinning at her like the Cheshire Cat. She finally began to laugh herself and said, "Oh, Nick, you're inhuman. He's young and full of enthusiasm."

Dad said, "Will I tell him to go ahead and write it, then?"

"You'd have a tough time stopping him," Nick said. "Let him go. We can put the brakes on here if it's too wild. Suzy, you'd better have something else lined up to drop into that spot, just in case."

She made a little face at him. "I have another article by Rosenberg I think could get us banned in Prague. Would that do?" She went back into her office, leaving Nick still grinning. But it was astonishing how quickly his expression changed after she had gone and he was alone. He kept remembering what she had said about Jimmy Race—"young and full of enthusiasm."

He was wondering what was youth and where it ceased, how one really knew when it was leaving one forever. And was enthusiasm the barometer? Was that how women, and others, too, distinguished between youth and middle age?

At forty-six Nick Strang was still trim and reasonably fit. He was a compact man of medium height who had managed to keep the fat from his frame so that he looked much younger than his years. He did have powerful shoulders—the legacy of his college wrestling days—and his head and neck were set into them with a certain air of truculence and strength. He had the stubborn, tenacious jaw of a fighter, but the brow and deep-set eyes were those of an intellectual.

He felt that he had preserved his enthusiasms but abandoned his violences. Yet Suzy's remark disturbed him, as it would not have done a week or so ago. He reviewed briefly in what manner, if any, this week differed from others and in passing noted that it was exactly eight days since the advent of Jimmy Race, sent on by the Chicago Bureau for further training as a European swing man, but he refused to admit that there was any connection.

Nevertheless, when Mme. Visson came in and said, "You have an appointment at the American Embassy at three, M'sieur Strang, and Monsieur Schuman is expecting you at the Quai d'Orsay at a quarter to four," he found that he was still entertaining a mental picture of Jim Race, his bulk, his overwhelming presence, and the irritating manner in which his thighs and hams moved inside his clothing when he walked. They gave one the same helpless feeling one had in the presence of a tank.

Nick called in to Suzy as he went by, "Back around five," and she waved her hand to him without looking up. He knew she was hard at work on the layout and content of the editorial page, which, since she had taken it over more than a year ago, she had raised to a position of eminence and prestige with her choice and display of material provided by himself and the Chicago office.

His mind went back to that August 6 of 1944, which would forever remain burned in the minds of every Parisian as Liberation Day, when French and American troops had entered the city, and he, a major in the Intelligence, but detailed to move *Yank* magazine into the *Sentinel* building, had come swinging down the rue Marbeuf in a jeep, to find Suzy waiting at the door with the keys.

She had been Suzy Vincent then. He had met her briefly in Paris, early in 1938, when he had been a rewrite and she was just breaking in as a leggy and not particularly noticeable girl reporter, after which he had been transferred to London. He had heard vaguely that when the Germans moved in and the paper had closed down, caretakership of the plant had been left in the hands of one of the French employees.

And he remembered how she had looked that day, with cannonading and burp-gun firing going on all about them, how he had cried, "Well, little Suzy Vincent!" and swept her into his arms, and they had exchanged a comradely kiss and hug of Liberation Day. It was only later that Nick realized that here was no longer a child, but a grown woman and heroine who had played out a deadly game right under the noses of the Germans in Paris.

Alone, her care of the newspaper property and her ingenious concealment of its vital parts from the Germans would have endeared her to him. Together they went over the plant while from behind books, buried in closets, hidden between floors, she restored the priceless and irreplaceable brass matrices for the Linotype machines, lead for the type pots and casting, composition mats for the stereotype machines.

She had ready names and telephone numbers of the old French crew who were immediately available, linotypers, make-ups, stereotypers, pressmen, and had them pouring into the building almost at the same time that Nick's G.I. staff was assembling and preparing to publish the first issue of *Yank* on the old *Sentinel* presses. Together Suzy and he had brought the dormant plant to life almost before the last tank gun and rifleshot had ceased to echo through the liberated city.

The war had wiped out the fifteen-year age difference between Suzy and himself. They had been comrades in arms and comrades in work. They adored each other. One day as they stood together on the composing-room floor, the smell of ink and lead in their nostrils, their ears attuned to the crashing, tinkling melody of the Linotype machines played against the bass of the presses rumbling below, they had suddenly looked at each other long and searchingly and had known that they were deeply in love. Three weeks later they were married.

Now she was his right hand, his other brain, his alter ego. Nominally her charge was the editorial page, but when he left the paper and she was there, he knew that nothing could go wrong.

Yet when he went out of the building into the rue Marbeuf and walked to his car, parked outside, Nick found to his surprise that what remained in his mind now was the empty space on the editorial page, the two-column hole Suzy would be reserving for Jimmy Race's think piece on the case of the imprisoned American businessman, Frobisher. The yawning gap seemed to glow in his mind like an image of light that lingers on after one has closed one's eyes to it.

4

MAN WITH A SCARF

In the editorial room, seated at a typewriter banging out some fillers to please Mitchell Connell, Janet Goodpenny was also thinking of the first time she had seen Jimmy Race, and, curiously, it had also been that marvelous, sunny, victory-throbbing day in August of '44 when American troops had marched through the Arc de Triomphe and down the Champs-Elysées on their way into the battle lines in pursuit of the retreating Germans. It was hard to keep one's mind on work with Jimmy sitting across the room from her.

Janet was a plain, dowdy girl with straight brown hair that fell somewhat untidily on either side of her face. Friends said that with her flat-heeled shoes, horn-rimmed glasses, sloppy clothes, and leather jacket she was always prepared to play the part of a creep. The truth was that Janet had long ago made peace with her lack of looks and glamour and replaced it with an ever-flowing well of kindness. She enjoyed doing things for people, and everybody imposed upon her shamelessly, sending her out for cigarettes or coffee, asking her to call up their wives to break the news that they weren't coming home, burdening her with black-market deals in money, getting her to turn out any dull and unimportant items that nobody else felt like writing.

She ripped the short filler out of her machine and stole a glance over to where Race was fuming and smoldering at his typewriter. And she saw him again as he swung his jeep out of line at the Rond-Point and came over to the Boston Unit of the Red Cross Clubmobile she was serving.

He was a captain of paratroopers then, dust-stained and victory-flushed, the excitement of Paris flowing through his veins, the prototype of the irresistible soldier with his helmet, the chin-strap hanging loose, set on top of his massive reddish head, the wall of his chest beneath his battle jacket, the great hams spreading over the narrow seat of the jeep, crowding the two French babes he had picked up somewhere. Janet had never seen anyone before who had filled her with such a sense of invincibility.

He had accepted coffee and doughnuts from her, grinning happily at her, shouting, "Ain't this some town? Believe me, when this is over I'm comin' back here and make it sit up and roll over." When he drove away he called back to Janet over his shoulder, "So long, sister.

See you back home after we chase these monkeys across the Rhine!"

She had never forgotten him. Nor had she ever seen him again until the day when Dad Lapham had brought him into the editorial room to introduce him as the new member of the foreign staff.

He had, of course, not recognized her at all and had looked right through her when Dad mentioned her name.

Mark Mosher, the city editor, flipped his telephone back onto its cradle, made a few notes on a sheet of copy paper, and then looked around the room, calling, "Has anybody seen Grisha today? Is Grisha around?"

The small, pale, Chaplinesque man with the villainous-colored neck scarf half rose from the bench at the end of the room. He had the stub of a cigarette impaled on a pin so that he could smoke it more closely. A shabby tan raincoat lay on the bench next to him.

Mosher picked him up with his eyes. He had a pencil poised. "Oh, there you are," he said. "What the hell was the name of that Rumanian who was kicked out of the government in Bucharest in 1946?"

It was astonishing to see the spine of the pale little man stiffen at being singled out. His eyes glistened as he stood up to reply.

"Papalescu. Jean Papalescu. He was Minister of Agriculture from 1945 to March 1946. He was of the Peasant Party."

Mosher said carelessly, "Okay, Grisha, thanks," and bent to his scribbling again. But the man, having secured an entering wedge, now was not to be denied, and with incredible swiftness, like a mouse slipping along the side of a wall, he moved from the bench across the room and was leaning over Mosher's desk. "I have little story about very important personage I can give you. Five thousan' francs. Nobody knows this but me. Please, you let me?"

The city editor looked up with distaste on his face. He

could never bring himself to care for these Central European tipsters, stooges, and informers who hung about the paper endlessly badgering to sell a piece of gossip, a reputation, or if need be a life for what they could get for it, though he knew the fellow called Grisha to be the most accurate of them. The man was hanging bent over his desk now, his moist eyes full of pleading, the Adam's apple in his throat quivering with eagerness. "It is about a priest in Czechoslovakia who was saved by the French Chargé d'Affaires and who—" Here he bent lower and brought his trembling mouth close to Mosher's ear and whispered for a while.

Mosher shook his head. "That's no five mils' worth. I'll give you two."

Grisha turned his unhappy eyes on Mosher for an instant, then shrugged his shoulders, leaned closer again, and talked while the city editor scribbled. Mosher's gaze roved again and picked up Janet Goodpenny, who was pushing her horn-rimmed glasses back up onto the high bridge of her nose, from which they always had a tendency to slip, especially when she bent over notes or a typewriter.

He called, "Hey, Janet, be a good kid. Look in the files and see if we have anything on a Father Resnicek. He was former assistant to the Papal Secretary in Prague."

Janet said, "Certainly, Mark," and dropped what she was doing at once. She got up and went over to the files and fingered through them. She did it automatically with her eye set to catch anything like the name that Mosher had given her. But deep inside her she was thinking of Jimmy Race, so huge that when he hunched over the typewriter on his desk he made it look like a portable, and the way he poked and punched at it, moving his head as he did so almost like a prizefighter shifting with blows, and thinking, too, of the fact that he hadn't remembered her at all.

She heard his roar as he looked up suddenly from the story he was beating out of the rickety machine on his desk. "It's got to be drugs of some kind, but how can you write a piece without knowing?" The rest of the staff remained silent to hear him out, for he was voicing many of the doubts and questions and uneasiness that had beset them ever since Frobisher had been arrested in Budapest.

"If it isn't a drug, or physical torture that would leave a mark, what is it? This guy was an American. But his confession had the same whine in it as Mindszenty's and those other Hungarians and Bulgars and Russians. And selling out pals! Boy, we make mistakes in G2, or the O.S.S., but we don't sell out. I can't see any of them making me confess to something I didn't do."

It sounded like a brag, but it wasn't, the way Jimmy Race said it, for he seemed to be considering the matter clinically and on the basis of the kind of person he knew himself to be, rather than emotionally. Still fingering through the files, Janet believed him. Even under the stress of torture, she found herself thinking it would take many months to break down this massive mountain of a man, reduce and pare away the flesh to get at the spirit inside. She found that quite suddenly the thought of Jimmy Race undergoing torture made her feel a little sick.

Felix Victor said, "Yeah, but what if they got you to confess to something you did do?"

"I don't see what that's got to do with it," Jimmy said. "We're talking about Frobisher, who wasn't a spy but said that he was. My God, some of these stooges around here ought to know something about how it's done." His eye was caught by Grisha, the tipster who had just finished with what he had to tell the city editor and was turning from Mosher's desk, his order on the cashier for two thousand francs, the equivalent of about six dollars, clutched in his nicotine-stained fingers.

"Here!" Jimmy Race shouted at him, brutally and directly, as though talking to a dog. "You! Where are you from?"

The little Central European stopped in his tracks, frozen by the impact of the assault. He was pale again, and his mouth twitched once or twice, but he recovered countenance and even a semblance of the small amount of dignity he had lost and, looking the big man in the face, replied, "Brassó!"

Jimmy repeated, "Brassó," and Mitchell Connell in the slot of the copy desk smiled openly because it was obvious that Jimmy had no idea where that was.

He could enjoy Jimmy's discomfiture, though not for long, for Jimmy flung his ignorance aside as he did any obstacle and said to Grisha, "Okay, you've been around all those countries. You must know or must have heard something. What about it? How do they go about getting a man to sell out his own mother without pulling his toenails out or taking his hide off in strips? Hey?" He was shouting at him because he was still victim of the misconception that the way to make a foreigner understand English is to yell at him, and to emphasize his question Jimmy got up and stood towering over the little man.

There was then a curious stillness for a moment in the city room. Nobody typed or said anything, everybody was quite motionless, watching the two men in the middle of the room.

Grisha was looking up into Jimmy's face, and his eyes were squinting and closing like one who has been looking into too bright a light. He appeared to be as transfixed and helpless as a sparrow. Still he did not or could not reply, and on top of the embarrassment of silence that seemed to grip them all was piled a deeper one, for now they could all see the beads of sweat that were forming themselves on Grisha's pale, narrow brow and on the space beside his upper lip not covered by his mustache. But most degrading and pitiful of all was the desperately haunted expression of his eyes.

He broke the spell finally with an effort and turned away. "I know nothing," he said. "I'm sorry. I cannot help you. Excuse me please." He turned and almost ran back to the mourners' bench, where he had left his shabby tan raincoat. He picked it up and scuttled from the room.

Jimmy said, "Now, what do you suppose got into that little rat?"

Connell took a half-dozen stories from the spike at his right and glanced at them. "Nothing much. They've probably had him in the boot at some time or other. You've just scared the pants off the best little stool pigeon we've got."

Mark Mosher said, "Oh, he'll come back. There's nothing he won't do for dough."

For the first time Jimmy Race felt a little foolish standing up there in the center of the room with no antagonist. He wished he could think of some way of getting back to his desk and typewriter without sacrificing dignity and face. That messy little Boston girl with the flat-heeled shoes and the stringy hair was striding along in his direction bound for the city desk with a folder from the clipping file in her hand and he would have to step aside to let her pass, which would make him look even more ridiculous. He turned and went out the back door of the editorial room that led to the elevators. . .

Outside in the lobby Jimmy felt like having a drink and thought he would go up to the small club bar on the top floor. But in the hall he encountered Suzy emerging from Dad Lapham's office, clutching her page proof. She smiled at Jimmy when she saw him, and said, "Hello, Jimmy. How's the piece coming?"

He was glad to see her, glad of an excuse to stop and talk to her, glad to be alone anywhere with her, even though there were doors ajar and typewriters clattering, people talking swift French on telephones, elevators humming.

He said a little savagely, "It isn't."

Suzy looked alarmed. "Oh, dear," she said and her eyes involuntarily dropped to the gaping hole in the editorial-page proof.

"Not that one," Jimmy said, "but there's another one I can and will write. We'll just singe the tail of the State Department a little and burn the rear of our Ambassador along with it. He hasn't even dared open his mouth to condemn the Hungarian Government. There's an American being railroaded and nobody cares. Not a single damn soul anywhere cares or does anything."

Suzy looked doubtful. "People care. Many people, and very deeply. They just don't know what to do about it." She was thinking about Nick and wondering what his reaction would be to a piece attacking the American Ambassador, who was an intimate friend, or the State Department, for whom Nick himself acted as a kind of ambassador at large on the Continent.

Jimmy looked down at her from his towering height. As always when he was in her presence he felt unsteady, unsure of himself, and in danger of losing his head. He said, "Suzy, will you have dinner with me tonight?"

She looked up at him tranquilly and half amused. "What, again? Last night. And two nights before—"

Jimmy asked, "Will Nick mind?"

Suzy made a reply that did not come from her French heart but rather from her overlay of American experience. She said, "I *am* married to him, you know." She would not have dreamed of thinking or saying such a thing if Jimmy had not brought up the question. She had not considered whether Nick had minded her going out with the newcomer from America to initiate him into dining at Fouquet's, the Vert Galant on the Ile,

Chez Anne, in Passy, and other places where the Parisians went to eat good food and drink perfect wines; she had not considered it at all. For that there was anything to mind in this act was to her unthinkable. But Americans, she knew, said strange and unnatural things and in return, she supposed, received the replies they wished to hear.

The deep and compelling intensity had come into Jimmy's eyes. "You know," he said, "the fact is that when I look at you, I don't feel as though you *were* married."

He spoke the literal truth. From the first time he had laid eyes on Suzy Strang he had refused to consider or accept the fact of her marriage to Nick. Curiously, in the professional field he could accept and understand Nick as editor and boss, the man who made decisions by which he was to a certain extent committed to abide. But as Suzy's husband he obliterated and abolished him. He did not exist. Jimmy had met him, sized him up physically and mentally; that is, he had estimated his forcefulness, ruthlessness, and acquisitive power, and had judged him to be the lesser man. Thereafter he had felt as free to court Suzy as though she were a girl of eighteen just home from boarding-school.

Suzy was half entertained. She said, "You mean *you* don't feel married to me. I can understand that."

"Suzy," Jimmy said, "Suzy! I wish to God I were."

Bon Dieu, Suzy thought to herself, *I should have known. This man is in love with me.*

She thought quickly of what she might have said, or have done. They were so difficult, these Americans; one could not coquette with them, or play at being a woman. They were like children. They either became hurt or took one seriously. There must be an end made to this. She looked up at him to make the obvious remark that would have turned the relationship back into the channels where she desired it and found herself caught up in panic.

She was frightened and at the same time attracted by the fear. She was afraid of his bulk, his power, his intensity and force of concentration. He was in love with her and would try to take her with the same crushing, slow-moving inevitability with which he brushed aside whatever stood in the way of what he wanted. The kind of man he was, the enormous force for self that he was, the Gargantuan range of his ego, so blind to anything but his own aims and ambitions, both repelled and attracted her, for they were so natural. He was probably not at all aware of the kind of person he was. He saw himself, she was sure, as kind and friendly as a tame bear, and his desire was to protect the downtrodden—those, at least, that he had not trod down himself because they had got in his way. His indignations and idealisms were genuine. If one left oneself unguarded even for an instant to such a man—

Dad Lapham came out of his office with the layouts for pages two and three. He smiled cheerfully at Jimmy and said, "You gonna have that piece of yours ready? It's getting on. Suzy likes to close her page at six."

That broke up the dangerous thing that had begun to fill the hall, that surrounded them like something thick and tenuous.

"Hell," said Jimmy. "I'd better get cracking." He turned and followed Dad down the corridor and back to the editorial room.

5

DUEL IN A CITY ROOM

NICK FLIPPED the right-turn signal of the Citroen 15 he was driving to make the turn off the Quai d'Orsay and across the Seine via the Pont de l'Alma, conscious of a nagging disquiet. He searched his mind to try to run it down.

Both the conferences at the American Embassy and at the Foreign Office had been negative and off the record. Nick thought with irritation upon the former, arranged by the American Ambassador to France to give some of them the chance to talk on the subject of the Frobisher case to Hugh Willicomb, American Ambassador at Large and emissary of the State Department to Europe. He reflected upon how few human beings understood and supported the basic, underlying tenets of a free press. Their motives were always of the best, and Nick could understand them, but the first reaction of a statesman, public servant, or politician seemed invariably to be: "Don't print it."

Willicomb's off-the-record conference with Nick, the *Time* and *Life* man, and several other big magazine correspondents and bureau chiefs had harped on that note. The international situation was delicate. Washington was looking bad on the Frobisher case. An ill-timed story might make things worse, or even endanger the Intelligence that was still functioning in Budapest. He also discussed the war risks, bringing from Nick the comment: "Flatly, then, we don't commit a hundred and fifty million people to war for one guy." Willicomb had smiled frostily and disclaimed meaning anything of the kind.

The Foreign Minister's press conference at the Foreign Office had not been much more fruitful. He had talked off the record of France's coming participation in the meeting of the Western Defense Pact nations. He had not even mentioned the Frobisher case.

Nick had been tempted to ask him what his policy would be if the Hungarians or any other satellite nation perpetrated such a challenging impudence upon a French national and then thought it wiser to refrain. Diplomats were never happy at being put on the spot, particularly in front of other correspondents. One of Nick's perpetual worries in his job was keeping diplomats happy, particularly French ones, inasmuch as his paper was a guest in France and, since its inception as the Paris Edition of the *Chicago Sentinel* twenty years ago, had existed and operated on the sufferance of the French Government. Actually, Nick felt no restrictions on his freedom to print what he wished, but he always had the feeling that the French were much more likely to resent bad manners or tactlessness or some thoughtless diplomatic gaucherie than an unflattering story.

He drove slowly down the avenue George V, past the two big hotels, the George V and the Prince de Galles side by side with their ever present groups of Americans on the sidewalks outside the entrance doors, just standing and looking and sucking on big black cigars, and the knots of uniformed chauffeurs endlessly waiting beside their big, flashy, opulent American cars. It brought up again an echo of the old nagging problem that seemed never to settle itself—for whom was he editing the paper?

It was another of the facets of his job that made it so entirely different from anything he had encountered in the papers he had worked on back home before the war. His circulation breakdown would have driven the average New York or Chicago publisher goggle-eyed. He sold his paper to the vast, quick-changing, sometimes fast, sometimes sluggish tourist stream, to the expatriates, and the core of the American colony in Paris, as well as the involuntary exiles, the businessmen, the ex-G.I.'s, and the students. It circulated in twenty-two different foreign countries and was a must in the chancelleries, ministries, and government offices of most of them. As always, Nick felt torn by the double duty of satisfying and entertaining the floating population of Americans as well as maintaining American prestige in Western Europe where it had been under constant assault and badly damaged during the cold war. Also in the *Herald Tribune,* the other American paper in Paris, he was bucking an older and longer-established newspaper.

He waited at the corner of the rue Bauchart for the blue-caped traffic policeman to elevate his white baton and wave him across the Champs-Elysées, and found himself near a newspaper kiosk. His eyes automatically sought the copies of the *Sentinel* and did not find them. He swore irritably. At other kiosks on the Champs it was the same.

There was business to be picked up at these kiosks and there was a circulation arrangement made with them for display. But the Communists went around from kiosk to kiosk, and depending upon the agent or proprietor thereof, bribed, bullied, threatened, persuaded, or forced them to bury the paper, thus losing sales to many English-speaking Frenchmen whose eye might be caught by some headline, or some story not to be found in any of the French publications.

For a moment he felt the same wave of helpless anger and resentment that always came over him when he thought of the Communists, the cold war, his country, and his own position, which was anomalous. Anywhere else he could have and would have fought them tooth and nail. In France, however, they were a part of the French Government, a minority party with elected deputies to the Parliament and officials appointed to public duty. And the paper that Nick represented and edited was a guest of that government, and under a law on the French statute books might at any moment be suspended from publication. It was unthinkable, many French statesmen and ministers had said, that there should be a Paris without this lively American newspaper, but Nick never forgot that the machinery existed by which it could become extinct overnight.

His little circulation tour ended, he approached the offices and plant and began the usual struggle to find a parking-space on the crowded rue Marbeuf. Nick thereupon came to the real cause of his deep-seated irritation. It was, of course, as he had known all along, Jimmy Race, the "new boy" recently sent on by the Chicago office to do a trick on the Paris Edition in preparation for a tour of duty on the staff of the Foreign Bureau.

He remembered now that his resentment had begun back in the office when Dad Lapham had told him that Jimmy was boiling up a think piece on the Frobisher case. They were all alike, these newcomers from the States, until they were halter-broken, got some sense and experience, or departed. Either they wanted to editorialize all over the place or they were scoop-happy kids who came over wanting to play cops-and-robbers. They all had a touch of *The Front Page* in them and were all for interviewing Tito, or penetrating the Kremlin with a list of six questions addressed to Marshal Stalin that were to shake the world.

Part of Nick's duties was to break them in and acquaint them with the facts of life and journalism on the European continent and particularly during the desperately precarious period of the mid-century. There had never been a time when huge and evil forces were playing more desperately for keeps than the years of '49-'50 with the pressure ever increasing. Nick, who had seen the tail end of the Nazi conspiracy before the war, knew that it had been child's play compared with what was going on now.

Jimmy Race was going to be even more of a problem because he had a great deal of ability, more than anyone else who had come over from the States in a long time. Nick knew that he could ordinarily count on the staff to cut any newcomer down to size in short order and rub the green off him. Nick had a smooth working organization that was geared to the needs of a paper with no French competition whatsoever; the work was not too difficult and the mood of the city room thorough if placid, and the young men did not particularly care to have their tempo disturbed by a fire-eater from Chicago wanting to rush about the city or country or Continent asking questions, pulling political beards, or digging up stories likely to embarrass any one of a number of important personages.

But it was different with Race, for the man not only had the authority of youthful accomplishment, but fairly exuded vitality, strength, and force. Nick knew that several of the younger members of the staff were already stirred up and impressed and were conscious of the restraints imposed upon them by the nature of the publication. He was aware that Mark Mosher, his city editor, was beginning to have doubts about local policy and coverage and was already looking for stories and angles that were a little more lively and sensational. It did not take much or long to infect a body of vigorous young Americans with the germ of slapdash, tabloid home-bred journalism.

What was really annoying him, however, Nick thought as he climbed out of his car and walked the few steps to the entrance to the building at No. 49, was that since the advent of Jimmy Race he himself had begun to have doubts as to his own policies and the kind of paper he was publishing. Was he a careful, objective, level-headed editor doing the job for which he was paid, or was he a stodgy, middle-aged transplanted American, overimpressed by European culture, manners, and tradition, who had forgotten his own youth as reporter, crusading editor, and war correspondent?

As he went up the steps to his office, Nick Strang was conscious that at least through all this he had been successful in keeping even so much as a hint of a thought or a speculation about Jimmy Race and Suzy out of his mind.

The Paris Edition always got itself to press in an orderly and gentlemanly manner and with a minimum of excitement, which is the mark of a well-ordered paper and particularly one on which the news editor and the chief of the copy desk know their business.

When Nick entered the editorial rooms at six o'clock looking for Suzy, the desk was practically cleared of work. The two reporters, Art Glass and Felix Victor, were preparing to finish up for the night and leave for their homes and their French wives. Cass McGuire was puttering with the mountain of notes and recipes he kept in his desk for a cookbook he was compiling in his spare time. Janet Goodpenny had gone over and was helping old Mr. Stafford of the travel department, who was struggling with a litter of material designed for the special spring travel supplement.

Nick could always estimate the state of his paper with his skin as well as his eyes. He could see Nan Millet in the recording booth with earphones over her head, which meant that the story from one of the correspondents in another city was being telephoned in late, but probably in time to make the first edition. The calm of the news and copy desks was soothing. The only sign of genuine activity in the room was the rattling of Jimmy Race's typewriter. He had evidently got into the guts of the piece he was writing, for he was pounding the machine so that the desk beneath it resounded to the battering.

Suzy was standing close to Race looking at several sheets of gray copy paper, the first few pages of his lead, and Nick tried to interpret the expression on her face. He was not quite sure whether she was looking troubled or impressed.

Mitchell Connell in the slot of the copy desk looked up as Nick came in, and said, "Hi, Nick, what do you want to do with 'hanging'? Dad didn't say."

Nick said, "Hanging?" and looked blank for a moment.

Connell passed a piece of proof over to him. "The Ordy statement," he explained, "about hanging the next American caught spying in Hungary."

"Oh," Nick said, picked up the story, and studied it for a moment. The impudence of it galled him, and he was tempted to spike it. But it was an emotional reaction, and he resisted it. It was a direct quote. The Hungarian Minister of Affairs had authorized the statement, and therefore it was news. He said, "One-column box with story. Stick it up in page one." Then he said to Joe Short, "There was nothing in the Ministry statement except background."

He went across the room to where Suzy was standing, smiled at her, and asked, "How's it going?" If Jimmy heard him, he did not look up from his typewriter, but continued the heat and fury of his composing.

Suzy did not make any reply, but silently handed him the three sheets of copy paper containing the first part of Jimmy's story. Nick questioned her with a glance, or rather it was little more than a thought directed at her, for they were so close and understood each other so well that they more than often anticipated one another, but Suzy refused to reply with look or word, or even so much as a change of her expression. Nick gathered that she wished him to read it without the prejudice a sign from her might induce. Nick had his own seismograph where Suzy was concerned, or thought he did, and he had the feeling that she was nervous, and even worried as to what he might say about the article. He sat down on the edge of the desk with his legs stretched out and began to read it.

It made a martyr out of Frobisher. Outrage and indignation burned from every line of the article. It speculated on the method by which an innocent American had been forced to stand up in court and confess to crimes in which he had no part, savagely indicted the United States for the weakness that made such compulsion possible, and as savagely attacked the French and British governments for failing as allies to stand together and by concerted action to bring about the relief of the imprisoned man.

Many of the ideas and opinions expressed in it were those which Nick had entertained at one time or another with considerable bitterness. However, his task was to reflect and not to educate. There was neither news nor interpretation in the article. It was a call to arms. He would, of course, not dream of publishing it.

He looked up and, with the sheets held in his fingers, made a brief gesture that he knew Suzy would understand. He thought he saw disappointment in her eyes, but was surprised when he glanced past her, over her shoulder, to find himself staring at Janet Goodpenny, who had raised her brown head with the lank hair falling on either side of her palish face and was looking at him through her dark shell-rimmed glasses with a kind of fixed desperation combined with a curious pleading.

Nick said briefly to Suzy, "Have you got something in type to fill the hole?"

Suzy nodded. "Of course."

"Prague? The Rosenberg article?"

Suzy said, "Would you prefer a cartoon?"

Nick wondered whether she was mocking him. She was not in the habit of doing so. But there was no hint of it in her expression, and her eyes were serious and clear. Yet he knew she wished that they were printing the Race article.

Jimmy Race stopped typing for a moment and looked

up at both of them. His eyes were alight and a little mad-looking, and he was breathing as though he had been walking fast. He said, "Hello. I'm sorry I'm so late with this." He glanced up at the clock and said, "I can wind it up in about another page if you want to send down the first takes."

Nick dropped his hand onto Jimmy's shoulder in a friendly fashion and said, "You can take your time. We won't be able to use it tonight anyway. Suzy's got something to drop into the spot."

"Why?" asked Jimmy Race, his voice sounding back upon itself in the sudden quiet that filled the room. "Is there something wrong with the story?"

Nick's glance measured Jimmy. They were all children, these writers, as vain of their work as any singer or actor, and they all had a certain amount of ham in them. He was wondering whether the capacity of the reporter's ego to bruise was in proportion to the great bulk that housed it, and decided to let him down easily, particularly in the presence of the others.

He said, "It's a first-class piece of writing, but it isn't right for us yet. It wants some talking over. Drop into my office in the morning and we'll discuss it."

"Why not now and right here?" Jimmy Race said.

Nick considered the matter in the light of Jimmy's challenge. He was never averse to a rousing argument; in fact, he enjoyed talking and threshing out both sides of a matter, and members of the staff, if they had any ideas, were encouraged to speak up and get them off their chests. Nick had a peculiar faculty of being able to argue without getting angry. If Race wanted a public debate on the demerits of his article, Nick had no particular objection.

"Certainly," he said equably, and repeated, "it's a first-class piece of polemic writing. But as it stands now it does not take into consideration my position as editor, the position of the Paris Edition publishing in a foreign country, and, above all, the known facts in the case. I probably should have placed my own position last, as it is the least important."

For the second time that day Nick found himself attacked on the Frobisher case. "Great Gehenna," Jimmy Race thundered at him, "you don't believe Frobisher is guilty, do you?"

Nick paused a moment to wonder actually what he did think and replied, "No, but I haven't any facts that tell me he isn't. We want to believe him a victim of a forced confession, but all we have to go on is hearsay and what people connected with him or who think they know him intimately say. The facts that are available are that he did stand up in court and confess, and that the Transoceanic reporter who covered the trial saw him and writes that he appeared to be normal and in good health. Outside of that we don't know a damned thing."

Jimmy said flatly, "Doesn't anybody around here ever try to find out anything?"

In the pause that followed the question Suzy said, "I'm going downstairs to make over, Nick." She walked the length of the room and vanished around the corner of the library. Jimmy Race made a gesture and opened his mouth as if to speak, apparently thought better of it, and refrained. Nick had the feeling that what he had been about to say was: "Don't go, Suzy. Stay here and watch me take this guy." And he wondered why Suzy had left so abruptly. Was it because she knew this was one that Jimmy Race could not win?

Nick said evenly, "We do, within our limitations, and they are many. Europe is a lot different from the United States when it comes to digging facts, or getting people to talk, or even printing what you have learned."

Jimmy asked, "Do you think that our diplomats have

done a good job?"

"No," said Nick.

"Then why not say so?"

"Because we don't undermine the prestige of our representatives."

"And of course we don't have a word to say about our gutless State Department." Jimmy's whole huge frame emphasized the sarcasm.

"You're in Europe now, Jimmy."

The big man exploded. "Good God, what kind of a place is this Europe? Is everybody a coward here? Hasn't anybody got a voice? It's only five years after Hitler, and we're doing it all over again."

The use of the word *coward* was not a pleasant one, and its effect lay thickly over the room. Mark Mosher pretended to study the late edition of *Le Monde;* Joe Short cleaned his fingernails elaborately, and Mitchell Connell clipped a weight to the box head on the hanging statement and tossed it down the copy chute at his elbow.

The door leading from the outer corridor flew open with a crash propelled by the waddling rush of the fabulously corpulent woman behind it, Thyra Addison, the fashion writer for the Paris Edition.

"Whooo! Darlings!" she shrieked. "Am I late? Am I just terribly late? Can you bear with me? We simply *must* get this into the paper. We must. There's never been anything so exciting since Christian cut the skirt length."

She was shaped like a pear and dressed like a scarecrow. Her head was too small for her and sat perched at the back of her shoulders, but her hair, showing beneath a preposterous hat with a bow like a sail on it, was done up in gay ringlets, and she had bright, merry, and tolerant eyes.

Her entrance snapped some of the tension that had

built up in the editorial room. Mitchell Connell said, "Scoop of the ages. Where the hell you been, Thyra?"

She cruised into the room like a blimp and took them all in with her smile and the electric quality of her ferment. "Why, Jacques Fath, of course, for their opening. Oh, dear, I simply must get it into the paper. It's too thrilling for words. And, of course, the dear boy would keep his surprise of surprises until the very last, just before the bride."

Joe Short rasped, "What surprise? Okay, Thyra, let 'er rip."

Her voice filled with the import of what she had to impart and, dropping several tones, she said breathlessly, fanning herself with her hand, "Sleeves! Sleeves are going to be detachable at Jacques Fath's this year. They come right out!"

Joe Short said, *"No!"* in a fair imitation of Charlie McCarthy ribbing Edgar Bergen. Mark Mosher looked up from his paper grinning and said, "You swear?" Cass McGuire, the night-club writer, got up from his chair, made Thyra a bow and a flourish, and said, "Won't you come in and take off your sleeves?"

Thyra said, "*You* may think it's funny, darlings, but if you don't think there'll be excitement in Paris, New York, London, and Chicago when *my* story gets out—"

Connell said good-naturedly, "Okay, babe. Get on the ball. Let me have it in takes. We'll make as much as we can for the first edition."

Thyra Addison waddled to her desk, her chair disappeared beneath her, she produced a voluminous wad of notes from an untidy handbag, and soon the keys of her typewriter began a surprisingly speedy rappity-tap-tap under the assault of her sausage-like fingers.

"Well?" said Jimmy Race.

Nick brought his mind back sharply into focus on the pages he held in his hands. He understood the younger man's indignation. They were all at the appeasing game again.

Nick handed the sheets back to Jimmy. "You may be right. A great deal of what you say is true. Nevertheless, I'm not going to publish this in its present form. We don't print intemperate pieces." He added, "You might as well learn that now," but he said it without rancor. He turned away and walked out of the door that led to the composing-room.

The reaction was immediate and violent. Jimmy Race, filled with rage and frustration as well as the wounded pride of authorship, tore the article into halves and then strips, and then macerated the strips and let them fall like snow into the wastebasket at his side.

As he did so, Janet Goodpenny, her odd little face quite white and strained, gave a little cry as though Jimmy were tearing a piece of her flesh. Jimmy did not even hear her. He got up, took his hat and topcoat from the peg on which they hung, and stalked out of the room without another glance at any of them.

Felix Victor remarked, "Here endeth the first lesson."

Art Glass, the other reporter, looked troubled. He said, "But the guy can write. I read his stuff. It's damned good."

Mark Mosher shook his head. "That Nick can really get rough. He'll ride over any guy that wants to do anything a little different."

Joe Short protested, "Oh, I dunno. I thought Jimmy rather asked for it."

Mitchell Connell said carelessly, "Oh, he's young. He'll get over it." Then he thundered, *"Hey, Thyra!"*

"Whooool" came her little scream. "Darling! I've got it all right up in the first paragraph."

6

INTRODUCTION TO PARIS

WITH ALL COPY out of the way, the editorial room had the happy faculty of going out of business during the supper period, and it was usually deserted between the hours of eight and nine. The chances of a local news break after eight o'clock were slim, and as long as there was somebody hanging around to answer the telephone and take a message, just in case of sudden riot or catastrophe in the capital, the staff could depart with a clear conscience for a leisurely dinner complete with *vin ordinaire en carafe.*

That particular night it was Mr. Stafford, the travel editor, and Janet Goodpenny who remained behind working in the corner of the empty city room. The old gentleman was somewhat overwhelmed by the amount of copy swallowed up by the spring travel supplement, and Janet was sacrificing her supper hour to help him.

It was shortly after nine o'clock when Janet completed an impassioned piece of prose over which she had typed the temporary heading: *Come to Beautiful Rapallo.*

The telephone on the deserted copy desk rang. Janet got up and went over and answered it.

"Hello."

She recognized Jimmy Race's voice at once, even though it was somewhat thick and blurred. Janet said, "Editorial room."

"Hello– Hello. Is Suzy there?"

"No. Have you tried her office?"

"Yes. There isn't any answer."

"I'm sorry. She's not here. Do you want to leave a message?"

Jimmy Race pondered this for a moment and then

said, "No, never mind. Is Dad there?"

"No. He isn't here, either."

"Is Mark Mosher or Joe Short around?"

"No."

"Cass McGuire?"

"There's nobody here but Mr. Stafford and myself. They're all out to dinner."

"Who is this speaking?"

"This is Janet Goodpenny."

"Oh. Hello, Janet."

"Hello, Jimmy."

There was a pause while it seemed as though the telephone had gone dead and Janet wondered whether they had been cut off, a not unusual event, or if Jimmy had just hung up in disgust, when his voice came again. "Had your dinner yet?"

"No. I've been helping Mr. Stafford. I was just going out."

"How about coming for a bite with me?"

Janet drew a deep breath and looked up at the ceiling. Her fingers tightened in their grasp about the telephone instrument as though she were making sure of the person who for the moment lived inside it so that he would not slip away. She was thinking, *He's asked me to go to dinner with him. He has. I mustn't let him know how much I want to go.*

Aloud she asked, "Are you sure you want me to, Jimmy?"

There was a long pause once more, and Janet's heart sank. She felt sick. She had given him the opportunity to say, "All right, if you don't feel like it, skip it."

But instead she heard his voice, deep, and for the moment filled with virtue. "Am I sure I want you? Hell, I'm calling you up, am I not? We'll go out and make a night of it, baby. I feel like getting a little tight."

Janet was certain that he was tight already, but she

didn't care. She said, "Okay, Jimmy. Where are you?"

"Across the street in the Jockey Bar."

"I'm not dressed–"

"You got clothes on."

"I'll be over in about ten minutes."

She wanted to fly across the street at once. She could have been out the door, down the stairs, and over in ten seconds. Ten minutes was all she dared allow in case he should suddenly change his mind, or forget all about having asked her and just go away.

She used the time to go out to the washroom, where she cleaned up her face and hands, put on fresh lipstick, and made ineffectual passes through her straight hair with a pocket comb. "Damn!" she said to herself in the mirror. "*Why* do I have to look like a zombie?"

She removed her glasses and examined herself. The effect was lessened. But she had a plain New England face. She supposed if she did try to do something with her hair it might be an improvement, such as having it cut and waved. But it was a nuisance then. She debated whether to leave her glasses on or off. Finally she put them back on. She was nearsighted and without them she had a tendency to peer and squint in order to see things clearly. She sighed and gave a little shrug as she went out. She was as she was and had been made, and there was no altering that. She put on her loose brown tweed coat, said good night to Mr. Stafford, and went across the street to the hangout, the Jockey Bar.

Janet found Jimmy holding up a corner of the bar, his face flushed. His mop of hair was standing up like a cockscomb, his blue eyes were gleaming, lighted by the fuel of liquor. His bulk and the way he leaned at the bar pre-empted the place of three. Janet thought again, as she had that day five years ago, of his invincibility.

He waved his half-empty glass at her, then tilted it to his lips, threw back his massive head, and finished it.

"Hi, Janet! What'll it be? Do you want to have a quick one here or shall we go to some other joint?"

Janet said, "I don't care. Whatever you like."

"Okay. I've had enough of this place. Let's beat it. I've got my car outside."

They went into the street, where he had a gray Ford vedette parked. "Okay, sis, climb in. Where do we go?"

"I know a little—" Janet began, when Jimmy broke in as though he had not asked the question nor she begun to answer it. "What do you say we go to Harry's Bar? You know this town better than I do. You tell me how to go. I suppose only tourists hang out there, but it's a spot I want to see."

Janet guided him down the faubourg and rue Saint-Honoré, then past the Place Vendôme into the rue de la Paix, whence they turned into the rue Daunou and parked across the street from No. 5.

"Sank roo de Noo," Jimmy said, grinning. "Boy, if I've read that ad once I've read it a thousand times. I was here once before during the war, but I was so stiff I don't remember much about it. Do you mind slumming?"

Janet minded nothing. Through error or accident or some queer set of coincidences, she had Jimmy Race all to herself for an evening. He had her in tow, she would go where he went, sucked along in his wake—his prize, his captive.

They went into the somber mahogany-and-gray smoke-fog atmosphere of the bar with its queer compendium of shields and coats of arms of British universities, American college pennants, and trophies on the paneled walls, the old and faded photographs of prize fighters, jockeys, horses, and bowler-hatted sports, the dried and shrunken boxing gloves suspended from the ceiling over the bar like desiccated human organs in a medical exhibit.

A *vestaire* took their coats. A scrawny cat at her feet made a half-hearted attempt to wash. The place smelled of beer and maraschino cherries. It was early in the season and there were not many people there, and those mostly at the tables. Jimmy liked to lean against bars. He was built for it. Janet moved gratefully into his orbit. They ordered Scotch. Jimmy said, "Well–" and gave her glass a slight bump with his, and they drank. Janet felt warm and happy, even though Jimmy was not paying much attention to her.

He raised his highball glass in a toast. "To the Paris *Sentinel* when it was a newspaper and not a poop sheet for an old ladies' home."

There was a sardonic rasp in his voice, and Janet turned her head so quickly that her long straight hair flew around her face and neck with an oddly graceful swing.

"You heard me, sis," Jimmy said. "You don't think that's a newspaper you're working for, do you? Those guys have all got fatty degeneration of the back porch from sitting around and reading the French papers and Transoceanic Press copy. Why, if a real story ever went by they'd fall on their faces from atrophied calf muscles if they tried to get up to follow it."

He was standing up straight at the bar now, his big paw wrapped around his drink, his features twisted in a grimace of half amusement, half contempt as he looked down at Janet.

"None of 'em have any guts, gimp, or gumption," he continued. "They're all as soft as mush in the go-get-'im department. They sit around on their hams and think because they're getting out a rag in Paris instead of Kokomo they're hot stuff. They can yawn themselves into their deadline and snooze themselves to press, and if they don't go in on the button, so what? If anybody comes up with an idea, there are five guys before Nick waiting to beat it to death before it can get around and cause them some inconvenience. And if it ever does get to Nick, he strangles it quick just in case it might hurt the feelings of some frog sitting in the Ministry or at the Quai d'Orsay. There isn't a reporter or an editor on that sheet fit to be called a newspaperman. Maybe they were once, but they ain't got it now. They're all chawing cud with Nick like mother cows, on both sides of the question. Hell, that's no way to run a newspaper."

Jimmy took another swallow of his highball, shoved the glass to the bartender, saying, "The same, and for Little Four-Eyes, too." Then he turned back to Janet and said, "Yeah, sissy. That's how it is. And did you ever stop to figure that out, or do you think they're all wonderful because they can answer a telephone in French, read French papers, and go home and sleep with their French wives?"

Janet was looking at him with her mouth twisted in an odd way. She said, "They have no right to hold you back. But they can't. They won't be able to. No one can."

Jimmy stared at her in total surprise. He even leaned down a trifle to get a little closer look. He saw that she was pale and passionate, with a touch of red burning in either cheek. But most marked was her mouth, which had taken on a softness and a mobility, of warmth and sympathy, like a small, red flower. It was turned to him and for him, and yet was lonely and forlorn. He said, "Kid, there's something to you."

She turned her eyes into his now, and for a moment he was deeply touched by the humanness, the worship, and the warm, womanly sympathy that opened out from her to him.

But then Jimmy's thoughts turned to Suzy, and he forgot all about Janet. He had been a fool to run out on her, and the whole office, too, for that matter, just because Nick had tied a can to his piece. He had felt hot enough on the subject about which he had written, but maybe the story hadn't been as hot as he.

Also he had led with his chin like a sucker, challenging Nick on his own grounds. He knew on whose side Suzy had been. She had walked out of the room because she did not wish to be present when he took a licking and witness his humiliation, and he loved her all the more for it. And then he hadn't had the guts to stick around and take his medicine. Instead he had flung from the building like a churlish child and started to bind a fine bun on and so now he was stuck with this little four-eyed candidate for spinsterhood from New England, who was sweet enough and apparently, as matters stood, on his side of the fence, but as a partner for a gay, infectious evening in Paris, or even as a companion on a good binge able to make him forget Suzy and what a sap he had been, not likely to go far.

Nevertheless he still felt kindly toward Janet for what she had said and he asked, "Another one, sis, or do we go and rout out some chow?"

"Another one, please," Janet said, "And then maybe another one after that."

"*Allons*, there, bartender," Jimmy said. "You have heard the lady. Set 'em up in line." He looked down at Janet with a new respect. Maybe the kid was going to turn out to have a hollow leg. Some of those plain ones very often did and would stay up and drink all night with you.

They dined later on Southern-style spareribs and New Orleans creole tomato rice at a place on the Left Bank off the boulevard Saint-Germain. They ate spareribs that were sweet and tender and then fried chicken and drank red wine by the carafe. The sensation of being hard-liquor drunk brought on by successive Scotches was beginning to leave Jimmy and was replaced by a wine-heady sense of expansion.

"What was it brought you to Paris?" Jimmy asked.

"Oh, during the war, I was here with the Red Cross.

A clubmobile unit from Boston. When it was over, I had to come back. I just couldn't bear not to. I fell in love with a city and a people."

Jimmy stared at her again. What a funny little widget. She looked like a drip, but she had a way of coming out with the damnedest things. "Well, what do you know?" he said. "Me, too. I took one look and said, 'This is for me. When the war's over, I'm coming back.' "

Janet bent her serious eyes on him. It was on the tip of her tongue to say, "I know, I heard you," but she refrained. It would only embarrass him. She wanted nothing to mar their evening. She was warmed by the liquor and the wine, but above all by the nearness to Jimmy.

They finished another bottle of wine. Janet had a sudden feeling of selfishness. She said, "It was good of you to come here with me. Where would you like to go now, what do you feel like doing?"

Jimmy replied, "I want to see Paris."

There was no clue in either his voice or his expression, and there were several ways in which the wish could be interpreted. Yet to Janet, at that moment, there could be only one, and she said without hesitation, "Very well, I will show it to you."

They went out into the street and got into the car. It was one o'clock in the morning, and the tempo of the city and the traffic had died down in the side streets and along the main boulevards. It was clear and light in the sky.

The engine of the car made a great roaring in the confines of the street. Jimmy did not know where Janet was taking him, but he had liked the temper and immediacy of her reply to his challenge and he permitted himself to be guided by her. He knew that they had recrossed the Seine, recognized by its acres of lights and its exquisite buildings, the deserted Place de la Concorde, and later the Madeleine and the familiar building of the Opéra, but thereafter he became bereft of all sense of familiarity and direction in the labyrinth of streets that went shooting off at star angles from squares and roundabouts. He only knew that after a time they were climbing steeply because he had to proceed in second gear. They drove through a dimly lit square finally, surrounded by sagging buildings that looked like backdrops for a stage set, and emerged on a terrace beneath a church with spire, minaret, and cupola of snow-white marble that must have been dazzling in sunlight, but now basked, a cool cream, in the milky light of the tilted half-moon that had crept a quarter way into the eastern sky.

Janet motioned Jimmy to stop, and when he did so, he got out of the car and followed her. The edge of the terrace looking south was railed. The city, glowing with light and infinite grace, lay at their feet.

"There is Paris," Janet said.

Jimmy grinned to himself. She had taken him literally.

"Where are we?" he asked.

"At the top of Montmartre. That's the Sacré-Cœur just behind us."

"But a hill this high, smack in the middle of the city—I thought Montmartre was just a section, you know, where the joints were."

It was as if Janet had not heard him. The moonlight was on her plain, colorless face and glittered from her glasses. She repeated softly, "Look! That is Paris."

The city was a soft gray by day, the patina of old buildings; she was deeper and softer color verging on blue at night, like the sky. And like a Frenchwoman she wore her lights like many-colored jewels, star bursts where the streets radiated away from some circle far below, diamond-studded brooch of the now distant Place Vendôme, rubies and emeralds reflected from the neon lights of the bars of the Places Pigalle and Blanche, the glitter of a silver ribbon where a bend of the Seine came into view.

It was an old city over which he gazed, huge, wise, surfeited with the knowledge and culture of the world. Many an ego, many an eye looking out over it from the same vantage point down through the ages, had felt itself diminished by its magnitude and its challenge. But not Jimmy Race. On the contrary, he felt himself swelling to match it.

"Oh, you great, big, beautiful babe," he said to Madame Paris, "how'd you like to have me for your sweetheart?"

Janet knew well enough to whom he was addressing himself and she did not even turn up her eyes to look at him. And yet the next moment he put his big paw and arm around her shoulder and drew her to his side and held her there, comfortably, comfortingly. He did this because of the canted moon, because she was a girl, feminine and soft despite the lack of sparkle in her looks, because the kid was so obviously stuck on him, because it felt good to have her warm little body thus pressed to his up there on the hilltop overlooking the city, but probably most of all because she happened to be there.

He was quite drunk now, was Jimmy Race, drunk on the fumes of accumulated drinking, drunk on himself, on his love for a girl who belonged to someone else, on the intoxicating night and the sensual sight spread beneath him. It made him feel big and strong and all-powerful, that thing that lived inside him inflating him like an enormous balloon and threatening to float him away in the sky over the sleeping city to look down upon it Godlike and terrible.

Jimmy held the girl to him tightly as though to anchor himself to her for the moment and began to talk. He was speaking to the winds that swirled down from the Sacré-Cœur to carry his words out over the city, but his words were for Suzy who was somewhere down there below; they were for the girl next to him because she had shown that she understood him and had climbed into his corner. They were addressed to Paris because she lay there decked out so coolly and impeccably beautiful, and they were for himself, too.

He said, "You're right, sis. There she is. Just like a woman waiting to be taken. And she makes it so worth while to try to take her. There's a saying, you know, 'You can't astonish Paris.' But she doesn't mean that. You can, and she loves it. She pretends she's seen everything, but she'll give herself to the guy who can hand her a little thrill, a new experience, a tiny bit of knowledge she never had before. That's me!"

He said, "I'll crack that Frobisher confession story if it's the last thing I do. And Mindszenty and Bulakov and Villaczek, and all those guys who stood up there in court in Budapest and Prague and Sofia and Moscow and swore and confessed themselves into dungeons and pest-hole jails and the firing squad and the hangman's noose. I'll find out how it was done, I'll write it, I'll lay it in her lap, and she'll love me for it."

Jimmy was conscious that Janet had stirred a little in the cradle of his arm, that she had turned her head and was looking up at him.

"God!" he said. "The guys who have been close to it and haven't had the guts or the savvy to get it. The T.O. guy in Budapest with his 'Frobisher appeared to be normal and uninjured—' *Appeared to be!* And the guy's on the spot and calls himself a reporter. We've got our own man in Vienna and he turns up sick. Nobody lifts a finger to get at the truth of how the trick is done. If I had been in Vienna—"

He paused and then went on. "When I get to Vienna or Trieste or Athens or Berlin, I'll be over the border within twenty-four hours. Hell, we used to drop into enemy-held territory during the war and disappear and live off the land. It's a cinch now compared to what it was, and nobody's had the guts to try it and nobody but me is going to do it." It sounded like boasting, but all it was actually was Jimmy's thoughts as they came into his head, and through the wine and liquor he had had they were turning into speech.

"They couldn't stop me," he said. "They couldn't then and they couldn't now, because when it comes right down to it, they're not smart enough. If they were smart, they wouldn't have to use cops and guns and terror and torture. If they were really smart they'd have figured out something else.

"Inside of two days I'd have somebody who'd talk, baby. There's always an underground, always somebody looking to get the truth out. Whatever they did to turn a man into a coward, I'd know. And once I know it, it's all up with the dirty game. They can't use it any more. By God, Nick would have to print that wrapped around his lousy travel ads. 'Come to beautiful Budapest. Read how the happy Hungarians turn a man into a phonograph.'

"How could they stop me?" Jimmy Race asked. "Who could keep me from getting what I wanted? Those punks?"

As though it were an echo, he heard a faint, breathless whisper from his side. "Nobody. Nobody could stop you. Nobody could ever stop you from getting what you wanted."

"You know," said Jimmy Race, "you're a sweet kid," and bent down, tilted her pale face upward, and kissed her on her lips.

They remained thus for what seemed like a long time, for it was Jimmy who found himself unwilling to relinquish the contact. He had closed his eyes to the soft moon and sky light, to the night glow of Paris, and to the small, trembling person who was at his side. It might have been Suzy. He had imagined that if Suzy gave her lips as an earnest of herself it might be like that.

7

EXIT THE MAN WITH THE SCARF

IT WAS ODD that even two weeks after Jimmy's walkout, and long after he had apologized for it, the emotions and irritations stirred up by his rebellion swirled about the paper and its staff.

Jimmy himself appeared to have calmed down and changed. He plunged into work with vigor and interest, did what was asked of him, and seemed anxious to be amenable and to learn in what manner this newspaper published on European soil differed from what he was accustomed to back home. He no longer talked about the Frobisher case. The think piece was never salvaged or rewritten and was forgotten.

But the things he had said and done, the immense force of his personality, half grating and irritating, half dynamic and attractive, had left its mark upon them all in the form of little islands of tension that appeared to have formed in the formerly placid waters of the daily work of getting out the paper. They showed themselves in such ways as the minor incident of the ejection of the little Central European stooge and tipster.

This began when Nick returned to the rue Marbeuf after an unpleasant half hour with a subminister at the Foreign Office over a story of a Catholic priest persecuted in Czechoslovakia who had been given shelter by a minor French diplomat, himself a Catholic, who eventually aided him to escape. Ordinarily Nick would have summoned Dad to him, accepted the responsibility for the story, and thrashed out its origin and history with him. But Dad wasn't in his office when he called for him, and Nick went into the editorial room to look for him.

He knew that he was irritable and that his nerves were raspy. He had not seen or read the story before it went into the paper and had not paid much attention to it afterward. It had appeared during the time of the Frobisher sentencing and the brush with Jimmy Race.

Nick saw Dad leaning over Thyra Addison's desk in deep conference. Janet Goodpenny was checking back files and making earnest notes on some kind of a job for somebody. Two or three heterogeneous characters, including Grisha, occupied the mourners' bench, and Jimmy sat at his desk next to the travel section in the act of overpowering his typewriter. The fixed stare, the hunched shoulders, the heavy breathing through the nose, and the hammer movements of the fingers and wrists assaulting the keys all brought to Nick's mind echoes of the episode of the Frobisher case. He had no way of knowing that Jimmy was engaged on a piece estimating the effects of the reduction of gas and water pressure in Paris in the event of a threatened utilities strike, and that that was just the way Jimmy wrote. Only Mark Mosher appeared to be unoccupied.

Nick went over to his desk and dropped the paper folded to the offending story before him. He said, "Where the hell did that story come from?"

Mark, shocked by the suddenness of the attack, said, "Why, is there something wrong with it?"

"Certainly there's something wrong with it. I've just had my ear chewed for half an hour by Ribeaux over at the Foreign Office. They're sore and I don't blame them. The Czech Government has lodged a formal protest. Ribeaux wants to take it out of my hide. I want to know who is responsible for it!"

Mark was still somewhat behind the pace and said, "Well, I got it from this fellow Grisha."

"Who the devil is Grisha?"

"He's one of those stooges, you know, those characters that hang around here, selling tips; he's been pretty reliable." Mark's eyes traveled across the room to the long bench at the far end. Grisha was there, pin-smoking a cigarette butt, his tan raincoat over his arm, the hideous snakeskin-pattern scarf gleaming from underneath his jacket. Mark said, "There's the guy now."

Nick looked where he was indicating. Grisha had heard his name and had half risen from the bench. But something in the attitude of the two men warned him, for he did not continue. He remained poised in that manner like a puppet with a broken string and then sank back on the bench again.

Jimmy stopped work on his story and looked up in unabashed interest, and Dad Lapham, too, disconnected from Thyra and straightened up, his bright little eyes roving about the room. Nick felt himself on a merry-go-round from which he could not get off. He said to Mark, "Why do you let guys like that peddle you stories? You ought to have more brains than that."

Mark began to experience a sense of injury. "Was the story untrue? I'm sorry—"

Nick cut in testily. "I didn't say that. That was the trouble. Apparently it was true. All the more reason for keeping it out of the paper. You should have known that."

Dad came over cheerfully from Thyra's desk and said, "It was my fault, Nick. I should have caught it and killed it."

Oddly, Dad's assumption of the blame only increased Nick's feeling of irritation, probably because he was aware that in the final analysis it was actually his own responsibility as editor-in-chief and that any other time he would have been the first to acknowledge it and take himself to task. But now instead he said, "The hell it was, Dad. It should have been caught long before it got to either of us. There are times when we can't read every line in the paper. That's what we've got editors for. Mark should have killed it when it came to his desk. Joe Short should have thrown it back at Mark when he got it, and Mitchell Connell should have questioned it when it got to him. That's three of you. It's time you chaps found out that quite often the story a paper keeps out of print is quite as important to it as the ones it gets in." He then swore irritably, slammed the paper with the story in it down on Mark's desk, and walked into the ticker room.

His rebuke lay like a pall upon the room, and Connell, Short, and Mosher were all three red-faced and angry because the scolding was half deserved, but not wholly so. It had been a pretty good story, and Mark was right to be attracted to it. Yet one of them might well have called it to the attention of Dad or Nick before committing it finally to print, or at least checked with one of them whether they had read it. But it was not easy to take a public bawling out.

Mark Mosher felt abused. After all, his job was to dig up stuff that would interest people, or what the devil was the use of his sitting at that desk? An office boy could do as well. He called out harshly, "Grisha!"

The little man was up as though the bench had been electrified and hustled over to the city desk, his raincoat dragging, an anxious look upon his narrow face. "Excellency—"

Mark Mosher said aloud so that everybody could hear him, "What the hell do you mean coming in here with a cockeyed story like that? You heard me. Here, this one. You know what I'm talking about."

Grisha looked down at the story. He had difficulty with English, but he recognized it from the headline. He stammered, "But, Excellency—" He began to sweat again, and his eyes mirrored hurt and surprise.

Mark mocked, "But, Excellency—" Joe Short and Mitchell Connell watched the two men, as did Dad Lapham. Dad said nothing. He knew what was in the air. There was a scapegoat needed, a whipping-boy. Maybe that would clear the atmosphere. What did it matter if a little Central European tipster got burned in the process? Nobody had asked him to come around.

"But the story was true. Did anyone say it was not true? Did I not warn you, Excellency, when I gave it to you that perhaps—"

Nick appeared again, coming from the door of the ticker room. He paused on the threshold.

Mark shouted at Grisha, "You talk too damn much. You and your damned stories. Go on! Beat it! Get out of here. And don't come back. If I see you come in that door again, you're going to get a shoe to the back of your pants. Come on, now. Outside."

It was a catharsis. It was also a wretched injustice. Strange, the thing that seemed to grip them all. Nick knew that what was happening was unfair, but he did nothing to stop it, for, after all, it did not matter too much, and that was how things sometimes went with men. They just got on the wrong track and stayed there.

Grisha was so pale that by contrast his eyes seemed flushed. He turned without another word, lifted up his raincoat from the floor, and tried to make an exit that contained some shred of dignity. His Adam's apple was working furiously in his throat, and his mouth twitched.

Jimmy Race watched him go with the contempt of the strong for the weak. A shred of a man, he thought, nothing human, with no will or resistance or spirit. That kind was made to be walked over. They were always asking for it and always getting what was coming to them.

Janet's heart ached for Grisha. She hated injustice

and she knew that one had been perpetrated. What had happened had not been his fault. He had fulfilled his part of the bargain. He had to pass her desk, the last one before he could attain the sanctuary of the door. She smiled up at him and whispered, "Never mind, Grisha." She felt so sorry for him. She wished she might have patted his hand.

Her feeling provided him with that little moment of support, the one friendly glance necessary to enable him to reach the door and escape from his tormentors.

He looked down at Janet, and his mouth twitched into a little smile of recognition and thanks. His dark and pained eyes were full of gratitude. Then he fled.

From the door of the ticker room, Nick was half tempted to call him back. But it was too late. The men in the room settled down again, a little ashamed. It had dissolved some of the tension. Nick was conscious of feeling silly as he walked through the editorial room, for Dad was grinning at him like an imp.

Joe Short said, "There was a note on the end of Klaussen's story out of Vienna tonight, Nick. They're going to have to open him up. He's going into the hospital tomorrow and will be out of circulation for about a month."

Nick said, "Oh, oh. His wife is with him, isn't she? Make sure they've got enough dough. How is Trans-oceanic Press coverage out of Vienna?"

Joe Short shrugged his shoulders deprecatingly, but Mitchell Connell said succinctly, "Steenks!"

Jimmy Race left off his typing and his head came up. He said, "Will you be in your office a little later, Nick?"

"Uh-huh."

"Be all right if I come in and talk to you?"

"Sure." Nick was thinking that the big guy at least could learn, and one of the things he seemed to have acquired was reticence about spreading business with

Nick all over the editorial-room floor, which was all to the good. He said, "Drop in when you're ready." He wondered what the big, restless man wanted of him.

8

BUILD-UP FOR DISASTER

SUZY ASKED, "Do you really think it is a good idea, Nick, to send Jimmy to Vienna?"

The query startled Nick for two reasons—that Suzy should not approve of his decision to grant Jimmy Race's request and send him to Vienna to take over and cover them during the convalescence of the regular correspondent, but mostly that she should break their iron-clad rule never to talk shop on their week-ends at the old made-over mill at Montfort-l'Amaury, once one of the seats of Anne of Brittany.

The old mill that Nick had bought lay sheltered in the valley at the foot of the once fortified hill on the other side of the village. He and Suzy had made it over into a retreat for themselves. The mill was their escape from the taxing duties on the paper, and they rarely asked guests, Suzy taking care of their heavy entertaining in their big rooftop flat in the Passy section of Paris. At the mill, while Nick fished or read, Suzy busied herself with her watercress beds, which she operated at a profit. She kept small, neat, Frenchwoman's account books on the project and was as delighted as a child that it was successful.

"I was just wondering—" Suzy began again, when Nick cut in with: "I know. I heard you. What do you suggest?" He turned to look at her. She was dressed in slacks and a flannel shirt open at the throat and was seated at the rustic table with her account books spread before her.

Suzy looked reflective. "Howard Akers might like to go down from Brussels for a month or so. Or if you're really worried about Vienna, Harry Franz could split his time from the Prague job and go there every other week. He really knows Vienna."

Nick thought, *How odd! She's been worrying about it. She has everything all figured out. I wonder why?*

"Well, yes," he said aloud. "I'd thought of that, but it doesn't work out. Howard has got the Belgian business at the tips of his fingers and there's due to be a hell of a row there. I don't like to pull Franz out of Prague. It means an exit visa and a new entrance visa and would give the Czechs an opportunity to turn us down. The trend is all toward keeping out Western correspondents once they leave."

"Still–" said Suzy.

"What's wrong with sending Jimmy?" Nick asked. "He isn't a kid. He can write. It will help to break him in. He's calmed down a lot since he's been with us."

Suzy said, "I'd prefer to see him remain in Paris," and then added her reasons. "I don't think he is ready yet to go to Vienna. I don't believe he has calmed down. I believe he is a stubborn man who will let nothing stand in the way of his getting what he wants."

"What do you think he wants in Vienna?"

Suzy reflected over this. Did she actually know, or was it one of those instances where because she was a woman she felt something intuitively that was difficult to put into words. Finally she replied to Nick. "I don't know. I only know it would be better for us and the paper if he didn't go." And then she found herself entertaining a thought that amazed and frightened her. It was: *Yes, and better for me if he did go. That young man upsets me. What is the matter with me?*

Nick was trying to use his reason and judgment. He understood, for instance, in one sense what Suzy was trying to tell him about Jimmy and yet he could not help considering her odd phrasing: "I'd prefer to see him remain in Paris."

He knew he was taking it out of context. And yet how often unwittingly people gave away some of their innermost thoughts merely by their choice of words or the phrasing of a sentence! "A stubborn man who will let nothing stand in the way of getting what he wants." And supposing that he wanted Suzy, that Suzy had heard the call of this desire from a man who was young, tough, and ruthless and had subconsciously expressed her reaction to this demand.

It was not jealousy in the accepted sense. It was Nick's devilish sense of objectivity and his own hypersensitive self-criticism that brought forth these phantoms. For Suzy was young, she was hardly past thirty, and the life she had led in the underground during the war had been filled with action and danger. She, as well as the men with whom she consorted, was prepared to be flayed and shredded by torture before being mercifully killed. They were all people of action, and something sang in their blood.

It no longer sang in his, or at least so he thought, and he had almost forgotten that it once had. For he too had been war correspondent, soldier, and intelligence agent. He remembered a glorious and harrowing three weeks behind the lines in Yugoslavia, the numberless stolen rides on bombing missions, the landing at Salerno.

What had remained of all the beautiful courage, sacrifice, and adventuring? The truth was that it had never really mattered except to those who were engaged in it. The world was never changed by young men who risked their necks to write a piece about their sensations. But sometimes, if one could pinion a thought, hold it, polish it, and print it where the right people, or for that matter any people, could see it and read it, one might move the tortured old planet just an infinitesimal fraction in the right direction.

And yet how dramatic and exciting were the young men with their challenge to danger, and always would be!

What if Suzy, without her being wholly aware of it, were in love with Jimmy Race because of this challenge? What could one do? Fight? Oil creaking joints, get aboard one's horse again and, as had been written, ride violently off in all directions? Or send the young man off to Vienna for a while and get him out of the way?

It was typical of Nick that he did not consider that he might be more attractive to Suzy than someone like Jimmy Race.

When he answered her finally, he was aware that he was not trying to understand too well what she was driving at, but he could not help himself. He said, "I fail to see your logic. A couple of weeks ago you were finding him young and full of enthusiasm and the paper in need of some of the kind of pep he could give it if turned loose. Now I propose to give him a chance and you want him held back."

Suzy considered this and wondered for an instant what had been God's scheme in creating men so stupid in their understanding of women. She felt entangled now and not quite on sure ground since she had had the alarming thought that *she* might be a good deal safer if Jimmy went off to Vienna and forgot about her as she had no doubt that he would.

But above all, since Nick had chosen to take this line, not usual for him, indicating that indeed something had happened to all of them since the advent of Jimmy Race, it closed off further avenues of explanation.

For Suzy was a Frenchwoman and a European, and she differed from American wives in that she would not risk offending her husband's pride. She considered Nick wholly an adult, able to look after himself. If he did not have the perspicacity to see that the change in Jimmy Race in the past two weeks was deliberately designed to put him off his guard, it was not her place to damage his dignity by pointing it out.

Suzy retreated. She clapped her hand to her mouth and looked like a little girl who had used a word she oughtn't. "Nick! I've talked shop! I've broken rule number one. Now, what ever do you suppose led me to do that?"

Neither one of them mentioned Jimmy or the Vienna assignment again.

Nick said, "It won't take you too long to find your way around. Vienna isn't as difficult as some of the other cities. After all, the Army is there. You will probably run into a lot of chaps you used to know in the war. How will you go?"

Jimmy replied, "I thought I would drive."

Nick nodded. "You'll find it useful to have a car there. You'll be staying at the Bristol. It's central and convenient and most of the other chaps will be there. Look up Behrens, the Oceanic man, and remember me to him. He's a nice guy and will give you a hand until you learn the ropes. If you're in doubt about anything, ask him."

Jimmy said, "Thanks, I will."

Mme. Visson looked in at the door to Nick's office. She said, "You wanted to see the Olivers before they went off on the Scandinavian trip."

Nick replied, "I did. If they are there, ask them to wait a few minutes." He consulted his appointment diary. He had a full schedule. The Olivers, a husband-and-wife writing team, were going to do a series on Denmark, Sweden, and Norway for the travel section and needed some briefing. A minor official in the business department of the paper in Chicago was on his way to Paris from London and would want some coddling. He had a meeting scheduled with the shop steward of the Printer's Branch of C.G.T. to discuss the new wage agreement in view of the French Government's decision on wages and prices. There was a note to talk to Cass McGuire about running a dictionary of food and French menus in his column, an idea of Suzy's, something the American tourist could clip and that at a glance would aid him in translating the bill of fare in the average French restaurant. Felix Victor, the better of the two reporters on the local staff, had submitted an idea for a new series on the work of the modern version of the postwar American student in Paris, the ex-G.I., and what he was doing to 1950. It was crisp and well thought out and researched, and Nick wanted to encourage him.

And yet he was lingering on here with Jimmy, wet-nursing him with advice and instructions like a kid reporter. He felt foolish, and at the same time as though if he sent Jimmy off to Vienna with anything less than explicit instructions, he might come to regret it.

Nick consulted his calendar and said, "This is Monday the 13th. If you start tomorrow it'll take you two days or so to drive down there, and you'll want some time to get settled, look around, and dig up a few contacts. Let me have your first story Monday the 20th, for Tuesday's paper. Did Dad give you your telephone time?"

Jimmy said, "Five p.m."

"Mmm-hm. Set the call up well in advance. If anything happens that the wires are down, or you can't get through, send us a telegram. You can also try getting through direct to either London or Rome, and they'll relay it. And," Nick concluded, lifting his head from the material on his desk and turning cool and steady eyes on the big fellow sitting opposite him, "keep out of trouble."

Jimmy laughed. "I guess there probably isn't much trouble I can get into there as long as—"

Nick snorted. "The hell there isn't. The old Wild West is puss-in-the-corner compared to what goes on there. It's a four-power town, it's full of Russians, and wherever there's Russians there's trouble. The last time I was there the average was one kidnaping or gun fight a day. We don't bother to report those any more. They're routine."

The big man was looking at him now with an odd expression on his face. Nick continued. "I'm sending you down there at your request because I think you can do us some good there and learn something about how things are done over here as well. I want a reporter there, a guy with eyes and ears and the intelligence to analyze and interpret what he is seeing, not someone who wants to play cops-and-robbers with the Russians and the M.P.'s."

Jimmy said, "I'm grateful for the chance you are giving me and I'll do my best. It shouldn't be too hard to lick."

Nick studied the younger man. The speech had sounded sincere, and yet he thought he heard little alarm bells going off. Something was bursting out all over Jimmy Race, something he could not conceal, a kind of triumph, an anticipatory excitement. The more Nick talked, the more like an ass he felt, and yet he considered that he must make Jimmy understand something of what he might be up against.

He said harshly, "It will be very hard to lick. You will have to forget everything you ever knew or learned back home. You've got no automatic prestige here just by being a reporter and connected with a big organization. They don't like publicity or care about it in the American sense. Any contacts you make and prestige you gain will be by your own efforts and on the basis of the kind of guy you are and the friends you can make. You can walk into any cop house in the U.S. and tell the chief of police, 'I'm Race of the *Sentinel,*' and he'll spill his guts and let you put your feet up on his desk because he'll take those columns of space he gets in the paper down to the city manager when it comes time for reappointment. There isn't a policeman on the Continent will give you the right time; the government officials are suspicious and scared to death to talk; to them a newspaper guy means trouble, a crook, and a chance to figure in the next purge. This isn't a crowd of cheap city-hall shysters, headquarters grafters, and municipal pickpockets. This is really tough. Everybody is playing for keeps because when they lose out over here the whole family—mother, granny, uncle, and the kids—go floating down the Danube or are dumped into the sewer in the same bag along with the original victims. There are damned few exclusives to be got over here. If you get one it's because some chap owes you his life, or because some smart guy who takes orders from and gets paid off by the Cominform wants you to drop a sixteen-pound shot for him that will land on the toes of somebody in Washington. You can talk, bluff, buy, or prestige your way out of a jam back home, but here you don't mean anything to anybody, including your own people in the Army, Navy, Air Force, and diplomatic corps. They will regard you as a damned nuisance who is trying to upset *their* applecart and ruin their pitch and kudos with the people back in the States.

"So—" said Nick, and drew a long breath. He lit a Gaulois and offered one to Jimmy, who smiled and took one from an American deck he produced from his pocket. Nick waited for Jimmy to speak, but he remained silent.

"That's all, then," Nick said. "You'll be out there on

the end of a wire, but back here we've got to get out a paper. I want to know I've got somebody I can trust to keep his head and stay out of damn-fool jams. I want to know that when I come out into that office at five o'clock the phone will be ringing and you'll be on the other end of it with a piece I can use. Okay?"

"Okay, Nick."

"Good luck, then. Drop in and say good-by before you pull out tomorrow."

9

ALWAYS KISS THE GIRLS GOOD-BY

ON THE WAY OUT from the paper, Jimmy encountered Suzy downstairs in the lobby and he pounced upon her with a big, lusty cry of: "Suzy! I was hoping I'd find you. I looked for you upstairs."

She was wearing a tailored suit of gray flannel with piqué flare-back cuffs and a loose coat. Her hat was a small white straw sailor, and the dark veil that held it in place emphasized the clean, strong line of her jaw. She had on white gloves with a tiny frill at the cuff. She was appetizingly, lusciously, impeccably, perfectly feminine, Eve after her departure from Paradise, clothed and sophisticated by Paris.

Suzy felt the assault of his presence. He hovered over her. For an instant she had the absurd notion that like a beast of prey he would leap, open his jaws, and she would vanish down his gullet.

"Nick is sending me to Vienna," Jimmy said.

"Yes?" Suzy said. "You will like that. It's quite different."

Just seeing Suzy there filled Jimmy with the sense of elation that he had worked so hard to suppress upstairs in the office with Nick. "You bet I will. Come on across the street with me to the Jockey and let's celebrate."

"No, Jimmy. I have work to do." She did not want to be alone in a bar, sitting across a table from him, his heavy, penetrating, compelling gaze fastened upon her.

"Then come for a ride with me just for a minute. We'll take a spin through the Bois. It'll make you dizzy. There's a green haze in the trees already."

She did not wish to be dizzy, Suzy thought. She did not need the bursting of buds in the leafy avenues of the Bois de Boulogne to turn her head.

"No, Jimmy."

"Then dinner tonight? I'll be leaving tomorrow."

. . . Nor dine with him, to sit in warmth by shaded lights, drugged with wine and food, to feel the silent importuning. "No dinner, Jimmy. I—we're having people tonight. A man and his wife from London." She determined immediately she reached her office she would call them up at their hotel and invite them.

"Well, then," said Jimmy, suddenly relaxing the pressure of his personality with which he had been trying to overwhelm her, "will you go for a walk around the block with me? There are things I've got to talk to you about."

It was as though he had read her mind and realized that she did not want to be alone with him where he might press his attack. Yielding to her in this was saying in effect, "See, nothing can really happen to you right out in the street with everybody going by." It was when he relaxed into boyishness and gentleness as he sometimes did that she was most vulnerable to him. She sighed. "Oh, all right, Jimmy. I'll walk with you."

He was still sensitive to her mood. He did not take her by the arm for fear the touch of his fingers at her elbow might alarm her again. Instead he walked soberly at her side down the rue de Berri to the faubourg Saint-Honoré, where they turned their steps to the right in the direction of the glittering shopping-section.

Suzy said, "Do you always get your own way like this, Jimmy?"

Jimmy was again filled with power and ambition, energy and anticipatory excitement and the sweet feeling of invincibility. Things were going well.

"Yes," he replied. "Because when I want something badly enough I want it with everything I've got. And then I keep pushing. And after a while people stop pushing back and give way and I've got what I'm after. I don't think about it. It just happens. Is that bad?"

"Like going to Vienna?"

"Sure, like going to Vienna."

They turned down the avenue Matignon and headed for the Rond-Point. It had been a very big block around which they were doing their walking, but Suzy had acquiesced in it because of the purpose she felt she was following out. She came to it now.

"Jimmy, why do you want to go there?"

He walked along a few steps at her side looking down at her. He was bursting with desire to tell her, to fill her with the dreams and ambitions that seemed to be too prodigious even for him to contain any longer, and to see the gleam of admiration light up her dark eyes. Yet he hesitated and in the end did not do so. He was not sure of her. The battle for her was still raging, and she was still Nick's wife and co-worker. It was conceivable that she would speak to Nick, drop some hint– The appointment in Vienna might yet be canceled.

He replied, "To wrap it up, tie the ribbon of the blue Danube around, bring it back, and drop it in your lap."

"Jimmy," Suzy said, with an odd kind of earnestness, "aren't you ever afraid?"

"Of what, Suzy?"

"Of being so convinced of your own rightness, of being so big, so contemptuous of anyone who isn't as strong as you? Of barging through life brushing everyone aside who gets in your way? Of taking whatever you want no matter what it might do or mean to anyone else?" She did not mean to let it, but a curious kind of desperation came into her voice. "Don't you think you owe the gods any humility ever? Aren't you even a little bit afraid of their jealousy?"

Jimmy breathed deeply and exhaled his breath in a gigantic sigh of contentment. The sky was a French-blue canopy, the sun was shining with the first false warmth and softness of coming spring. He was in Paris walking beside the woman he loved, who had just confessed his strength and her weakness, who in effect had sent up a cry to him: "Spare me, but if you must, then take me quickly."

They were approaching the opening to the wide spaces of the Rond-Point and the Champs-Elysées. Standing on the street, almost at the curb, blocking their way for a moment, was a young couple kissing. One saw them all the time in Paris. The street was roaring with traffic, the pavements filled with pedestrians hustling about their business, but they were oblivious of anything and anyone but each other. Their lips parted for a moment, and Jimmy saw the eyes of the girl swimming with delirium and the gleaming moisture of her mouth, mobile and shaped with longing.

A great bubbling laugh rumbled from the cavern of his chest. "Paris!" he cried. "Nobody cares or bothers if you're young and in love in Paris." Then he took Suzy by the arm and drew her into the doorway hard by where they were.

It was a cobbled entrance through the building to a courtyard, a shaded tunnel half denied to daylight. A single light gleamed behind the glass door of the concierge's quarters, a huge striped tomcat washed its fur in the parting of lace curtains in the window. Jimmy took Suzy in his arms and bent his mouth to hers, until he felt the warm quiver of her lips through the fine fabric of her veil and for a moment, too, he was aware of the touch of her gloved fingers on his face.

He felt dizzy and shaken almost beyond control and he uttered her name in a kind of groan. "Suzy— Suzy—" And then again, his voice trembling so that he hardly knew it: "Suzy—when I come back from Vienna—"

A door banged, and Jimmy jumped away. His Anglo-Saxon blood and temperament were not, like the couple on the pavement, conditioned to disturbance. It was the concierge emerging, a rosy, cheerful little man wearing a blue cap with a glazed brim and a large watch chain across his middle. He grinned at them and said, *"Ne vous dérangez pas,"* and went out into the street.

But the spell was broken, and Jimmy did not try to recapture it. There would be time later. He knew that now. He looked down at Suzy, but she did not return his glance. Instead she had opened her handbag and produced a mirror and was examining the exquisite line of her mouth. She made a tiny repair with the corner of a wisp of linen handkerchief. Jimmy self-consciously wondered whether he had lipstick on his mouth and reached for the handkerchief in his breast pocket.

In silence they walked up the Champs-Elysées, past the big movie signs and huge show windows of motor-car companies, back to the rue Marbeuf and the entrance to the *Sentinel* buildings, where Jimmy said good-by to Suzanne. "You'll hear from me from Vienna," he said.

She said, "Good luck, Jimmy," and achieved a parting smile for him before she turned and walked up the single flight to her office. She was angrier at herself than she had ever been in her whole life.

Acquisition of visas to enter the American and Russian military zones and automobile-club carnets and other papers necessary to crossing European borders with his car delayed Jimmy's departure, and it was not until midafternoon that, packed and ready, he parked his machine in front of the paper and went upstairs to say good-by.

He went barging into the editorial room, where most of the staff was at work, grinned at them impudently, and said, "So long, you desk commandos. Race is off to do a little field work."

Some of the staff had heard rumors and already knew; some did not. Mitchell Connell said, "Okay, Richard Harding Davis, Jr. Where are you off to now?" and when Jimmy replied, "Vienna," added, "Haven't those poor people got trouble enough without that?"

Thyra Addison shrieked from her corner. "Darling, do take a look at what the women are wearing and drop me a line I can use in my column. Viennese women used to be *so* chic before the war."

Mark Mosher said, "Boy, I envy you, getting out of this dump. That's the place to be. You're really right in the middle of it there."

Art Glass looked impressed and remarked, "You'll be able to get a lot of material for another book," but his partner Felix Victor, who was embittered because he found himself compelled to compile a statistical report for Mark Mosher on the percentage distribution of American tourists on the Continent per boatload debarking at Cherbourg and Le Havre, merely remarked, "Keep your nose clean. There are some very nasty guys on the other side of the railroad tracks." Cass McGuire offered a list of night clubs.

Only Janet Goodpenny said nothing at all; she sat at her desk, her hands in her lap, staring bleakly at her typewriter. She had not heard anything about his assignment to Vienna. Except around the office she had not seen him since their night out together. *He was going to Vienna!* What was it he had said he would do when he got there? It all came back to her, and suddenly she felt sick at heart and frightened. Time then was rushing past her with a kind of blinding and doomful speed that made her incapable of making any move, or saying anything that could halt or slow its passage. At any moment Jimmy might turn and go out through the door and then it would be too late. Numbly frozen in her chair, Janet could only hear his words passing through her head, repeating like a cracked phonograph record, time after time, after time: "When I get to Vienna, I'll be over the border within twenty-four hours."

And then what? What if something happened to him and she never saw him again? Had he told anyone else of his design? Nick or Dad or Mark Mosher, or anyone who was responsible? Had he meant what he had said, or was he only drunk and boasting a little, the way men did? Was she the only one who knew? Supposing Jimmy were to vanish and would some day be found floating in the Danube with his wrists bound with wire and a bullet through the back of his head, like the American correspondent Allen who was found dead in the harbor in Greece?

"Well–" said Jimmy, and shifted his topcoat onto his arm. Janet forced herself to look up. Their eyes met for an instant.

Jimmy had completely forgotten about Janet. But he remembered now. The memories were going off like alarm bells in his head, the night at the top of Montmartre, the drinks he had had, the way he felt, big enough to jump over the moon without straining a seam in his britches, and the things he had told her about what he was going to do.

He remembered, too, that she had been stuck on him. He had tried to ease her down by keeping away from her after that and not leading her on, because she was a good kid and decent and he didn't want to make her unhappy. She was okay for an evening when you were lonely or disgruntled and wanted company, or an ear into which to funnel your frustrations, but she wasn't the type with whom you'd want to take it any further. But supposing she was still moonstruck and hadn't got over it? Supposing she told someone what he had said and it reached Nick's ears? Nick would cancel the assignment on the spot, or if he had already left, call him back.

He saw her frightened eyes and how pale she was and that her lips trembled and seemed to be trying to frame his name. There was a fire there and it had better be put out. His reaction was instinctive. He held her eyes with his until his gaze became long and melting, and for her alone. Then at the end he made an almost imperceptible movement with his head in the direction of the door. He saw from the sudden look of hope and relief that came into her eyes that his signal had been received.

"Well–so long."

He went out and waited by the elevator in the corner of the stairs. Janet followed almost immediately. He said, "I wanted to say good-by to you alone, baby," and drew her down with him a quarter flight of the stairs where they would both be screened by a turn in the landing.

"Jimmy–Jimmy," she whispered, "I didn't know you were going. I'm so frightened. You aren't going to–you won't–"

He took her hand in his and laughed and then bent over her. He was deliberately concentrating upon her the full force of his ego; he used his eyes, his will, and his touch. "Baby," he said, "you can't hold a guy to what he said when he was a little drunkee. Me, I was a whole lot drunkee when I shot my mouth off, but it doesn't mean I can't take care of myself and keep out of trouble. I probably talked a lot of stuff I didn't even mean. Just file it away under the Vino-Mixed-With-Scotch Department, get it? I wouldn't want anyone to get a wrong impression. So be a good kid and keep mum and forget about it, will you?"

He was taking her into partnership again and asking her to protect him and not expose his weakness. All men talked big when they were drunk, she supposed. But for the moment the pang of fear persisted. She was so helpless in her entanglement. He meant so much to her.

"Jimmy—you will take care of yourself, won't you? Promise me?"

"Sissy, you can bet on that!"

In a movement that was touching in its naturalness and sweetness Janet reached her arms up around his neck and lifted her face to be kissed. Jimmy responded to her with a kind of brotherly and easy acquiescence, since there was nothing to lose by it. But again, as before, he found himself suddenly shocked and surprised by the tenderness and comfort there was in the touch of her mouth, the feel of her straight, smooth hair against his cheek, and the gentle surrender of her body to his. He lingered for a moment, giving himself up to the sensation. Then he parted from her, gave her a genuinely affectionate kiss on the temple, and went. Janet heard him go down the steps two at a time and waited until she heard the bang of the outer door. Then she started slowly back to the editorial room, where her absence had not been unnoted.

It was Mitchell Connell, who missed very little, because of his central position in the room, who had caught the look between Jimmy and Janet and her subsequent following him from the room. He said, "Oh, oh —what goes on, an office romance? Don't tell me that little Janet has succeeded in nailing that guy!"

Mark Mosher said, "Yeah, he practically lifted her

out of her chair."

But, as usual, it was Felix Victor who had the last word.

"Boy, but you guys are observant, for a lot of newspapermen," he remarked. "Who Mr. Bigpants is in love of, and good and hard, is nobody but the boss's wife. Ain't you birds got any eyes?"

10

NO CALL FROM VIENNA

It had been a week since the departure of Jimmy Race. It was the afternoon that he was due to telephone his first story from the Austrian capital. Janet knew that he had been assigned five o'clock as his calling-time. She had been watching the clock since four. She was lovelorn and at the same time she was nervous and worried. If she might only hear his big, rich, booming voice. If only the time would come when his call would be through and she would know that he was safe and that the fears that haunted her were groundless.

At ten minutes to five she could bear it no longer and went into the transcribing-room and offered her services to Nan Millet in monitoring calls, which Nan willingly accepted. Calls often overlapped, or did not come in exactly on time. Janet studied Nan's schedule sheet: *Brussels, 4:45; Vienna, 5:00; Rome, 5:15; Berlin, 5:30; Istanbul, 5:45; London, 6:00; Prague, 6:30.*

The telephone rang, and Janet's nerves jumped. It was five minutes to five. Nan picked up the receiver and said, "Yes . . . yes . . . Yes, Mr. Akers. Right away. . . ."

She turned to Janet. "Brussels is a little late. It's Mr. Akers with eight hundred words. Do you want to take it?"

Janet's mouth felt dry, and she tried to make her

voice sound natural. "I'll take the next one."

Nan nodded without comment, picked up a spare green celluloid recording-disc and went out to the city room, where the two telephone-recording booths were located. Janet felt she could have wept with relief and gratitude. Jimmy's call would be next. She would be there to take it, would hear his voice. He might even be pleased when she told him who it was monitoring his first story.

At five o'clock Janet's nerves were stretched like violin strings, but there was no call from Jimmy. At ten minutes past, the telephone rang. With an enormous sense of relief Janet picked up the receiver. Her ears were already filled with the memory of the sound of Jimmy's voice. But it was the switchboard operator announcing the call from the Rome correspondent.

Janet said, "Very well. This is Janet. I'm helping Nan. I'll take it right away." She went out, entered the second booth, talked for a few moments with the man in Rome to test the clarity of the connection, and then switched on the recorder. She saw Nan leave the other booth with the record. The Rome man had a thousand words on an inflammatory speech by Togliatti on shipment of American arms. She would be there forever.

When she finally finished she met Nan Millet on the way to take another call. Nan said, "Was yours Vienna?"

Janet shook her head. "Rome."

Nan said, "Istanbul's coming in ahead of Berlin. I'm so glad you can help. I'm all jammed up tonight. I suppose now Vienna and Berlin will come in at the same time. It always happens that way."

But it didn't. At least, Berlin called, but not Vienna, and shortly afterward Prague was on the line, and a long call from London.

At seven o'clock Nan said, "Oh, dear. I suppose I ought to stay here for Vienna if and when it comes in, and I promised to meet a boy from home–"

Janet offered, "I'll stay. I don't mind."

Nan said, "You're a darling. You needn't wait after eight o'clock. If they haven't come in by that time, they never do unless they send a message." She went out leaving Janet sitting by the two telephones that did not ring, nor would any more that evening.

Shortly after half past nine, when Dad Lapham returned from his supper and went into the news ticker room to check on the late copy emerging from the teleprinter machines, he was surprised at hearing movement from the recording-room beyond. He listened for a moment, then went on through and opened the door.

There was only a hooded desk lamp burning, and above it almost like a ghost hovered Janet's pale face with large frightened eyes behind her spectacles glowing out from it.

He said, "Hello, sis! What are you doing here in the dark all by yourself?"

Janet said in a voice that trembled, "I promised Nan I'd stay here and take–Jimmy's call from Vienna–if it came."

"Hell," Dad said, "if he hasn't called by now there won't be anything. You been here all this time? Go on out and get yourself some supper. He probably didn't have anything to file or we'd have heard from him by now."

Janet seemed to sag a little. She put her hand up to the side of her face, her eyes closed, and her mouth twisted curiously; her limp hair hung down into the typewriter keys. Dad Lapham watched her for a moment, then went over, picked up her chin in the cup of his hand so that she was forced to look up at him, and said, "Sissy, I guess maybe you've got some trouble. Maybe you'd want to talk about it a little to someone."

Janet took his hand in both of hers and held it tightly for a moment. Then she whispered, "Dad—I'm frightened. I'm afraid that something's happened to Jimmy."

Dad laughed reassuringly and perched on the edge of the desk. "Now, what would be happening to a hunk of man like that in *Wien* except to move up against a little drink the Viennese call *Pflumli* which gets you taken all over drunk so quickly that a little thing like calling up and filing a story becomes practically unthinkable."

But now Janet surprised Dad with the passion with which she spoke. "Oh, if it were just that, if he were drunk, or just didn't give a damn, I wouldn't care. Dad, I've got to tell you something, and will you promise not to tell anyone if I do, because I promised *him* I wouldn't ever. I couldn't bear it if anything were to happen to him and it would be my fault for not saying anything."

"Sure," Dad said easily, "what's the big monkey been up to?" In the back of his head he was making up several paragraphs he would exchange with Jimmy Race for tampering with a kid as straight and decent as Janet and therefore he was not prepared for what Janet had to tell him about their night out, Jimmy's outburst against the paper, his ambition to solve the mystery of the Communist confession cases, and his boast as to what he would do should he ever reach the border of a country adjoining the iron curtain. "He said that if he ever got to Vienna, or any of those countries, he would be across the border within twenty-four hours."

"The hell you say," Dad ejaculated involuntarily before he recovered himself and said, "What makes you think he could get across anybody's border?"

"Because nobody could stop him. Don't you see? Nobody can keep him from anything he wants to do. He—he's too big. He just goes and does it. But afterward—if there were too many of them. If I'd told someone before he went to Vienna maybe Nick wouldn't have let him go. But he swore he was drunk when he talked like that and made me promise not to say anything to anyone. And now if something awful has happened to him it will be my fault, and I can't bear it, Dad, I just can't—"

Dad Lapham was no longer feeling easy, but he said, "Oh, nonsense, sis. Forget it. Go out and have some supper and go home and get some sleep. We don't start to worry about guys with the tank capacity of Jimmy Race until they've been missing at least a couple of weeks. The boys probably gave him a welcome to Vienna at the Balkan Grill or filled him full of *Heuriger* at Grinzing and he won't be really conscious for four days and able to operate for three more. That's awful stuff, that *Heuriger*. I once lost ten days out of my life with it."

He had her up from her chair as he was speaking and was propelling her out into the city room, where he helped her into her leather jacket and accompanied her to the stairway.

Janet said, "Dad, you're a dear. You're sure—"

"Sure as I am that this is Monday and I've got to get out a second edition. Forget it. If that gorilla can't take care of himself, who can?"

But he was not sure at all. He thought that he knew a newspaperman when he saw one, and, for all Jimmy's arrogance and self-assertion, he was an old enough hand to know what a deadline meant to the men back in the office charged with getting out a paper, and to respect it. Drunk or sober, he would have got a story through or, lacking one, there would have been a message to that effect.

He went at once to Nick's office, where he learned that Nick and Suzy were dining late and were not expected back until ten o'clock. He left a message to be notified immediately upon their return and went into his own room, where he placed a number of long-distance telephone calls. He studied a map of Europe that hung in his office and re-examined the boundaries of Austria. The Germans and the Czechs to the north and the Italians and the Yugoslavs to the south. But due east lay the Russian zone and Hungary. Dad remembered from his visits to Vienna before the war that from the dining-terrace atop the Hochhaus, Vienna's one skyscraper, one could see the low hills of Hungary rising from across the Danube no more than twenty-five miles away. He said, "Damn!" and chewed at a fingernail. "Do you suppose the guy would be big enough boob to–"

At half past ten, when Nick and Suzy came in, Dad laid it on the line. He said, "I guess you know there's been no call, file, or message from Jimmy Race. I've been talking to Janet Goodpenny, who is worrying herself sick because the big clown got drunk with her a couple of weeks ago and told her if he ever got to Vienna he'd be over the border within twenty-four hours. I'd kiss it off as a guy with a lot of liquor in him flexing his muscles to impress a mouse, except that he made her promise not to tell anyone. That sounds like maybe he was serious and was afraid if she cracked he'd be recalled from the Vienna assignment. He's been gone a week now, just long enough to get into trouble."

Suzy said, "Oh, la la," took off her hat, and sat down.

Nick thought a moment, then said, "You've called the Bristol, I suppose."

"I'm waiting for it now," Dad replied. "I've got one in for G2 in Vienna, and Major Mannix, the P.R.O. officer. Jimmy must have checked in with him at some time or other. Maybe that's one of them coming through now–" as the phone rang.

He said, "Hello–Hotel Bristol. . . . Give me the *portier* please. . . . This is the *Chicago Sentinel* in Paris calling. Will you please check whether Mr. Race, James Race, is in his room or in the hotel, or if he has left a message where he can be reached. I will wait. . . ."

They all looked at one another without saying anything as Dad held the line. Nick was not one to borrow trouble before it was upon him; nevertheless he wondered what Suzy was thinking. The telephone in Dad's hand came alive again, and he spoke into it. "Yes, I'm here. . . . Not in his room. . . . Yes—his key is in his box. . . . You say his bed has *not* been slept in? Since when? . . . No, when did you last see him? Eh? . . . Three nights ago? Did you say *three?* And you've been on duty every night? . . . Will you find out if his car is about? I'll be calling you back later. A gray Ford vedette, License No. 74TTX 382. . . . He left no message of any kind? Will you check on when he was last seen and if possible with whom? . . . His luggage *is* still in his room. Yes—yes. . . . Leave word if he calls or comes in, to call his office in Paris at once. . . . Yes, Lapham, Elysée 12-87. Thank you."

To them Dad said, "He hasn't been in for three nights. The concierge remembers him particularly, but he's going to check with the day man—" Dad began, when the phone again cut him short. He answered it and then said, "We're through to the Army in Vienna. It's Major Slater of G2 coming on."

"Oh," said Nick, "let me speak to him," and took the instrument. "Hello, Ed? This is Nick Strang in Paris. We're a little disturbed about a new guy we've just sent in there. He doesn't know the ropes too well and may have done something foolish. He should have checked in with us today and hasn't. The Bristol reports he hasn't been in his room for the last three nights. Yes . . . yes . . . uh-huh . . . yes. . . ."

And thereafter Nick talked to the major for what seemed an interminable period during which he said only "yes" or "I see," but when he hung up finally, he was as troubled as Dad.

He said, "I dunno. He didn't check in with any of

them since his arrival, but Ed says the boys put a tail on him for a couple of days just for routine and to keep in practice. He's been to some places where he oughtn't to have gone and talked to some characters G2 doesn't like. His car is still in the Army parking-lot next to the Bristol. It was checked in there Friday night, and according to their records hasn't been out since. So wherever he went it was on foot or by bus or in another vehicle. Ed will put a couple of the boys on it and really run him down wherever he is. He said he'd call me back when he hears anything."

Dad said in the voice of one who doesn't believe it for a moment, "He could have got drunk maybe and is sleeping it off."

Suzy's eyes were grave. She said, "He might have met with an accident of some sort and be in a hospital–"

Or with a Viennese blonde and be holed up in somebody's apartment, Nick thought, but kept the thought to himself and was disturbed and angry with himself for doing so. Ordinarily he would have voiced it to Dad and Suzy, but he had the feeling that to do so would almost seem like an indelicacy–if Suzy had been fond of him.

Suzy knew that her allusion to a possible accident was a wish that there had been one, that he had fallen, or had been struck by some irresponsible Viennese, Russian, French, or American driver, that something simple and physical had happened to him and not what she had been fearing ever since Dad had reported his conversation with Janet.

Nick said savagely, "He couldn't have been such a fool as to go over the border without first checking in with our guys and letting them know how he was going to–"

The telephone on Nick's desk rang again, and they all twitched nervously at it and then pulled their hands back. Nick smiled wryly and picked it up. Race's power to upset them from almost a thousand miles away was only too apparent.

He said, "Strang talking. . . . Yes, hello, Bob. What do you know. . . . *What?* . . . The hell you say. Okay, we'll be right up."

He dropped the receiver back on its cradle with a hard click and said to them, "Bob Stokes of Transoceanic Press upstairs. He says there's a story coming in now over the telephone from their correspondent in Budapest that concerns us and that we'd better come up."

They squeezed together in the tiny lift that took them up to the fifth floor and the T.O.P. offices and went in. There was only Stokes there, a small dark bureau man who smoked cigarettes nervously, and his wife, who did rewrite and doubled as secretary and who was sitting at a typewriter with a pair of earphones clamped on, and hitting the keys with the desultory attack of one who is taking slow and indistinct dictation over a long-distance wire with a bad connection.

Nick asked in a strained voice, "Is it about Jim Race?"

Stokes fiddled with his cigarette and said, "Yeah. I'm sorry. It looks like a bum rap. But I figured it would be better your getting it this way than having it come in over our wire."

They went over and stood behind Mrs. Stokes and read over her shoulder what she had already taken down. *The Chief of Police of Budapest announced today that an American spy and saboteur had been captured and arrested in an attempt to enter Hungary illegally. He gave his name as James Race, an American citizen, and claimed to be a representative of an American newspaper. However, no passport, or credentials of any kind to substantiate this claim were found upon his person. He is being held incommunicado in Andrássy Prison for further examination.*

They were up with the dictation now, and the subsequent words they read as they materialized before their eyes beneath the hammering keys.

In a brief statement, Minister of Affairs Andreas Ordy declared the American to be a spy, that he would be tried as such and if found guilty of conspiring against the Hungarian People's Republic, would be handed—

Here Mrs. Stokes stopped typing for a moment and spoke into the chest mouthpiece she wore. "I beg your pardon, Mr. Vargy, I'm not certain I got that last. Would be what? . . . Oh!"

She thereupon exed out the word *handed* and in its place wrote *hanged.*

"Oh, *bon Dieu!*" said Suzy Strang.

11

BRIEF LESSON IN DIPLOMACY

NICK HAD HAD NO DOUBTS as to the hullabaloo that would result from the Race case, and it had come up to expectations. For one moment as the bad news had been tapped out on Stokes's typewriter he had found himself wishing desperately that he could suppress it, and phantasy sentences had formed themselves in his mind in which he asked Stokes whether he could not sit on the story for a few days until one had time to look around and decide what to do.

Of course he did not do so, since he knew very well that the Hungarians would spread the story through every agency, but Nick had time for an inward sardonic laugh at himself. When unpleasant news hit home the first tendency was to suppress. What became of his objectivity now?

And again, later, he found that he had lost similar objectivity with regard to his attitude toward the apparently lackadaisical procedure of the State Department in dealing with the affair, Suzy's words regarding a great nation that seemed no longer to have either the chauvinistic interest or the power to protect a national in difficulties in a foreign country suddenly began to take on meaning, and he could no longer brush them aside as he once did.

Diplomatic protest in Budapest was proving ineffectual, and in Washington the State Department, goaded by the demands of the *Sentinel,* editorially as well as by political pressure, was twisting and squirming and evading, using diplomatic double talk, and counterattacking by placing the entire responsibility for Race's predicament on the shoulders of Nick.

Nick had talked on the overseas telephone with the home office and convinced them that Race had been assigned to Vienna under strict orders to keep out of trouble and had deliberately disobeyed them, but he knew that the people in Chicago were smarting under editorial attacks by several of the New Deal papers that chose to regard Jimmy's escapade as a deliberate attempt to embarrass the Administration. Despite his superior's knowledge to the contrary, they were inclined to hold Nick responsible, and he knew they were right in doing so. For he was the sole editor in charge. He had assigned Race to Vienna and he knew that emotion had been present to outweigh judgment in making the assignment.

The G2 report from Vienna did nothing to improve Nick's peace of mind. However Jimmy had managed to get himself into Hungary, he had acted with incredible folly and haste in failing to contact the Army, which through its intelligence channels and connections with refugee organizations remained in touch with what was practically a two-way traffic stream between Budapest and Vienna in a kind of deadly game played with electrified barbed wire, land mines, and border guards with machine guns.

But Jimmy had apparently sought out the worst rascals in Vienna to make contact with—Austro-Hungarian gangsters, kidnapers, black-marketeers, all of them more or less in the pay of the NKVD, the Russian secret police. Working in the manner of a Chicago police reporter who has nothing to fear from reportorial association with the underworld, he had left himself wide open for betrayal.

Under the strain, Nick's temper flared up easily this day, and he forgot himself so far as to quarrel with Hugh Willicomb, the Ambassador at Large, with whom he had an angry interview in the Ambassador's suite at the Crillon next to the American Embassy. It was a week after Jimmy's arrest, and the State Department had been unable to elicit so much as a reply to their queries about the fate of Race, much less get a representative in to see him.

The interview had begun badly for Nick when he realized that in his own cold, intellectual, and dispassionate manner Willicomb was almost as angry at him, and his paper, as Nick felt himself to be at the representatives of his government. There is nothing quite so disconcerting to one who is attacking full of righteous indignation to find that he is being counterattacked with equal indignation and as righteous, and Nick spent the first half hour with Willicomb convincing him that neither he nor the paper had deliberately sent Race into Budapest as a journalistic stunt.

Thereupon the diplomat moved Nick into another untenable position by asking, "Is it, then, your suggestion that some hundred and fifty millions of Americans and all of Europe be plunged into a new and immediate war because of the immaturity and total irresponsibility of one fool?"

Nick said, "I am only suggesting that we take off the

kid gloves and act like a people with guts. Pick up a Hungarian of some importance in the States and hang *him!*"

"Would that bring your man Race back to life after he had been executed? Or the next American they would seize and kill in reprisal?"

Nick's irritation was rising, for he felt that, but for circumstances, he would be arguing on the side of Willicomb, and to a man who prides himself upon being dispassionate nothing is so disturbing as to encounter the quality in another. He said, "Every Hungarian official or diplomat in the States is nothing but a spy or pay-off for the Cominform. Seize one of sufficient importance, turn up the F.B.I. evidence on him, and put pressure on the Hungarian Government to release Race in exchange."

A look of distaste passed momentarily over the thin lips of the American Ambassador. He remarked, "Surely, Mr. Strang, you realize as well as I that we are not the kind of people who 'seize.' "

"And how long do we keep up that pretense?" Nick replied bitterly. "Diplomats and the great shrine of the crease in the striped trousers! The other side doesn't give a damn what kind of a fight they get into. They wear the baggy pants, and a diplomatic roughhouse doesn't do them any harm. They would dare anything to help one of their own, but your kind won't risk the crease in his pants."

Willicomb was able to muster a frosty smile. He said, "This was not exactly your attitude during our discussion of the Frobisher case, Mr. Strang."

"There is this difference besides the fact that Race is an employee of our company and I am responsible for him. I don't know what Frobisher was mixed up in, or who he was, or anything of his background, but I do know that Jim Race is no more a spy than I am."

Willicomb said, "Do you know how and under what

circumstances he was arrested? We do." He selected several reports from a briefcase on the table, glanced through them, and said, "He thought he had bribed the Hungarian captain of a coal barge bringing a load of coal from Germany to Budapest to take him aboard and conceal him. He had been under NKVD surveillance from the very beginning of the negotiations with a notorious Central European agent, a former Nazi. Apparently when the barge put off from Vienna there were two members of the Hungarian secret police on board. Race was arrested immediately when he disembarked in Budapest. He had, of course, no visa or proper credentials of any kind."

"That doesn't prove him a spy. It only proves him an ass," Nick said, and again swallowed the bitter self-reproach that he had put Jimmy in the position to play such a fool's trick.

Almost as though he had read Nick's mind at that point, Willicomb said, "I understand your position and it is most unfortunate. Washington has taken a most serious view of this. The Cominform has been looking to inflict a really damaging blow to our prestige in Western Europe. If Race hadn't existed with his military and civilian background, they would have had to invent him. As it is, we have made it easy for them, and you can be sure that they will not fail to exploit both Race and the weakness of our position."

Nick felt utterly defeated. To his surprise, Willicomb's frosty expression changed to something more human and warm as he continued.

"I wish to say that in a sense there is a burden of guilt upon all of us, Mr. Strang. As you very well know, the force of diplomatic protest is the weight and extent of the power behind it. When that power is weakened or diffused by cupidity, stupidity, political indolence, or national disunity the diplomacy that represents it then begins to take on the aspect of the faintly ridiculous. If we protect ourselves now it is only because the American people have seen fit to withdraw the physical protection that once we and every other American citizen abroad was afforded. Search for the blame for this weakening and diffusion might in the end lead us into every American home, for the American people are politically responsible for the actions of their government. If for whatever reason they force or have forced their government to withdraw a powerful and victorious Army from the European continent leaving the vacuum to be filled by a greedy and imperialistic power, they must be prepared to accept the responsibility for the consequences of this act."

His face congealed again as he concluded. "Rest assured that with regard to Race, we will make every possible representation."

12

LODGINGS FOR A VISITOR

Andrassy Prison, at the center of Andrássy Street in Budapest, is a great square, gray, malodorous pile with barred windows and iron doors leading to the courtyard guarded by members of the People's Police equipped with Tommy guns. Inside it, a warren of departments, offices, interrogation rooms, cells and dungeons. It stank of damp, of bureaucrats, disinfectant, human excrement, human suffering, human sweat, and human cruelty.

Since his arrest Jimmy Race had occupied a single cell, which, paced off by himself, yielded about nine feet square. Built into one side was a wooden bunk with some dirty straw scattered on it. There was no other piece of furniture. There was no sanitary facility of any kind. Once a day, at six o'clock in the morning, a guard came with a shovel, a broom, and a pail of water and ordered Jimmy to clean up his cell. Twice a day he was fed. In the morning it was a weak bean soup with a piece of black bread, in the evening a pan with a few scraps of meat, dumplings, and vegetables. It was unappetizing, but it was subsistence.

Jimmy had been offered no personal physical harm or indignity beyond being forced to live in filth and unable to wash himself except for brief interludes when he was removed from his cell. His passport, his money, wallet, rings, cuff links, shoelaces, and necktie had been removed from him; otherwise he wore the clothes in which he had been arrested.

There was a small window in the steel door of his cell through which an eye inspected him at irregular intervals. Jimmy had tried timing them until it was obvious that the inspections were deliberately uneven. There might be twelve in an hour, or three, or twenty-three.

Four times during the week, or at least what Jimmy judged to be a week, also at irregular intervals, he was summoned from his cell by guards and marched to an office where there were other prisoners like himself seated on a bench, guarded by men with automatic weapons. There was a rail in the room behind which were several desks at which sat uniformed officials and clerks.

They spoke only Hungarian. During the entire time Jimmy never heard a word of English spoken. Occasionally an official would summon one of the other prisoners from behind the railing to some kind of interrogation or filling out of papers at the desk, but the summons never came for Jimmy. Several times an official entered with a large sheaf of papers and conferred with one of the men about the desk, obviously about Jimmy, for they often looked and nodded their heads in his direction, but at the conclusion the visiting official would pick up his papers and go out. One day he waited there five hours and another seven. But during those times he was allowed to go to the toilet and even snatch a brief wash at a basin with running water.

The third time the suspense, the frustration, and the waiting suddenly became unbearable, and he got up and shouted at the official behind the desk, "Why the devil don't you take me? How the hell long am I supposed to wait around here?"

The official merely looked up at him with the air of a man who does not understand a word that is being spoken, as was probably the case. The guards motioned him angrily back to his seat on the bench, and he went. He tried it again on one of the police officers who arrived with a new sheaf of papers, and received the same treatment. When the two guards came forward a few steps and motioned him back to his seat he decided to risk defying them to see what would happen.

He said, "Nuts! I'm staying right here until somebody sees me," and planted himself. The official at the desk said something to the guards in Hungarian, and they returned to their post at the door without any further gestures in his direction. To dive past them through the door would be suicide. He had no idea of what level of the prison he was on. Before he got very far in that warren, he would unquestionably be shot down.

The guards simply left him there. Nobody paid the slightest attention to him. First he began to feel foolish standing there with traffic going on about him as though he did not exist. Then a sudden wave of truculence arose in his throat that made him want to rage, to tear down the rail, seize the officials by the scruffs of their necks and upset them, hurl inkwells, and bellow at the top of his lungs.

He caught himself just in time. *Whoa, kid. Don't be a sap for them. This is treatment A. It's supposed to make you want to blow your top. That's what they want to see.*

Don't fall for it. He managed the difficult steps back to the bench and sat down again.

He was elated over his triumph over himself and them. He felt strong as a bull and mentally as well as physically alert and capable. This was kid stuff, and he could wait as long as they. Eventually someone would have to talk to him, and in English.

And yet each time a door opened and an official entered he could not, to save his life, keep from looking over expectantly as did the other prisoners. Being talked about constantly in a foreign language he could not begin to understand, whose words contained not a single familiar root or clue, also began to work on his nerves again. There was no way of stopping his ears to keep it out.

The waiting when they returned him to his cell and left him to himself was worse, for he could not keep his phantasies from working.

He was as yet far from alerted to his real peril, and most of his thoughts were of Nick and Suzy back in Paris. By now they must both know what a fine sap he, the great reporter, had been to walk into a secret police trap without taking so much as a single safeguard in case something went wrong with his scheme.

The Hungarians would surely have issued news of his arrest. He could see the expression of contempt on Nick's face, and it murdered him. Suzy would at least know why he had done it, and admire him for his guts. He wondered how long it would be until Nick, or the U.S., or somebody started the machinery to get him out. Sooner or later he would be able to get to tell someone his story. They would probably try to scare the hell out of him first, but eventually they would have to turn him loose since he had committed no serious crime. They would usher him across the border and that would be that. He wondered whether he would have the guts to go back to Paris and face them all.

Only occasionally the thought popped into his mind—what if nobody ever came for him? What if they just let him stay there and rot until he got sick and died, or went off his nut and banged his head against the stone wall?

He did not at any time think of himself as another Frobisher, an innocent man about to be railroaded and forced to a confession, he did not think of the incongruity in his being about to accomplish the task to which he had set himself, to find out how the Reds achieved the confession of all whom they arrested and tried. He was Jimmy Race the unconquerable, who had got himself into something of a jam through his overeagerness, but who could eventually get out of it as soon as he came in contact with somebody who could understand English. He had been in jams before and had never had the slightest doubt of his ability to extricate himself.

He even made excuses for the State Department. If they had failed in the case of Frobisher, they would not in his, for he was different. He was Jimmy Race. Perhaps there had been some reason why they had not been able to get Frobisher out. Besides which there was always the power of the newspaper to bring pressure.

It was eight days after his arrest, as nearly as he could judge, when two guards came for Jimmy and marched him off, this time in a different direction from before. They took him into a dingy office where at a large desk littered with papers sat a man with a close-cropped bullet head and bad teeth. His shirt was soiled and his tie splotched, his fingernails grimy. He was writing when Jimmy was brought in, and did not look up for several minutes, leaving him standing there. The two guards ranged themselves on either side of the door.

When he finally looked up, Jimmy noted that his eyes were exceptionally brilliant and alert, and when he spoke, his English was excellent. He said, "Oh, yes. You are Mr. Race, the American spy who was arrested a week or so ago. I am sorry we have been unable to get around to your case until now. Please sit down," and he indicated the chair on the opposite side of the desk.

"Look here," said Jimmy Race, and bent his heavy, compelling gaze upon the smaller man while force and the will to make him comprehend emanated from him. "Let's get this straight right from the start. I'm no spy. I'm a reporter for an American newspaper. I came in here to do a job for my paper. Maybe I shouldn't have used the methods I did to get in, but in my country when you go after a story you've got to be ready to take a few chances. I'll talk to you on that basis, but cut out the spy stuff."

The man with the bullet head nodded and smiled, showing his sick gums with their decayed teeth. "Naturally you are not yet ready to admit that you are a spy; nevertheless we know you are, Mr. Race. But we will have discussions about this later." He consulted a paper and said, "I am sorry about your accommodations, but for the moment that is the best we can do. At the present we are badly overcrowded."

Jimmy thought, *He is talking exactly like a hotel keeper.*

"It is really astonishing the number of conspiracies against the People's Republic that are uncovered," the man continued, "and the kind of people that take part in them, when we are doing so much for them. That is why we are so busy here. Still, I assure you there are much worse places in Andrássy Prison than your present quarters. Let us hope you will not have occasion to visit them."

Jimmy was struck by something else, and it gave him a queer feeling of unreality. The little man was absolutely and utterly sincere in what he was saying—as sincere and honest as Jimmy. He believed it. He believed that Race was a spy and that every miserable victim dragged out of his home and into the Andrássy was plotting against the Red Government. Another thing that astonished Jimmy was his mildness and the politeness of his address. He was not being treated as an enemy, but rather as a visitor with whom the little man had some business to discuss.

The official now searched through the disorder of papers on his desk, found what he was looking for, said, "I have here a letter from your Ambassador," and handed it across to Jimmy.

He took it eagerly, too eagerly, but he could not control it at that moment, it was so unexpected, and so welcome. It was real. Written on official Embassy stationery, it took cognizance of the arrest of an American national, James Race, who was being held by the Hungarian Government on a charge of espionage and attempted sabotage and requested recognition of the right to have him seen and interviewed by a representative of the Embassy. It was couched in the usual heavy and circumlocutory diplomatic phrases, bowings and scrapings.

Nevertheless, it was there, concrete evidence that his country was aware of his predicament and had initiated action and had got results in so far as it had reached the desk of the prison official assigned to his case. That this was but the beginning of his interrogation and that the man might be but a very minor link in the prison hierarchy did not strike Jimmy at the moment. It felt good just to finger the paper with the seal of the United States of America.

The official was regarding him placidly and in a not unfriendly manner. He now asked, "Would you like to write a letter to your Ambassador, Mr. Race?"

Jimmy said, "You're damned right I would."

"Very well. You may do so." He pushed a tablet of blue-lined writing-paper over to Jimmy and handed him a pen.

Jimmy wrote avidly and with a sense of relief. He told honestly of the circumstances of his arrest, shouldered the blame for his action, and asked for representation. He indicated that his treatment in the prison had not been too bad, all things considered, but that he thought he had had enough in view of his obvious innocence of the offense and that the Embassy could afford to take a strong line with the Hungarian Government, as his paper, the *Chicago Sentinel,* would back him up since, after all, he had done no more than any American reporter would in search of a story.

When he had finished he handed the three sheets he had covered to the official, who accepted them gravely and said, "I may read this?"

Jimmy grinned. "You will anyway."

The official smiled and began to read. Several times during the course of the letter he nodded his head as though in agreement with the contents. When he had come to the end, he looked up again and said affably, "Very good, Mr. Race, though, of course, it is all a lot of lies." And thereupon, still in the most pleasant manner, he tore the letter in two, then in four, and again into eight and sixteen until his stubby fingers could tear no more.

Choler reddened Jimmy's neck and rasped his voice. He leaned forward, causing the two guards at the door to stir, and bellowed, "What the hell is the idea of that? You told me I could write the letter."

The man was contemplating him blandly, and his eyes were alert and peaceable. He reached over and took next the letter from the American Ambassador and with the same calm and methodical movement tore it likewise in two and four and, like Jimmy's missive, reduced it to paper snow. When he had finished, he took the collected bits and let them drift like carnival confetti through his fingers into the wastebasket.

He said gently, "Let us call it a little object lesson, Mr. Race, the first of a great many to which I am afraid you will be exposed if you continue to compound the error of your temerity in entering Hungary with stubbornness in refusing to reveal the truth about your mission. This will remind you, just in case you did not already know it, that the Government of the United States does not reach into Andrássy Prison, and never will. Good day, Mr. Race."

He spoke sharply in Hungarian. The two guards stepped forward.

Felix Victor came into the editorial room and everyone stopped working and looked up expectantly. He had been assigned to the American Embassy on the Race case to report on any developments. Mark Mosher said, "Did you see Willicomb?"

Victor shook his dark, shaggy head. "No. He's in Lyon, making a speech. But his secretary talked on the phone with Budapest. The Ambassador sent a third note, but the Hungarians haven't paid any attention to any of them. He hasn't been able to see anyone of any importance, either. Same old run-around."

Janet came from her file cabinets and stood by Thyra Addison's desk where she could hear. She had kept her troubles to herself, but was thin, pale, and tired from the strain and had lost weight. In the ten days since the announcement of Jimmy Race's arrest she had never ceased blaming herself for his plight.

Cass McGuire said, "What do we do next, whistle up a B-36 and drop That Thing?"

Art Glass looked up from his typewriter and grunted, "Boy, are you funny."

Cass bristled. "Oh, yeah? Are you anxious to climb back into your soldier suit on account of a windbag like Race?"

Joe Short contributed, "It does seem like he kind of stuck his neck out, doesn't it?"

Glass ripped out the story he had been writing, glanced at it, and passed it over to Short. "Three hundred on forthcoming *Figaro* riot," he said in one tone of voice, pertaining to office matters, and then continued in another, the personal and argumentative. "Oh, I don't know. If he'd got away with it, he'd have been a hero. At least he had the initiative and the guts to take a chance."

Mark Mosher, as the youthful executive, chose to enter the office bull session from the editor's point of view. He said, "Sure, the guy had a right to do what he wanted with his own neck, but in the end it's Nick who's going to have to take the rap for this."

Nate Krine had been reading copy with his practiced eyes, but his ears had been following the conversation. "I can't see that," he said. "How the hell can they hold an editor responsible if one of his men turns out to be a triple-plated boob, especially since they wished Race on him from Chicago and ordered Nick to train him?"

Mark Mosher snorted. "Oh, can't they? That's what you guys think. Wait until you do a trick on a desk. They hold you responsible for everything. That's why Nick's the boss. It's part of his job to know men. He should have smelled out the kind of a guy Jimmy was and kept him away from trouble. I could have told him."

Felix Victor said amiably, "Well, then, why didn't you? He might have listened to you. I knew the guy wanted to get his tail in the sling first crack out of the box, but a reporter's supposed to keep his bazoo zipped. What do you suppose they'll do to Nick for this?"

Ferdie Hoffman, who'd had long experience on newspapers on both sides of the water, came out from behind a French racing paper and said, "Well, right now when nobody knows much what will happen, the home office is sending him be-brave-we-are-all-behind-you messages on the leased wire, but as soon as it is decided one way or the other they will yank him back to Chicago and give him a nice job as automobile editor for the Sunday supplement, or toss him right out on his royal ear for getting the paper into a bad spot. They don't never forgive nobody nuthin', especially when they think they've been let down. You might say that unless Nick manages to pass a miracle somehow and spring James out of that Hungarian cooler, he's a cooked goose liver."

Art Glass said savagely, "Oh, to hell with Nick. He's not sitting in a stinking jail behind the iron curtain. What do you suppose is going to happen to Jim?"

The stage had now been set for Mitchell Connell, who liked to move in when the time was ripe and hold the floor with his flair for the dramatic and his prestige, which could always command the attention of the city room and give him an audience.

"Well," he said, using a copy spindle to emphasize his points, "for one thing we're going to find out just how tough the guy is, by the length of time it takes them to soften him up to the point where it's safe for them to announce his trial. He wanted to know what it was they did to innocent guys that made them get up and confess their heads off. He's finding out right now. You can bet all the tea in China they've got him on the griddle right this minute. Let's see, they've had him about ten days now. He'll probably go a couple more weeks because he's tough and full of fight, though I dunno. Sometimes it's those big burly guys who crack easiest.

"Okay," he continued, "so when they announce the date of his trial, we'll know they've busted him and that he ain't a man any more. Then they'll walk him into a court fresh as a daisy, without a shiner or a mark on him, where he'll proceed to confess his head off—with music, if they ask for it. And after that, just to show the Western democracies what they think of the power of Uncle Sam to protect them, they'll march him out into the yard a couple of mornings later and up onto a platform where they'll drop a noose over his head and—"

Janet's piercing scream shocked them all into silence. "Stop it! For God's sake, stop it!" She put her two hands up to the sides of her head to cover her ears and ran from the room, banging into the desk and the coatrack as she did so.

Mitchell Connell said, "What the deuce has got into the mouse?"

Cass McGuire undertook to enlighten him. "Brother, you're hot at uniting a split infinitive, or killing the point of a paragraph, but you wouldn't recognize a human emotion if it came up and bit you in the ankle. The poor kid's been blind crazy about Jimmy Race from the first day he walked into the office."

13

INVENTION OF A CRIMINAL AND A CRIME

AT A QUARTER TO TWO in the morning Nick and Suzy sat at a table at Fouquet's, on the Champs-Elysées, and sipped *eau minérale* while Nick smoked nervously. They had been dining at Coq Hardi with the Gregorys, an American businessman and his wife who had just come out of Budapest. Suzy was wearing a wide moiré skirt by Dior with a halter bodice of white piqué and looked like a page out of *Vogue*.

The businessman had turned out to be one who had apparently used neither his eyes nor his ears in Budapest and had little in the way of help to offer in the matter of analyzing Jimmy Race's predicament. His wife had chattered endlessly about the poor accommodations and the cost of living in Budapest, and the evening had been a bore and a strain.

When they had finally got rid of the pair, neither Nick nor Suzy felt they wanted to go home yet and dropped in at Fouquet's to cool off and find themselves again.

But of late it had been more and more difficult for them to get back to a basis of the kind of free and quick-witted and understanding exchanges between them that had cleared up so many difficulties and problems in the past. Nick's phantasy that Suzy was deeply concerned with Jim Race's arrest and imprisonment for personal reasons was becoming more and more difficult to dislodge. Suzy on her part felt limited in the amount of sympathy she felt she could extend to her husband without diminishing his position and his self-esteem.

She had never felt quite so helpless or at a loss. She knew that her husband was being badgered from all sides and that if Jimmy were executed it would mean the end of his career. But she had also a severe and balanced sense that it would also mean the end of Jimmy, the Jimmy who was one of their own, this man they had all known with his vitality, courage, enthusiasm, and talent who would be led out and butchered like an animal. The life, gaiety, energy, and ambition would be choked out of him, after which the useless clay would be dumped into a lime pit or a common ditch, and that would be an end to something that for all its faults and weaknesses was yet admirable in its strength and swashbuckling desire to succeed and cut a figure in the world, whether with a story or a woman.

Because she had once been a part of an organization that had operated clandestinely and performed miracles in the face of a determined and deadly opposition Suzy yearned for action even though her intelligence told her that there was nothing that could be done under the circumstances and that the boy was cut off from them as though he was being held a prisoner on the moon. And she also knew that the efforts that were being made to free him were as useful and valid as dogs baying at that selfsame luminary.

Nevertheless, she emerged with a sigh from the thoughts into which she had fallen deep-sunk, and said, "I get so discouraged, after I spend an evening with a man like Gregory. He has been over here for years and learned nothing. If Jimmy's life were to depend on men like that—Nick, it's true, isn't it? The government will let them hang him. Nick, what will we do?"

He looked at her, and his eyes were clouded. He felt tired, discouraged, and emotionally unstable. Was this the Suzy who had been devoted to him ever since he had come back to Paris with Leclerc's liberating armored forces that August in 1944 and had found her guarding the keys to the Paris *Sentinel* building as well as all the equipment she had managed to conceal from the Germans, and they had fallen in love on the spot? Or was this a woman pleading for her lover?

He said gloomily, "You know it as well as I do. The government has written him off. It's my mess, not theirs. Washington is prepared to take the further damage to prestige. They'll send notes and protest to the end, but Willicomb as much as told me they wouldn't lift a finger to do more. If anything is to be done, it's up to me. And I haven't got an army."

Suzy hesitated for a moment and then decided to speak about it. She said, "Nick—some of the men were talking among themselves this afternoon and one of them told me about it. Joe Short, Mark Mosher, the Glass boy, and that tall young man on the copy desk, and Sam in the circulation department. They were all in the war together. They were talking about having a lot of friends in the Army stationed in Salzburg and Vienna both, some of them in G2. They were saying that if nobody else was going to do anything, they would be willing to try to get a group together, cross over into Hungary, and make an attempt to break Jimmy out. They were saying that if a man like Skorzeny could spring Mussolini out from under the noses of the Allies, they would be willing to make the attempt. I thought—"

"My God, what *did* you think?" In a sudden and unreasoning outburst of temper Nick pounded the table so hard that a Perrier water bottle fell over onto the floor, where it bounded about like a ninepin. "What on earth could you think? Are you serious, Suzy? Am I surrounded by nothing but boy scouts and adolescents who want to play cops-and-robbers? Haven't we got enough trouble? This isn't Steve Canyon, Terry-and-the-Pirates kid stuff, out of the comic strips. This is serious."

Oddly, Suzy did not yield ground to Nick this time on his attack. She only said gravely, "Don't I know? But at least they were willing to try, and you shouldn't be angry at them for that."

Nick felt the justice of her reply. But he could not escape or immediately throw off the wave of bitterness that followed. There they were again, the two worlds, the world of the young and adventurous that he had left behind him, inhabited by young and crazy kids who would go off on a deal half-cocked like the bunch that tried to kidnap the Kaiser after the First World War, and his own, where men considered the pros and cons of a problem and gravely and dignifiedly accepted defeat where their intelligence showed them they were outnumbered, outgunned, outmaneuvered in advance, the sphere in which the temperature of boiling blood was reduced by the cooling showers of exacting and frosty intellect.

Nick turned and caught sight of himself in one of the many mirrors the Fouquets had installed so that entering and departing feminine guests might admire themselves. He saw nothing that he found admirable. He looked well scrubbed, neat, middle-aged, and ineffectual in his dinner jacket, neither more capable in this crisis nor more dramatic in appearance than the headwaiter in the same uniform. He thought that if he should be called upon to fight someone, he would make a very bad job of it and that if he should have to run or give pursuit to a person or a cab or a bus his breath would give out before he had covered fifty yards.

His mind recoiled angrily from this masochistic indictment and he told himself that man had managed to use his mentality to excuse all of these deficiencies, that you did not have to be twenty-one to press the trigger on a chopper, and that if you really meant to set out after something that was trying to get away, there were vehicles for the purpose, and that there was nothing, no problem or situation, that could not be solved by an application of intellect which could be set in motion sitting behind a desk.

The bitter taste returned to Nick's mouth. He was building pretty dream castles of mental heroism to reawake Suzy's admiration and conceal the fact that he was an ageing failure who had got a fellow American, himself, his paper, and everyone connected with him into one thundering bad mess.

And besides he caught a glimpse of Suzy in the mirror sitting beside him. Black-white-black, the dark skirt, the white bodice, dark eyes and hair surmounting, and between them the rose-and-white flesh of youth, the fine skin hardly able to contain the vigor and energy that burned within. Five years ago and she would have been a part of an attempt just as adventurous and dangerous as that which those crazy kids had proposed.

What was there, then, to appeal to her in a pale fellow whose beginning second chin was just commencing to dewlap his black tie, whose mind could only dryly appraise the realities of life, as against the big, burly, pink-

and-gold swashbuckler who like a blind Bayard had blundered his way into peril because of his convictions about his profession—or the other youngsters, all of them willing to lay their lives on the line to take a chance on going in and getting their guy out of the jam. It was all beautiful, enthralling, and utterly useless, but women loved it. Yes, and men, too. And therein probably lay his greatest failure, he told himself. There was no poetry in the contemplation of both sides of the question, or the slow, tedious spinning of the cerebral web. It was almost as though Nick were bidding farewell to Suzy and did not even have the energy left to cry.

But aloud he said, "I know. I'm sorry I yelled. It was good of them to offer it, but it isn't a very realistic solution. I guess my nerves are shot." He lit another cigarette and continued. "I'm wide awake. I can't bear to think of going home, getting into bed, and putting out the light. Let's go on back to the paper for a little."

They left the car parked in front of Fouquet's and entered the deserted rue Marbeuf. The electric sign of the Jockey Bar opposite was still blazing, but the *Sentinel's* display was dark and inside it would be as asleep and deserted.

They climbed to the second floor and Nick let them into their offices with his key and threw the light switches. They shed their wraps. Several copies of the final edition of the Paris Edition were neatly stacked on Nick's desk. From force of habit each took one and began to read it mechanically. Suzy, sitting as neat and elegant as a mannequin at the long glass-topped table, studied her editorial page. Nick, his short-cut, graying hair—curled close to his skull in the manner affected by college men—just showing over the top of his paper, checked over page one. At first there seemed to be no sound but their breathing and the rustling of the newsprint in their fingers. But before long they were both aware of another singular sound that seemed to be present in the room.

Suzy first looked up from her scanning of her page and listened, and even while she was doing so and cocking her ear, Nick put down his paper, looked over inquiringly at her, and asked, "What is it?"

Suzy said, "It sounds like someone crying, but I don't understand–" Then her sensitive ear located it, and she said, "Oh–from there."

They both looked simultaneously at the ventilator marked in the form of a small grating just beneath the ceiling. The sounds that emerged from it were unmistakably of someone sobbing. Nick asked, "Where does it lead to?"

Suzy replied, "The editorial room. There's someone in there."

Nick was out of his chair and leading the way with Suzy following. They could hear the sound now as they approached the door opening into the editorial room, and it was a woman's weeping.

It was pitch-dark inside the room, and Nick flipped the nearest switch that illuminated the far end of the L where the file cabinets were located. It furnished sufficient light to reveal the small, dark, hopelessly disheveled and miserable figure of Janet Goodpenny slumped down with her head on her arms at the desk that once belonged to Jimmy Race.

Nick flipped another light on, and Janet looked up in alarm. She had not heard them come in. Her face and eyes were swollen from crying. Her lips were thickened, her hair an unkempt and tangled mass, her cheeks streaked. She looked like nothing human.

Nick asked, "Janet, what on earth is the matter? What are you doing here by yourself at this hour? Why aren't you home?"

But Suzy went to her at once, bent down, and put her

arms about her, called her *"pauvre petite."*

The touch seemed to bring back Janet's self-possession. She mopped her face, blew her nose, and said, "I'm sorry. I didn't mean to make an exhibition of myself. It was no use trying to go to sleep, so I came here thinking I could do some work. When I saw his desk and remembered how he looked when he was working at it, so big, so invincibly big—"

"Uhuh!" Nick said, and wondered whether the same picture that was in his mind had crossed hers—this big man full of vitality and energy kicking and jerking his life away at the end of a rope.

"And then it all came back to me how it was my fault. He made me promise not to say anything to anyone, and I was silly and childish and stupid and believed him when I knew in my heart all the time that he was going to do something foolish and dangerous."

Nick went to her and put his hand on her shoulder gently. He said, "Yes, I know. None of us have been too good at this business."

She looked up at him quickly, surprised that he, too, should be shouldering some of the blame, not knowing how he accused himself, how filled he was with guilt on his own account for the motives that had impelled him to let Jimmy go to Vienna.

She seemed to take comfort from the presence of them both and looked from Nick to Suzy and again to Nick with an appealing kind of smile. The sturdy, powerful figure of Nick, his broad brow, intelligent eyes, and truculent chin, seemed to imbue her with hope. She said to him in a half-whisper, "Please, Mr. Strang, don't let it happen. You could get him out."

Nick looked at her uncertainly and asked, "What makes you think I could?"

She answered him with the fierce fervor of the young and loyal who believe. "You can do anything."

To this Suzy added her soft, low voice. "You can, Nick. Please try."

He stared at them both, startled because of their appalling conviction that there was something he could do and their joining of woman forces to make him share this conviction. He sought for a hint of mockery in it, but there was none. In Janet's plea there was nothing but anguish and despair. In Suzy's? Was there anything more than a simple declaration of faith and trust in his powers? Again the familiar, dizzying confusions arose in him. Were these two women banded together, drawn by a mutual grief and understanding?

Nick turned away from them, thrust his hands deep into his pockets, and commenced to bang about the editorial room in odd and half-exasperated jerks of movement that brought him up against the bulletin board, which he studied, the copy desk with its residue of unused late material on the spike, the long rows of steel file cabinets at the library end of the room, and the stacks of files of French and other Continental papers as well as the heaped-up back copies of the Paris Edition of the *Sentinel.*

But inside himself he felt suddenly a strange sense of peace and power that belied his movements, as though at any time he chose he could do what they had asked. It was there, so close to the surface, the idea that had been nagging at him for days. He had only to remove the last layers of irritation and suspicion that kept him from thinking clearly and that he knew had kept him from doing so for so long. He studied the labels of the drawers of the file cabinets, *A–Asta, Asto–Bere, Beri–Budo,* for a moment and then turned around to look at Janet and Suzy. They were sitting there exactly as he had left them, watching him with a kind of fascinated intentness, and in the poise of Suzy's head and the expression of her eyes he thought he saw a kind of a cheer for him, a belief in his powers.

He had an idea now and held fast to it. For one sickening moment as he contemplated it the whole thing appeared to him such a shriveled and forlorn seedling of hope which in all probability would never grow that he was tempted to abandon it before ever beginning. But in the next he knew that he had to hold on and develop it. It must be nurtured with all the fierce vitality he suddenly felt alive in himself and made to live beyond all probability of failure.

Nick cried harshly, "Janet! All right, now. Come over here and get busy. I need your help. Get me the obits on Fogos, Mezy, Borsa, Ordy, Szenes, and Halasz," naming the top six in the Hungarian Cabinet. "I want the current files on them, too, and all cross files, but you can get me those later."

His sharpness had the effect of pulling Janet out of her semihysteria. She got up and went to the files, made a list of names for which Nick had asked, and began to pull out drawers.

Suzy, too, came over. Her eyes were shining, and all her fine nerves and intelligence seemed to be centered in her expression. She had tuned herself to him and was as receptive as an antenna to whatever might come from him.

She said, "Yes, Nick?" It was partly a question and yet she already more than half understood him and what he might be after.

He said, "Blackmail, of course. We've got to develop pressure of some kind. It's all you can count on today on this sick Continent. Who's got something on whom, and on whom can the screws be turned? It's all government by who peeked over the transom in Central Europe, anyway. Only we haven't got anything as yet."

He took the envelopes containing the obituary biographies of the men called for and was pleased by their thickness. One thing Nick had insisted upon when he had taken over the paper, and that was the building up of the library at considerable expense. He had ordered not only that every item from the Paris Edition be properly filed but that French papers be read and clipped as well as the weeklies and he had even bought up the files and library of a Paris paper that had gone out of business. Nick was of that breed of editors who know that a solid foundation of research and reference material is the backbone and spinal column of any good newspaper and particularly one published in a foreign country where frequently one or two lines of flash news or press copy must be expanded into a four- or five-hundred-word story.

Nick gave half the envelopes to Suzy, and they sat down on the benches that ran alongside the long library table. He said, "You understand what I mean. We're just beginning. It's impossible that one of those six hasn't been a crook of some kind or hasn't done something that he has to keep hidden. It ought to show up in their biographies. Our first job is to pick the candidate."

Janet was standing there, her wet, swollen eyes fixed on him. Nick barked at her. "Go make us some coffee. Make some for yourself, too. It might turn out to be a long night. Coffee's in the cupboard in my office. You know where the electric stove is. Jump, sister." He was not meaning to be unkind, but he thought it best to keep her occupied.

He and Suzy began to comb through the biographies, lifting out items that seemed significant and making notes of them.

Suzy said, "Borsa was arrested once and sentenced for a bank shortage of two million pengös."

Nick threw back at her, "In the Communist Party in Hungary that would be a virtue. Look, it isn't what they got caught at. We're looking for what they didn't get grabbed for. I mean, as an example, here's this fellow Szenes, the agriculture man whose job it is to collectivize the farms. He was farm manager for the Esterházys back in 1928. If one could find out just how easy he's going on the old Esterházy crowd— But the guy's too small a potato for us."

Suzy remarked, "Halasz taught philosophy at Harvard for a year on an exchange professorship."

Nick grunted and said, "Only useful for blackmail if he tries to get into the Yale Club." Then he picked up another biographical typescript with renewed interest, glanced over it quickly, and came back to the beginning again, saying, "Oh, oh—"

Suzy dropped hers and said, "Nick—you've got something?" Janet came in with the coffee.

Excitement began to creep into Nick's voice. He said, "It's Andreas Ordy, the Minister of Affairs, the guy who said he'd hang the next American they caught. A very zealous fellow. But why? You always want to watch those zealous chaps who are out to prove what hundred-percent Commies and Stalin-lovers they are. When they lay it on thick they've usually got a reason. Anyway, the idea makes sense, doesn't it? Listen to the guy's record."

He ticked it off. "Andreas Ordy, son of a peasant in the Balaton region, country lawyer, member first of the Peasant and later the Agrarian Party, and again later still is found representing the Catholic Centrists, and the following year he appears standing for the Social Democrats. He's right in there pitching for whichever party is at the top. Notable Fascist who acted as an assistant prosecuting attorney under the Nazis and ended as a judge of the criminal court. Aha! Quits and joins the Communist underground in 1944 and turns up in Moscow, taking instruction. So he knew what was going to happen *that* far ahead. Subminister of Affairs in Hungary in 1946 to 1948. Then out of the government for a time and returns eventually in 1949 as Minister of Affairs. A man can't wear that many political coats in a lifetime and not have something to hide somewhere along the line. Janet! Hand me the clips on Andreas Ordy. And I want pictures, too. Sometimes you can get more out of a caption than a two-column story. Get me photographs of Renard, Angelotti, and all the other big-shot Communists, and that horse-faced Rumanian babe, Lila Baladru, too. Because when a guy's got something he's sitting on, there's usually somebody knows about it and will sell it if the dollar is big enough."

The space in front of Nick and Suzy began to fill up with envelopes and folders as Janet, working like a machine and with a kind of devoted fervor, plucked them out of the cabinets and whipped them over.

Suzy took a share of them and asked, "What are we looking for, Nick?"

Nick replied, "I don't know exactly yet. I know, but I don't know. I'm almost afraid to look for fear it won't be there. Ordy's record shows that he's spiritually a crook and an opportunist. We've got to find evidence in his past of something he wouldn't like to have turned up. We'll start with a chronology. Where's he been these past years—when? Why? With dates wherever they're available. *Anything* about him, understand? God, I wish Dad were here with that memory of his."

From the doorway, Dad Lapham said, "Somebody asking for me?" It was a quarter to three in the morning.

Nick yelled, "Dad! What are you doing around at this hour? Talk of the devil!"

The managing editor replied with enormous gravity, "Been over to the Big Ben watching the new American reverse stripteaser. She starts from scratch and puts *on* her clothes. Believe me, it's quite a shock when she stands there at the end with every stitch—"

Nick said, "Yes you were. You're around here like

the rest of us because you can't sleep. You're the guy we need."

Dad blinked his little eyes and regarded the piles of clips and pictures on the table. "What are you cooking up?"

Suzy said with a kind of calm authority and finality, "Nick is going to get Jimmy Race away from the Hungarians."

Nick threw her a look, but his heart felt good. He caught Dad up on the doings and concluded, "We want a chronology on Ordy. Everything you can find and everything you can remember. Every scrap. Dredge up every single item you can. You can never tell which one is going to be the one we're looking for."

Suzy kept the chronology, writing in the dates, names, and events connected with Ordy's movements as reflected by the press of Europe. Nick and Dad fingered the clippings, photographs, and files and fed her information. Janet, color coming to her face for the first time as she skipped back and forth bringing more clips, as cross-filings sent her off on new searches, bound volumes of back numbers, files of French papers, and when she had got a little ahead on these, more pots of black coffee.

Every so often Nick looked up and stared across to the sheets of copy paper Suzy had spread out before her. Suddenly the editor pushed the clips and folders aside and pounded his fist on the desk. "Hey!" he shouted. "Suzy —Dad! By Jiminy! Do you begin to see it showing up?"

They stared at him. "There it is," he said, pointing to the next to the last page. "It's as plain as your noses. We've got some item or other on him that tags his whereabouts for almost every month, and what he was up to. But there's a gap between February and August of 1948. Don't you see it? That's damned near six months of no Ordy. Where the hell was he?"

The three of them put their heads together and studied the sheet. Nick was right. Occupying the post of Vice Foreign Secretary of Hungary, he was reported on February 10 of 1948 in Prague, where he made an important speech that was partly carried in the Paris Edition because of its jingoism. And thereafter he vanished from the news completely until August of that year, when he was briefly reported as recovering his health in a sanatorium on the Albanian coast.

"Recovering his health," Nick repeated. "Recovering his health from what? What was it made him sick, and why wasn't there a story that he was taken ill—politically or otherwise? Those 'sick' yarns always get a play. And why in Albania instead of Hungary, where he belongs?

"And look here," Nick continued. "See his trail after that. He's in Italy with Angelotti, and here's a picture of him in France with Renard in which he is referred to as the *former* Vice Foreign Secretary. So he's been fired. Why? Okay. Next Suzy has him in London with Jimmy Smith, visiting the slum section of Liverpool. That takes us into October, when he's in Switzerland. That's the spot you go to when you begin to run out of other countries you're welcome to visit on the Continent. But in December he is back again in Budapest and is appointed Minister of Affairs when the Cabinet is reshuffled and the moderates are thrown out. He's got the job that nobody is too crazy about—hatchet man."

He scratched his head. "But where was he from let's say the middle of February to August?" he repeated.

Dad said, "He might have been anywhere—or sitting in his office in Budapest."

Nick shook his head and said, "Unh-uh. Not that guy. Look at his pattern. He's a bearcat for publicity. If there hasn't been a story about him for five or six weeks, he pulls something and makes one so that he gets back into print, with either a statement or a threat or a treaty designed to stiffen the satellite axis. Go back over his record and it's plain– Wait a minute. Look at the map."

They all turned to the wall map of Europe with Nick. With a crayon he traced the line. Praha–Brno–Budapest–Belgrade–Albania. They saw what his pencil showed. There was no direct way to enter Albania by land from Hungary or the iron-curtain countries, of which Greece was not one, except through Yugoslavia.

Nick said succinctly, "My bet is that the guy was in Yugoslavia. Probably Belgrade. Don't you see?"

Suzy gave a sharp little cry. "Nick! It was in June of 1948 that the Cominform broke with Tito and the heresy hunt was called. That falls within that time. Could that mean that Ordy–"

"He's acting like a guy on the lam, isn't he?" Nick replied. "Or anyway like someone who for some reason or other doesn't want to go home. Look! If he was in Yugoslavia when the blowup came, he doesn't go back to Hungary, but nips over the border into Albania, where it turns out he was 'recuperating' from an illness in a sanatorium. Next we find him in Italy, France, and England, mending his Communist fences, but keeping out of Cominform countries. Remember he's an opportunist. Then he goes to Switzerland, which is political sanctuary where nobody can touch him, and sits. Then in December he gets a come-home-all-is-forgiven message, goes back, and grabs off the job of Minister of Affairs."

Dad said, "What do you think he was up to in Yugoslavia?"

"What they all were doing in those days–cooking up some sort of nationalist deal with Tito behind the back of the Kremlin. At that time the satellites were still laboring under the delusion that they were independent countries. We know Ordy is an ambitious guy. He's been Vice Foreign Secretary for two years. He wants to be number one. Supposing he slips secretly into Belgrade and rigs a deal with Tito that's good for Hungary. It comes off, he is revealed as the author of it, and bingo, he's boss, maybe prime minister. But right in the middle of it Tito is named Communist enemy number one, and Ordy is sitting in the one place he oughtn't to be if he wants to keep his head on his shoulders. If it leaks out where he has been and what he has been cooking up—good-by Ordy. He can't get back into Hungary and explain his absence. But he nips into Albania, buys himself enough Albanians at a seaside sanatorium to establish an alibi, and lets on he's been there all the time recuperating. And he's in a good spot to get across the Adriatic to Italy if the heat really goes on."

Suzy said, "Nick—I think you've got it." Her eyes were shining with excitement. From the corner of the library Janet was regarding him with awe and devotion spread all over her plain features.

Dad was more skeptical. "Okay. It's possible. But supposing it's true, where does that leave us? It doesn't put us any nearer where we can put the screws on Ordy. By the time we can get somebody into Yugoslavia and Albania to run down Ordy's movements—"

Nick was shaking his head. "No—no. To hell with Ordy's movements. We've got those right here. All we'd get would be verification. To hell with Ordy. We've got to find the other guy."

"What other guy?"

"The man who was with him."

14

INVENTION OF A STOOL PIGEON

THEY ALL STARED at him. Nick said, "All right. For the moment I'm making him up. I'm inventing him. But he's got to be, don't you see? There usually is. He's a secretary or a friend or a confidential adviser. A guy like Ordy would never go into a deal like that alone where it would be only his word against Tito's, or the Yugoslavs'. Someone's got to be along to do the paper work, to advise, to witness and to corroborate when Ordy makes the pitch for the foreign minister's spot, if that's what he's after. More than one would be likely to spill the beans, but a trusted secretary would be the most likely to accompany him. Does that sound so far out of line?"

Janet shook her head violently in the negative and Suzy, who was following Nick's reasoning breathlessly, said, "It ought to be like that."

Dad Lapham hated his role of dispenser of cold water, but he also knew that someone had to do it. He said, "There's no secretary or companion mentioned in any of the stories of Ordy's movements. The piece we carried on his visit to Paris would have had the line 'accompanied by his secretary,' if there had been one. I suppose we could still check his hotel."

Nick said, "That's right, Dad. But supposing when the Cominform ruckus broke, the guy went the other way—back to Budapest?"

Suzy drew a deep breath. "Oh—Nick, if it were only so, if he only really exists!"

Nick said stubbornly, "He's got to. We'd all better pray to God that he exists."

Janet Goodpenny said quietly, "Please, God, let it have been that way."

Dad said, "How do we find out?"

Nick blinked at them for a moment without answering. He felt himself in the grip of something that was so ephemeral that it must be held fast with all the force of his own mind and energy and pursued with full play of imagination. It was a thread so tenuous that it could be broken and dispelled forever and with it would go Jimmy Race's life. But he would not let it be broken. He would and must follow it believing that it would lead him where he wanted to go.

He picked up the telephone and spoke to the night operator. "Pierre! This is Nick Strang. Look here. I want you to get through to Belgrade with a call for Vaclav Borvitch, the Minister of Services. Get him out of bed at his home. . . . Yeah, I know. You'll have to fake a high priority. Tell them it's U.S. Embassy or Government or anything you like. At this time of the morning they won't be inclined to ask too many questions, particularly when it's to an important government official. Get it? You've got to get me through. I'm depending on you."

He turned to them, grinning. "I've got a boy friend in Belgrade," he said. "He owes me one. He won't like the idea of paying off, but sometimes when a guy gets on the telephone out of a sound sleep, he talks before he knows what he is talking about."

They were all silent while they waited for the call to come through. To hold onto her nerves, Janet busied herself refiling envelopes with which they were finished, and making more coffee. Dad leafed through files aimlessly while Suzy rechecked and filled out her Ordy chronology. Nick paced the office. In twenty minutes the telephone rang. Janet, who was nearest, got to it first and passed the instrument to Nick, her hands shaking.

Nick said, "Hello, Vaclav? . . . Nick Strang, *Chicago Sentinel,* Paris Edition, calling. Sorry to wake you. Matter of life and death. I want some help. You know the spot we're in with Race, our reporter who is in prison in Budapest. I want some information on Ordy, Andreas Ordy, the present Hungarian Minister of Affairs, at the time he was in Belgrade in June, back in '48. . . . Never mind how I know he was there, I know. And I know why, too. . . . No, I'm not publishing anything, but I've got to know. . . . I see. . . . I understand." He put his hand over the mouthpiece and said, "The bluff worked. Ordy was there." Then he continued with Borvitch. "I know it never came off. It was interrupted. . . . I see. . . . I see. . . . It actually got that far. . . . *He* was committed, but you weren't. Look here, what I really want to know is did Ordy have anyone with him, a secretary, or an assistant. . . . A secretary, eh?"

Suzy drew in her breath sharply. Janet began to cry quietly. Dad was grinning and pounding his fist into the palm of his hand.

"Do you remember, was there any trouble between them at the time, did anything happen that— He did? . . . I see. . . . I get it. . . . With all of Ordy's stuff . . . yes. . . . Do you remember his name? . . . Certainly I understand. Or what he looked like? . . . Naturally not. Yes, we know where Ordy went after that, but not the other man. No . . . no. . . . You have my word. Thanks, Vaclav. We're square now. Next time you're in any kind of a jam where you need me or the paper, we're here. Good-by."

He hung up and looked at them triumphantly. The wispy, tenuous, spider-spun thread had suddenly thickened to a cord. "It's just the sheerest, blindest kind of luck," Nick said. "I was sure there had to be a guy with Ordy who would know about the deal, but I never dreamed that he might have gone rat on him when the showdown came and got away taking the evidence with him. But he did. He blew with everything that was on paper one day when Ordy was away from the suite in the hotel. The secretary must have got a phone call from Budapest that the heat was on. Ordy was scared to death."

"What was the secretary's name? Do they know where he went?"

"Borvitch said he didn't remember his name. He was

an insignificant sort of chap. Secretaries don't get introduced. He got away into Hungary. After Ordy began to holler, the Yugoslavs tried to have Mr. Secretary stopped at the border, but it was too late. He had a diplomatic passport and he had got over. For reasons of their own, the Yugoslavs didn't want anybody on the loose with proof of the deal that had been negotiated any more than Ordy did. Ordy felt safe from that source."

"What happened then?" Suzy asked.

"Just about what we know," Nick said. "Ordy didn't dare go back to Hungary as long as the guy had that valise full of dynamite, or until he knew what his secretary meant to do with it, whether he stole it for a purpose or just got the wind up when he realized their position, tossed everything into a bag, and dusted in a panic."

"But by December–" Suzy began.

"He's good and damned sure–" Nick continued.

"That the secretary's good and damned dead," Dad concluded morosely. "As long as the guy was alive and had the stuff, Ordy wouldn't dare go back in, would he?"

Nick groaned. "Oh, God! I suppose you're right."

They were all deflated and sagging around the table. It smelled of cold coffee, stale cigarettes, and Suzy's perfume. It was close to five in the morning. The cord seemed to have been snapped.

Nick banged the table again with his balled fist. "No! I'm damned if I believe it." He reached up and flipped Janet's chin up from where it had sunk behind her folded arms. "We don't believe it, do we, kid? Come on, let's work this out." He got up and commenced to pace. He felt Suzy's eyes on him again and it gave him courage.

He said, "You say he's dead, but it isn't the actual truth. The truth is that he is either dead or alive, only we don't know which. If the man is dead, Ordy is safe in returning provided the documents are destroyed or haven't been handed over to someone else. Under what conditions would Ordy dare go back to Budapest and into a big job if the guy is still alive? Either they caught him and sweated the stuff out of him, or something happened to make the papers worthless and therefore harmless. Or the guy managed to get out of Budapest and, once out, Ordy felt reasonably safe that he would not be able to get back in without his knowing it. As Minister of Affairs and head of the secret police he had the means of protecting himself." Nick turned to Dad with a kind of desperation. "He could be dead," he concluded, "but we don't have to accept it as so because there are so many other possibilities. If we could only get a sniff of something that–"

"Okay," Dad said quietly, "I'll quit being a pain in the neck. I've got something for you. Something came back to me. Maybe I'm getting just as screwy as you are on this. Janet, get me our files for December '48. There was a kidnaping story out of Vienna just about that time. Kidnapings were a dime a dozen then, but I remember there was something screwy about this one that made it a little different."

Nick shouted, "Criminy!" and snapped his fingers. "There was. I remember we discussed it. There was an angle that was different. Shake it up, Janet, baby."

She dumped the file in front of them, and Nick and Dad tore into it until they found what they were looking for, a story under a small two-column head out of Vienna in the issue dated December 18, 1948. Nick read it aloud. He could not keep exultation from getting into his voice as he did so.

" 'Vienna, December seventeenth. American Military Police here shot it out early this morning with an armed kidnap gang in a high-powered car and foiled what appeared to be a daring and brazen attempt to kidnap a native of either Viennese or Hungarian extraction from the streets in broad daylight.

" 'The intended victim, a man, crossed into the American sector in an effort to elude his pursuers, four armed men who piled out of a car not far from the Ring district, just as an American patrol happened by. Under strict orders from General Forbush to keep the American sector clear of any foreign nationals bearing arms, the Americans challenged the would-be kidnapers and when shot at, returned their fire in a brief exchange which saw one of the invaders fall wounded in the thigh. The other three escaped. During the excitement caused by the brief battle, the man, the object of the gang's attentions, also vanished.

" 'Questioned later in the hospital, the wounded man admitted that he was a member of the Hungarian secret police and that his comrades were likewise members of this force, but refused to reveal anything further.' "

"That's it," Dad cried. "I knew I remembered something. The guy was a Hungarian. Up to then it had always been Russians—and afterward—but this once it's a Hungarian."

"And our guy's alive," Nick yelled. "He's alive and he got away. Look! Ordy is reported back in Budapest and installed as Minister of Affairs on December 3, 1948. The heat was off him, he had received assurances that he was in good standing in the party. And he must have had word from private sources that his one-time secretary was no longer in Hungary.

"We can guess what happened to the secretary. He got back to Budapest all right and hid the contents of the suitcase, but he knew his life wasn't worth a nickel if Ordy ever got back in power. It must have grown pretty hot for him, and he became scared. Maybe the secret police suspected something and had him in for a little exercise. Anyway, he got out and across the border and into Vienna. But he wasn't bright. He didn't go far enough. He stayed in Vienna.

"Two weeks after Ordy is back in Hungary in his new job a mob of Hungarians—for the first time Hungarians—try to pick up a guy and even risk going into the American sector. Why? Because it hasn't taken Brother Ordy long to find out about his precious secretary and where he went. As long as he was in Vienna it was still possible to snatch him. And he had to have him alive on account of the whereabouts of the documents. That's why his thugs chased him instead of shooting him down from the car. Our guys break it up in the nick of time, and Mr. Secretary takes it on the lam again. He's on the loose and he's still got what it takes to stand Ordy in front of a firing squad."

"Only Vienna's too hot to hold him," Dad said.

"I know," Nick said. "He's got to move on. That's a year and a half ago, a little less. Where did he go? Where could he go?"

To their surprise it was Suzy who answered the question, firmly and briefly and with complete conviction. She said, "Paris."

They stared at her. Nick said, "Paris! Suzy! What is it, intuition?"

She looked troubled for a moment. "Partly," she said. But then she rose and, as Nick had before, faced the big wall map of Europe. "Where would he go—where could he go where he would be safe, but Paris? See, he must follow the refugee stream out of Hungary. Vienna—Salzburg— The same people who got him out of Hungary would direct him across the Russian zone of Austria and into the American zone. From Salzburg he could get into Switzerland, but he would not be able to find a job when he got there. But it is not at all difficult to cross the Austrian border into Germany and across Germany to France, which has the longest unsealed boundary in

Europe today—anyone who wants to and has a little money can cross."

She stopped and looked at them. Nick rubbed his chin and urged, "Go on, Suzy."

"Where else but Paris could he hide and make a living at the same time? What other city in Europe today has so many opportunities for a man who doesn't want to be noticed? Holland and Belgium? Too small and compact. England? It is difficult to get in. The Scandinavian countries—there are language barriers to overcome. But a trained secretary to a diplomat must speak French and either English or German as well as his own language. It's— Oh, he must—the line is so straight. He could cross the Rhine anywhere between Kehl and Karlsruhe. The river is so narrow there he could row himself across on a dark night. And after that he had only to walk or hitchhike into Strasbourg and get on a train for Paris—"

"Where he was found hiding in a washroom and arrested by the French Security Police, who check the trains between Strasbourg and Paris, for failing to have either a passport, papers, or visa," concluded Dad Lapham.

Nick spoke to him sharply. "Are you being sarcastic, Dad?"

Dad said, "I wasn't kidding. I think Suzy's got it. There was a little story around that time. It was either in *Le Monde* or *Figaro*—we didn't run it because it was too local and besides the guy got away."

Nick bawled, "Janet! Get the *Monde* and *Figaro* files, for December '48 and January '49."

Dad said, "It was either the guy or somebody like him who had come over the same route. The French police have taken to inspecting papers of people on the Strasbourg express, so many of them have been coming over. As soon as he heard about the inspection he'd have headed for the washroom, but the flics are used to that and would have got the conductor and routed him out."

"If only the time is right," Nick said.

They began to pore through the heavy bound volumes that Janet brought, Suzy joining them. Because the papers were printed in French it was a longer and more tedious task, as Nick's and Dad's eyes were not as accustomed to picking up the sense of a story from the headline. They finished '48 and had started on January '49 when Dad let out a whoop. "Got it! I knew it!" The story was in the *Figaro* for January 3.

Nick yelled, "Fifteen days from the kidnap attempt in Vienna. It used to take from two to three weeks for a refugee to make it from Vienna to Switzerland or France. Suzy, you translate it. You're faster."

Suzy read. "There was a disturbance at the Gare de l'Est yesterday afternoon when a Hungarian refugee, a stateless person who was being taken from the Strasbourg express in custody of the police for entering France without proper credentials, made his escape amid a scene of general confusion."

"Escaped!" Nick interrupted. "Did it again, you slippery little devil."

"And how!" Dad said. "Wait until you hear the rest of it. Sounds like our guy."

Suzy continued. "His handcuffs had been removed by his guardians to enable him to pay a visit to the toilet. As he emerged, accompanied by one of them and before the irons could again be fastened to his wrists, a refreshment wagon bearing coffee, cognac, and sandwiches most unfortunately passed between them. Like a flash of lightning, the prisoner leaped and upset this wagon, sending hot coffee and cognac in every direction, the cognac igniting from the spirit lamp of the coffee heater and causing a near panic. When the flames had been extinguished and order restored, it was found that the prisoner had disappeared. Police have a dragnet out for him."

"And never got him!" Nick shouted. "He's on the loose in this city."

Dad Lapham yelled, "Bingo! Now all we got to do is find him."

Janet said, "I'll look. I'll help. I'll look every day—"

Nick said, "No you won't. You'll go home and get some sleep first of all. But there'll be plenty of others who will." He glanced at the clock. It was just going on six in the morning. He said, "Get on the phones and start routing 'em out. I'll get hold of Mosher. Suzy, you get Cass McGuire out of bed, Dad, you get started on Art Glass and Felix Victor, and put Ferdie Hoffman on this, too. Where can the guy hide? What can he do? He's got to sleep somewhere, to eat and live. He can't work a regular job because sooner or later he'd be turned up without papers. So it's got to be something on the shady side and that narrows it. We know what we're looking for—a Hungarian of medium height, undistinguished-looking, who has been in Paris since January 3, 1949. That's not so far back to remember when a new guy came into your neighborhood and began to work a pitch. He'll speak French with an accent and maybe a little English. He'll be shy of cops, but at night he'll probably look for his own kind for company. Since he can't make any money legit he's got to be in some racket or other, maybe around Place Pigalle—that's for Cass McGuire to comb through—or the race track, or the boxing pits, or he's in the black market or the woman trade. Get the boys out and asking questions anywhere where there's any kind of racket going on. Give all the Hungarian joints a good going-over; check up with the secretarial bureaus, because he might risk doing some translating or secretarial work. He might be doing car-watching, or some steering or shilling for some tourist trap. And whatever they do, tell 'em to keep away from cops. There's probably still a paper out for the guy, and if the gendarmes lay their hands on him before we do, we're sunk because we'll never get to see him again. So they can't ask the chief of the precinct houses in the *arrondissements,* who'd be most likely to know if someone new had moved into his bailiwick. We've got to dig him up ourselves and quickly. Time's against us because we don't know how long Race can hold out. But if the guys know that, it'll put fire under their tails. They all wanted to be old-time, hot-shot reporters. Now let's see them get on the ball. If we can't run that guy to earth in this town in three or four days, we have no right to call ourselves a newspaper, or newspapermen."

He said to Janet, "Go home, sis, and catch up. Give the office a miss today. After you're rested up I may let you in on this hunt if it will keep you from brooding because you believe it's your fault that big slob got himself into this rat trap. It isn't. It's mine. Okay scram."

They all reached for telephones.

15

WHO AND WHAT IS A SPY?

Before his arrest and interrogation and when he was contemplating the subject and trying to reconstruct the feelings, thoughts, and sensations of a man undergoing the Communist pattern of preparation for court confession, Jimmy Race had always imagined that no matter what the technique of the inquisitors, there must come a time when a man alone and in some possession of his faculties could retrace steps he might have taken down the path toward involuntary submission and build himself back onto the road of firm resistance.

He could consider man only as a reasoning animal and

therefore master of his wits and his tongue. He would have been willing to wager that while scientifically applied torture resulting in the destruction of bone and tissue might very well break him and lead him to admit to crimes he had never committed, a psychological or psychiatrical attack upon his mind and will could never lead to the same result. He believed one of two things—either Mindszenty and the others were weaker than he, mentally, or the enemy had discovered something entirely new and were applying heretofore unheard-of methods. Neither of these things was true, but by the time Jimmy was aware of it, it was also too late. He had already become the victim of the pattern and he saw his vanished capacity to ratiocinate as something in the distance and but vaguely remembered, and even as something to be rejected because of its interference with an entirely new set of thoughts, emotions, desires, and credos which was slowly but steadily altering his personality.

His original and immediately fatal slip was his Western approach to a problem that was conceived by Easterners—that is, men whose minds were far closer to the Orient than to the Occident. It was a long time and again too late before he realized that he was not in the hands of stupid bureaucrats or brutal Nazi-type torturers against whom a man of courage, spirit, and faith in himself and his philosophies might reasonably be expected to make a determined stand, but that instead he was being handled by a team of clever and competent doctors, psychiatrists, neurologists, and clinical experts in psychology and psychiatry originally trained to recognize the symptoms of the sick mind and make it well and who now in the name of Communist discipline, fear, or fanaticism were engaged in a simple reversal of the process and concentrated upon making a well mind sick.

None of the things one imagined, Jimmy Race found,

was quite like that in reality. For one thing, the imagination did not encompass the ticking clock, the rush or deadly lag of the passage of time, the physical discomforts of places of incarceration, the calls of nature, the hunger, the continency, the bustle of the comings and goings in a jail or bureau of interrogation, the smells, sounds, temperature changes, the absence of daylight, the total lack of privacy. All played their immediate part in the disorganization of the process of continued and logical thinking. One fell all too quickly into the routine of interpreting or trying to interpret each noise, or summons, or change of situation, or trifling incident that happened around one in the light of whether it could be expected to bring an increase or a diminution of immediate discomfort. Footsteps approaching the corridor to his cell might be those of someone come to fetch him to begin the slow process of release. When they passed, it was a minor disappointment, but a disappointment nevertheless, since by no known process had Jimmy been able to hit upon any means of stifling hope. He was to find that the steady battering of the mind by hope aroused and cast down could be more punishing and destructive than truncheon or rubber hose crashing against skull or jaw.

After the first day or so he was not even able to see the carefully calculated patterns of furious activity, questioning, photographing, fingerprinting, measuring, moving from one to another of the series of low gray buildings that, connected by internal passages, stretch from Numbers 60 to 68 Andrássy Street, visiting this office, that police official, this medical examiner, in addition to the periods of solitary confinement. He had no concept that he had been studied and examined and reexamined by doctors and psychiatrists who had prescribed a course of treatment for him as they would for a patient, that his treatment was written out and charted and hung in an office where it could be consulted, and that the prescriptions recommended were being carried out by trained teams of men with all the emotionless thoroughness of male nurses in a hospital.

Thus it was two weeks after his arrest that four guards came into his cell and ordered Jimmy to strip. Jimmy's first instinct was to struggle against the order, to fight, to have it out then and there, but he conquered the impulse. There was no room in the cell to fight. Big as he was, they were four against one. In the end they would overpower him and take his clothes away for whatever purpose they wanted them and he would have gained nothing but a headache and possible serious injury. As an ex-soldier Jimmy knew all about the futility of getting hurt when it isn't necessary. He was not aware how habit-forming the decision not to fight in a particular instance can become, how more and more easily the mind accepts the decision and curbs instinct.

He removed his clothes, and a guard took them away. Then the cell door was unlocked, and they marched him naked through the corridors, past hurrying police, officials, clerks, guards who gave him not so much as a glance, past offices where secretaries were typing and working at steel files and card indexes, and into an office where a team of four interrogators in civilian clothes awaited him.

They sat around the four sides of a large table desk, their papers in front of them. There was no chair for Jimmy. The leader of the interrogators was the man with the bullet head and the bad teeth, whose name was Vajos. All of the men spoke English, though the others had accents.

Vajos said, "Ah, yes. Here you are, Mr. Race. Just stand over there by the wall where we can all see you and please answer our questions to you truthfully and without any delay." And then he looked at Jimmy's nakedness and smiled. The others looked, laughed, too, and one of them put his hand to his face and made a remark behind it in Hungarian to his colleague, and the other laughed and nodded.

"Now, Mr. Race, we will begin. By whom were you ordered to enter Hungary as a spy and saboteur?"

Shame, rage, the humiliation of his ego and indignity to his person, standing nude, ridiculous, and helpless before dressed men who looked at him as though he were some kind of strange animal, forced a bellow of anger from Jimmy, followed by a string of curses and obscenities. He bawled at them like a wounded bull elephant. He demanded his clothes and called them every foul name he could muster. He raged at them until his voice broke with hysteria and tears of helpless anger blinded his eyes. But he did not attack them physically because he could not overcome the shame and fear of his own nudity.

Vajos said, "Come come, Mr. Race, stop that infantile outburst and answer our questions. If there is anything more ridiculous than a man without his clothes it is one who has lost his temper as well. You look and are behaving like an ugly little child, and if we laugh at you, you have only yourself to blame. Afterward, perhaps, if you become more co-operative, we might be persuaded to give you back your clothes."

Later, when he was back in his cell, still naked and shivering in the dampness, his mind was occupied with thoughts of revenge, with rage and the memory of shame and helplessness, and with a kind of desperate searching for what he *could* tell them that would be the truth but would be considered more co-operative and would win back his clothes for him, or at least some garment with which to cover his hide and return to him the aspect and feelings of a human being.

Up to that point, the interrogations had not been too

difficult. They had been conducted with him seated at a desk opposite his questioner and had consisted in his telling his story over and over again, apparently in the hope of catching him in a variation. Sometimes Vajos was opposite him, sometimes there would be three or four different inquisitors before he saw Vajos again.

It always began in the same manner with an invitation for him to furnish them with the details of his purpose in spying on the Hungarian people. Carefully, with all the patience and force of conviction he could muster, Jimmy would reiterate that he was not a spy, but a reporter, and that he had entered Hungary for the sole purpose of collecting material for a series of articles on life behind the iron curtain. He felt forced to admit this much, since he was maintaining his stand and defense as a newspaperman. Sometimes it seemed almost as though he were getting somewhere when he caught Vajos in a good mood and elicited from him several replies to queries.

Jimmy said once, "Look here, Vajos, you have correspondents from Hungarian papers in other countries, don't you—for instance, ours, the U.S.A.?"

"But of course."

"You do not consider them as spies, do you?"

"But certainly not. They are on legitimate business. Besides, the Hungarian People's Republic has no need to employ spies since her only desire is peace."

"Then you recognize that a man may be a reporter on assignment in a foreign country and not be a spy."

"But certainly, Mr. Race. That is self-evident in the case of our Hungarian correspondents and reporters."

Jimmy drove his point home. "And why not equally self-evident in mine?"

Vajos smiled at him in a not unfriendly manner and went on to re-examine Jimmy on his military background.

But subsequent questionings showed that the comparison had made no impression whatsoever, and when Jimmy raised the point with Vajos, the little man said, "Mr. Race, I beg of you not to be so naïve. I thought you were joking with your comparison. Our newspapermen are welcomed by the democratic countries and are given visas. Information is put at their disposal. They break no laws in securing their reports. You, on the other hand, are not welcome here. There is a law against your entry without invitation, and an even more severe one against entering the country without proper credentials and a visa. No such invitation has been extended, no such visa has been granted you, therefore your presence here opposite me and the manner of your arrival brand you *ipso facto* as a spy of the Western imperialist warmongers. And the sooner you are prepared to give us the details as to who sent you and the full purpose of your mission, the better it will be all around and the quicker this matter will be brought to its conclusion."

"And what will be the conclusion?"

Vajos smiled his half-friendly smile again, one that seemed to say, "After all, we are men of the world and understand one another," and said, "Surely, Mr. Race, a man engaged in intelligence work knows the price of error or failure, of falling into the hands of the enemy. You will be tried, found guilty, and hanged. If you cooperate I can promise you that this end will be reached more quickly and less painfully than if you continue to be stubborn. Surely you were aware of this when you started out on your mission against the Hungarian people."

Jimmy felt sick to his stomach, and all the more because the little man was being so temperate and complacent about it, like nothing so much as a banker regretting that he must call in the mortgage.

Jimmy said, "Supposing I were a spy. It is not customary to hang intelligence agents captured in peace time."

"In Hungary it has become the custom," Vajos interrupted blandly. "We have passed a law making it a capital offense for anyone convicted of spying or sabotage against the Hungarian People's Government. You have broken several Hungarian laws in entering our country in the manner in which you were caught and arrested. It only remains for us to prove that you have broken the new one against espionage."

"Brother Vajos," Jimmy Race said earnestly, turning his heavy gaze upon the little man, "all the rest of your teeth will have rotted out of your mouth before that happens or before you get me to admit on the stand or anywhere else to anything but what I have told you."

Vajos said, "Well, perhaps." He had the exasperating quality of never becoming offended no matter what Jimmy said. "But at any rate we must try to change your mind before that happens. That will be all for today, Mr. Race."

Thereafter had occurred the episode of the loss of his clothes. And thereafter began a slow and gradual change in the manner and method of his interrogation. The questions were always the same. But now he had to fight physical discomfort, pain, humiliation, and extreme fatigue as well as their subtle prying and suggestions.

He was removed to a cell where there was no bunk or furniture of any kind. Powerful spotlights fixed in each corner illuminated it with a bright and stabbing glare that pierced the skin of the eyelids as though it were not there and lanced the eyeballs. They were never extinguished, night or day. It was impossible to escape their glare. He could catch a few minutes' sleep by lying on his stomach on the floor and burying his eyes and face in the crook of his arm, but at the first movement or shift of position, the terrible lights bored through his skin and awoke him.

There were times when he spent what seemed to be days under those lights, and others when he was questioned eighteen and twenty hours at a stretch by teams of inquisitors working in relays. He was no longer permitted to sit during these sessions, but was forced to stand upright, his hands behind his head, or to squat on his heels. The things they told him to do and enforced by the presence of their armed guards seemed to be childish at first, like the hazing of a high-school secret society, until the long hours wore on and each enforced position brought its torture and agony to his limbs and to his mind.

Eventually he had been given a garment to wear, a kind of white cotton prison pajama. It covered his nakedness now, but opened him to a new kind of indignity. When he asked to go to the lavatory, permission was refused him. They made a filthy animal out of him.

Physical strain and fatigue were something that Jimmy could combat with his truculence, his strength, and his belief in himself. But the degradations left him weak, trembling, and confused and without any weapons, physical or spiritual, with which to fight back. Some one of his opponents had divined the chink in his armor unerringly.

He had not yet been beaten, or offered violence in any form, but he had been given to understand that if he made any serious attempt to escape, or did not obey, he would be shot on the spot. The will to live was strong in Jimmy. While he was alive there was still hope, but after a week he was no longer certain of what that hope was, but merely that it existed and that he must be careful to remain alive.

The steady drain on his stamina was telling on him until he was a mass of aches, stabbing pains, and screaming nerves. He suffered agonies from muscular cramp that he was not allowed to relieve and he learned the true nature of the torture of not being allowed to rest or sleep.

When he thought of Suzy or Nick Strang or the gang back on the paper, they seemed to be so remote as almost to have become creatures of his imagination who had never lived. But his mind turned to them rarely, because he was so concerned with the horror of the immediate, the bustling, stinking prison building, the disgusting men charged with questioning him, foul food, dirty water, and the dawning realization that he had been abandoned, that those who held him were not only stronger than he but more immediately powerful than his friends and compatriots as well. There was never going to be any help or rescue forthcoming, there was never to be surcease of the torture of his body.

Hardest to bear were the swift changes that could take place any moment in the attitude and treatment accorded him, a sudden relaxation of the deadly regimen, a chair, a cup of passable coffee, a cigarette, permission to go and clean himself, and, above all, the sympathy of the ugly little round-headed police official, Vajos, who seemed to be pleased when he could extend one of these moments to Jimmy and who would say, "Mr. Race, I hope you realize that this is very painful to us. We are a modern and civilized people with a very ancient culture. Your stubbornness makes it necessary for us to use methods that we deplore. We hold nothing against you personally. You have your business and we ours, but they happen to have come into conflict. It is you who have made the original error and not we. Since you have lost the game by it, why do you continue to make matters more difficult for yourself and for us?" And at those moments when they showed him what seemed to be a softer and more human side, Jimmy caught himself wondering, indeed, why he did and what was the use of holding out against someone who had all the tricks in hand.

The trouble was, what with the pain and the fatigue, he would forget exactly what he was holding out for, whether it was an ideal, or something he did not want them to know, or a promise he had made to someone. Sometimes he had the courage and clarity to sit there, argue, or call Vajos obscene names, and at others he would merely sit there, mumble, and shake his head as though he had been asked something he could not rightly answer, from its not being very clear in his own head.

Each time after one of these "reconciliation" periods the next trial and session would be more severe and of longer duration. Several times he collapsed and fainted during the questioning. Buckets of water were sloshed over him. He was pulled erect and forced to go on until he collapsed again.

The interrogation had subtly changed and he was not aware of it. They had ceased asking questions, they were telling him now during his periods of recuperation, "We know you are a spy. We know why you came to Budapest. We know who sent you. We know in whose employ you are. We know what your mission was. We know whom you were supposed to contact here. Your Government has abandoned you for committing the crime of being caught red-handed in espionage. You have been written off. We have given you the facts. Confess and revenge yourself upon them." The endless accusations droned on. "We know . . . we know . . . we have found out . . . you are . . . you are . . . you did . . . criminal . . . spy . . . saboteur . . . plotter . . . Titoist dynamiter . . . capitalist bandit and warmonger. . . ."

What did stick in Jimmy Race's mind was that they would not bring him to trial until they had a confession and that they would not dare bring him into court showing marks of physical violence. He had strong recuperative powers, stronger than his captors suspected. During the long periods of sleeplessness and bodily exhaustion Jimmy often felt like giving in to end the useless struggle, and that he understood its hopelessness was in itself symptomatic of what was being done to him.

But during one of the "ease" sessions with Vajos, with a cigarette between his fingers, Jimmy said, "You're going to lose this one, Vajos. You could make me give in, seeing I'm only made of flesh and blood, but you'd have to tear me to pieces to do it. You'd have to break my arms and legs, bust my jaw, and smash in my teeth, pull out all my finger and toenails, and burn me with cigarette ends, or peel off hunks of my skin like they used to do to those guys at Belsen or Dachau; but then you could never produce me in court so that I could look pretty for the correspondents, the observers, and the foreign press when I stood up to sing—if I could stand up. That's the only way you'll ever get a confession out of me."

Vajos regarded Jimmy with seriousness and almost with something close to pity in his dark, intelligent eyes. He said reflectively, "You are probably just enough of a masochist to enjoy such a martyrdom, Mr. Race. Many genuine patriots would. But the methods you discuss are old-fashioned, out of date, and of no use to us whatever except in the case of eliciting information from someone for whom we have no further use afterward. We have therefore evolved new methods of persuasion that do not leave any external mark whatsoever, one of which I am thinking at the moment. We prefer not to use it because of its weakening effect, and men have died under it. A small demonstration of it would, I think, be valuable at this point."

He picked up a telephone, dialed an interior number, and spoke rapidly in Hungarian, then nodded and hung up the receiver. A few moments later four guards appeared at the door. They were accompanied by a tall man with a narrow face and a small mouth, of the AHV, the Hungarian secret political police, who saluted Vajos and then looked inquiringly at Jimmy.

Vajos said, "In a moment, Janos. Finish your cigarette, Mr. Race, and relax while you may. In a few moments I am afraid you are going to be a very sick man. I regret that you are going to have to accompany Janos and his glockenspiel quartet into room 27. Do you know what a glockenspiel is, Mr. Race?"

Jimmy replied, "No!" For the life of him he could not understand the allusion.

"You might imagine," Vajos said, "but you would never guess. It is most ingenious. You would not wish to change your mind perhaps at this point and co-operate? We have your confession all prepared and written out for you. You have only to agree to repeat it in court and–"

"Go to hell, you ——" Jimmy said, and called Vajos an unprintable name. "Make me!"

The policeman signaled to the guards, who ranged themselves alongside Jimmy in the manner to which he had grown accustomed so that now he automatically fell into step between them.

"Good-by, Mr. Race," Vajos said. "And you might remember this. Before we are through with you, you might very well be calling upon me and begging me to *give* you the opportunity of confessing."

They went clattering off down the corridor that led from Vajos's office, which was in one of the administrative ends of the block of buildings devoted to the business of AHV, toward the prison section, where the wood floors turned to stone and the tramp of the soldiers' boots of the guard and the rattle and clinking of their accouterment echoed from the walls. They went up to the second floor and paused before a small wooden door on which was painted the number 27.

The man called Janos opened it and strode in, followed by the two leading guards. Jimmy paused on the threshold for a moment and looked inside, but what he saw did not look very terrifying. There appeared to be nothing but a chair standing in the center of an otherwise apparently empty room, and next to it a large, galvanized-iron pail. He felt only a consuming curiosity. Even though he had sampled the tortures of fatigue and nerve and muscle strain that can be applied without visible physical damage to the victim, it was too difficult to be too apprehensive of something that was *ipso facto* guaranteed not to break bones, tear his skin, or leave otherwise recognizable marks upon his person. Neither the chair nor the pail looked very formidable. He had quite forgotten the name that Vajos had applied to the game about to be played with him there.

But when, a half hour later, the door reopened and he emerged from room 27 between the guards, it was not the same Jimmy Race. His features appeared to be puffed and swollen, not as from an outward beating, but as though there had been some unendurable pressure from within. His hands hung loosely at his side and he did not have entire control of his legs, for he shambled and stumbled at times and at others he seemed rooted in his tracks and unable to move forward until the prodding of the guard set him going again. And all the time his head was moving from side to side in a kind of uncontrollable negation like an animated Charlie McCarthy with a swivel neck.

This thing, the guards accompanied or rather propelled into the office of a Dr. Istvan Soldessy, who under the Hungarians before the war and later under the Nazis had been a society psychiatrist who used hypnotism occasionally to release the libidos of his wealthy clients, and who under the Communists, for the sake of his skin and his considerable fortune, had reversed his techniques and practices to bring about the destruction of men's minds. He looked up from his desk as they came in and said in Hungarian, "Ah. This should be Mr. Race, the American. Well, now, this should be most interesting. Very."

16

BACKGROUND TO CONFESSION

IN PARIS, the available staff of the Paris Edition, sparked by Nick Strang and driven by Dad Lapham and Mark Mosher, combed the underworld haunts of the great gray city of light and pleasure, looking for a stateless, paperless Hungarian who had arrived on the scene on January 2, 1949, who, lacking working permits or proper identification, could not accept a regular job, and who at all costs must keep out of the way of the police.

Inquiries had to be made guardedly for both Nick and Suzy were certain that at the first indication that he was being looked for the man would be certain that it was the police on his trail and would vanish. And time was of the essence; he had to be found quickly if at all.

Ferdie Hoffman, who immediately turned to the race tracks around Paris—Auteuil, St. Cloud, Longchamp—as the most likely place where a foreigner might get himself a spot of odd work sufficient to keep him alive without too many questions being asked, was the first to draw a blank. He had run across the trail at Auteuil of a little Hungarian who had arrived in France around the beginning of the past year and about whose presence it was whispered at the track there was some irregularity. Eventually he had been pointed out to Hoffman, a wizened little jockey with treacherous eyes and a wrinkled, cynical face. It was the first of many let-downs. The jockey had obviously not been secretary to a Hungarian diplomat, or anyone else.

They turned up Czechs, Rumanians, refugee Austrians, Bulgars, Albanians, and occasionally Hungarians, but never one who could fit the specifications of the Man Who Knew Something about Ordy.

Nick, hovering between the press-association newsprinter machines, which would be the first to carry any news that Jimmy's trial had been scheduled in Budapest, and the editorial room, wore Dad Lapham and Mark Mosher to frazzles with ideas and assignments. He was on the job eighteen hours a day and drove himself more relentlessly than he did them. He left the editorial side of the job to Suzy, who took it over in her quiet, effortless, efficient way, and established himself in the city room at a telephone opposite Mosher and proved once and for all that he had not forgotten how to be an editor who could keep an investigation going and make things hum.

But the tragic and disappointing pattern that was emerging from the mass of material being telephoned or brought in by the reporters showed that none of it was yielding so much as the slightest break or clue to what they were after.

They had done a thorough job, and Nick from experience knew that something should have been turned up from such an exhaustive inquiry. It was becoming more and more clear either that their man had left Paris after a brief stay, finding it too hot to hold him after the episode at the Gare de l'Est, or that he was a better hand at concealing himself than they were at finding him.

Time was running out. Chicago was on the telephone every day, fretting and wanting to know what Nick was doing at his end to procure Jimmy's release, reporting their own lack of success with Washington, making suggestions that could not possibly be carried out, nagging, and wasting Nick's time and energy. Nick's nerves and temper were growing more strained, and the tension at the office was mounting to boiling-point as he drove them ever harder.

•

Dr. Istvan Soldessy was an affable, rosy-cheeked man of some corpulency. He had frosty-white hair and extraordinarily keen and analyzing blue eyes that looked out at and through clients with too much comprehension and understanding. Except for his eyes he looked more like a successful stockbroker than a fashionable psychoanalyst and clinical psychiatrist.

In his elegant prewar practice in Budapest it was his custom to give an hour a day to each patient as he or she reclined on a couch in his office and rattled off the stream of consciousness for his comment and analysis. Now he was devoting five hours, two in the morning and three in the afternoon, to the task of breaking down the mental resistance of the American spy, James Race, at the behest of his new masters, the Cominform, via the AHV, the Hungarian secret political police.

He was not concerned with the actual guilt or innocence of his "patient." Dr. Soldessy knew very well why the American had been turned over to him. Men confessed under three sets of circumstances—under extreme agony and torture to gain a cessation of pain, and then they were likely to repudiate their confessions when their wounds healed and the memory faded; to save the lives of their families or some loved one held as a hostage; and finally, they confessed because they had been made to feel their guilt. This was the chosen basis of confession because it looked and sounded most natural in court. Psychiatry had long been used to cure men who suffered from guilt feelings when there was no real cause of guilt other than their masochistic desires to feel guilty. It had taken the devilish Communists to set the learned doctors to the task of instilling a genuine guilt feeling in a victim where there was no genuine basis for the emotion. They had worked out a technique whereby the subject was "prepared" before he was turned over to the doctor. It varied with the strength, the intelligence, the I.Q., and the tested ego of the individual, and was never quite the same in two instances.

Dr. Soldessy examined the card that accompanied the big, unshaven, glassy-eyed man in soiled prison pajamas who stood before him now, and he muttered approval. Eight days' "hard" interrogation, a brightly lighted cell, which meant that he would be suffering from extreme fatigue and lack of sleep, a half hour's trip to room 27. He turned over the card and noted the report of the physician in charge of two injections of scopolamine after an attempt of the prisoner to do himself injury. The physician noted that he did not believe it was a suicide attempt but rather a try at keeping them from producing him in court. He had administered the scopolamine both as a sedative because of its befuddling effect upon the mind and to prepare the patient for Dr. Soldessy.

The doctor looked up at the big man and said in the tone of one who talks to a small, recalcitrant child, "Come, now, there must be no more attempts at suicide or self-injury. This is quite the most infantile of all emotions, to try to project a hurt to another by inflicting it upon yourself. You understand this, don't you?"

Jimmy said, "Yes. Won't do it again." He knew that his speech and his tongue were thick, but he thought that his mind was quite clear. The doc seemed like a nice guy, the nicest he had encountered so far in their damned prison. At least he looked clean. "Can I sit down?"

Dr. Soldessy said sharply, "No, you cannot. You are

to remain standing. We are not on such terms yet."

From force of habit now, Jimmy did as he was told because in the end it was easier. But he felt a kind of numb hurt in his breast. The doc had disappointed him.

Dr. Soldessy began, "Now, Mr. Race, tell me something of your efforts during the war. I understand you were a paratrooper. What were your duties?"

Jimmy thought, *Oh, criminy, this guy, too.* They were always trying to make something of his war record. Well, he knew that routine by heart. He said, "I was a captain of paratroopers. We were dropped inside enemy lines."

"I see. For what purpose?"

"Reconnaissance, diversion, the cutting of telephone lines, bridges, and communications."

"Spying and sabotage, in other words."

Jimmy's legs were beginning to ache again and he knew his left calf muscle was going to ball up again and give him agony. He thought dully, *Just like all the rest,* and aloud he said wearily, "I was in uniform. There was a war on. I was fighting the same guys you were—I mean the Russians were."

"Do you really believe, Mr. Race, that it makes any difference to an act what clothes you were wearing when you committed it? Or that it in any way could alter its aspects?"

Jimmy looked at him bewildered. "I don't get you, doc," he said.

"Then let me put it this way. What counts is neither the intent nor the circumstances but the nature of an act itself. You could have been clad in a bathing-suit or tennis flannels, or in nothing at all at the time. But what you did was to go behind enemy lines for the purpose of gathering information and destroying property. Divorced from war, from clothes, from who the enemy was, or what his purpose was, the act itself still remains spying and sabotage. Is that not so?"

Well, the way the doc was putting it, you had to admit that it did sound about right. He said, "Gosh, I never thought about it that way, doc—"

"You must think about it in this way, because it is the truth. Will you try to do so?"

Jimmy said, "Why sure, doc, if you want me to." The doc was pretty reasonable, after all. The others had all been shouting at him to admit that he was a spy and a saboteur. The doc was only asking him to think and believe something that, now that he thought of it, was pretty obvious if one didn't dress it up in a lot of language.

"If I let you lie down on this couch and sleep for an hour, will you concentrate on what you have just said and promise to repeat it to me when you wake up?"

"I'd do anything for a sleep, doc."

"Very well. Then you may do so."

The doc was decent, after all, and Jimmy tried hard to play the game with him before he dropped off to sleep. He had been a spy and a saboteur . . . it didn't matter what clothes you wore . . . it was the act . . . the act . . .

When his breathing was quiet and regular, Dr. Soldessy went to his desk, extracted a prepared hypodermic syringe, and administered it with such skill that Jimmy never even stirred. The drug would have taken full effect by the time Jimmy awakened. It was the beginning of the interviews and the implanting of the fundamental concepts in the mind of the patient that were so important. In his practice Dr. Soldessy had used hypnotism at this stage. The drug that unhinged the moral values of the patient, confused and unsettled his mind, and made it completely amenable to outside suggestion was better for the immediate purpose at hand, though it wore off more quickly. But eventually, if the seeds were properly sown, the ideas and emotions grafted on the personality of the patient at the moment of his greatest weakness would become a part of him and remain in his consciousness without further recourse to the drug, once they had been initially understood and accepted, say long enough for the victim to stand up in court and deliver himself with total conviction of the burden of the guilt imposed upon him.

That, the doctor thought to himself with quiet satisfaction, was why they needed him, and the further they went, these rascals whose bidding he did, the more they would need him and the safer he would be. There would never come a time when they could leave off the distortion and corruption of human souls once they had started on that downward path; never afterward, having used him, could they free themselves from *him*. They would always be afraid of him because of what he knew and understood about them and their twisted, evil, guilt-ridden mentalities.

When the hour was up, Dr. Soldessy went over and shook Jimmy on the shoulder. "Very well, wake up. Get up. Stand over there. Remember your promise to me. Now, then. What were you in the war?"

There was a queer taste in Jimmy's mouth. The sleep had then done him little good. He felt more tired and bewildered than ever. He began to say, "I was a paratrooper, a jumper–" when Dr. Soldessy's voice beat through the numbness.

"No–no–*no!* Remember what we agreed–"

It came back to Jimmy then, and he grinned foolishly because it was silly of him not to have remembered it. It was the idea they had worked out together that had so pleased the doc he had let him sleep for an hour.

He said, "I was a spy and a saboteur."

"That's better. Repeat it, please."

"A spy and a saboteur."

"Exactly. And you know this to be the truth."

"Yes."

"Good. Now tell me something about your profession. You were, I gather, a reporter for a newspaper, or several newspapers. Is that true?"

"Yes." Jimmy felt at ease. The doc was regular, after all. He, Jimmy, had been a spy and a saboteur during the war, but at least the man knew what a reporter was and wasn't trying to make him out a spy afterward.

"What are a reporter's duties in America?"

Jimmy stared. It was so hard for him to concentrate, had been for so long, ever since what had happened in room 27. But he did not want to think of *that.* He had almost managed not to think of that too often. Aloud he said, "About the same as they are here in Hungary, I guess."

"I do not think so. The duties of a reporter in Hungary are to carry statements handed out by officials of the government to his newspaper and give them to his editor. Answer my question. What were your duties?"

Jimmy fumbled for the words. "Well—to get stories—facts, information about people or things that happened, go out after things that happened, find out and write them up—"

"Are the people about whom you are trying to get information of their private affairs always willing that you should have it?"

Jimmy thought about this for a moment. It all seemed so remote and far away and, now that he considered it, even faintly ridiculous. Of course they didn't want you to come prying into their affairs. What you got from them you had to work for, or steal, or force, buy it from someone else, or pick it up in spite of them. He felt that Dr. Soldessy would be amused to hear that and he told it to him.

"In other words," said Dr. Soldessy, "in your country

a reporter fulfills the function of a police spy in ours."

Again Jimmy stared at him. The doc had a way of putting things so clearly that had never occurred to him before. And yet how could it be exactly so? He said, "Yes, I guess so, but it isn't quite that way. We only want to get a story to publish so that people will know the truth."

"Remember what you have learned, Mr. Race. It is not the purpose, the circumstances, or the results, it is the act itself. The actions you have been taught to perform and have been performing are those of a spy. Is that not so?"

Remotely, Jimmy felt that there must be a fallacy somewhere, that this was not the answer, but he was too tired, jumbled, and confused to look for it, and, besides, why bother when what the doc said really made sense?

"That's right," he said.

This was the beginning of his education in guilt, in which, his resistance lowered by fatigue and nerve strain, and his mind and judgment weakened by injections of the drug, he was brought slowly but certainly along the path where he was no longer able to distinguish ethically and morally between the actions of a paid spy or intelligence officer and his own purpose and action in entering Hungary illegally to get material for a story on the secret of the torture trials. More, under the skillful guidance, planting, and short-cutting of the psychiatrist, who would lead him down long and devious alleys of sophistry only to bring him up sharp with a remark that cut away all the unnecessary ideas and adornment and left only what seemed to be a bare, ugly truth sticking out, Jimmy came slowly to implicating not only himself, but Nick, Suzy, the paper, and his country.

The doctor steered Jimmy to a discussion of Nick's own Army background in G2, and then quietly showed him that one intelligence officer had simply given orders to another. He laughed at Jimmy when he tried to assure him that Nick had had no knowledge that he would try to get into Hungary, and with one of those swift attacks that swept away all evasions and half-truths asked him whether he really believed that Nick, or his wife either, was that naïve.

He gravely listened to Jimmy's love for Suzy, which came pouring forth under the influence of the drug and the pseudoanalytic treatment, and then turned the medallion about and showed him the other side—two clever people, Nick and Suzy, who had conspired to make him their tool in espionage without having to shoulder the responsibility if anything went wrong. Step by step he led him to the conviction that he had committed acts of espionage and intended sabotage against a foreign government with intent to harm that country to the advantage of his own. For the secrets he managed to pry from the Communists, published or unpublished, had he been successful, would have finished as a complete report to the Army, the President, or the State Department in Washington, and Jimmy knew this to be true. The line between what he was and what he thought he had been was being narrowed.

Sometimes it was being achieved by hectoring, bullying, and shouting when he was in such agony of fatigue and physical exhaustion that he was ready and even eager to admit anything in order to obtain surcease. At others, a quiet, friendly chat, the reward of a snooze on the couch, or a cigarette and a remark of the doctor's such as "Surely you are aware, Mr. Race, that every patriotic man is a government agent when he is visiting a foreign country." Even had he been one-hundred-percent normal, Jimmy would have had to admit the truth of the statement.

And just as the analyst, bent on effecting the "cure" of a patient in the grip of neurosis, brought about a tenuous personal relationship between himself and his client, so Dr. Soldessy fostered a similar one between Jimmy and himself based on his analysis of Jimmy's character. The normal, subconsciously defensive Jimmy, who found it necessary to ride roughshod over all opposition, became, when he was abnormal, weak and dependent upon Dr. Soldessy, anxious to please him at times, hurt and upset and worried when the doctor appeared to be angry or out of patience with him. And yet as his corruption proceeded, all of these things appeared to be quite normal to Jimmy and as though that had been how he had felt always.

He had had lessons in "conditioning." When he was fractious they did not beat or maul him beyond the humiliation of slapping him in the face as a vulgar parent maltreats a fractious child, but once when he had been particularly recalcitrant and despairing to the point of not caring whether they shot him or not, they had simply overpowered him with numbers, dragged him below stairs, and dumped him into a dungeon. Or stuffed was the more appropriate word, since the space was so narrow and confined, low-ceilinged and pitched at such an angle that he was able neither to stand up nor to lie down. Here they left him for forty-eight hours without food or water, light or fresh air. Here Jimmy died mentally after suffering excruciating agony from his cramped position and entered his final tomb, for the damp rock was pressing all around him. He was too big, active, and strong a man thus to be able to bear confinement for long. When his evil jailers came finally to take him from this torture cell he could not but look upon them as his deliverers.

He was being trained like an animal being put through a scientist's maze in order to learn what things could win him a moment's respite from the daily routine of planned horrors. His subconscious was carried along with his physical and conscious being. Here was the real deviltry of the Red torture pattern, for it led man to the wholly unconscious betrayal of himself.

Still, somehow he managed to fight. There were moments of clarity when he was free of the drug, when the timetable and chart of his destruction were at variance with some sudden, unsuspected recuperative power, and he saw the abyss into which he was toppling. Then he could refuse to write his confession, even though they had shown it to him ready-written in his own writing, brilliantly, expertly, undetectably forged from specimens obtained of his calligraphy. He would again deny the whole filthy phantasy of spying, and then they would have further recourse to battering at his sanity and sending him dangerously close to the line from which there would be no return once he had crossed it, with yet another trip to the horror of room 27.

To let him savor fully his punishment and to rouse his dormant instincts to protest against it and sell him out, they would always tell him when they were going to take him there and reduce him to weakness and whimpering. "Oh, God, don't do that to me again. Please don't do that to me again—" And even though under the threat he would agree to what they wanted, they would not let him off any more than a dog is let off his whipping because he hides his tail and turns appealing, guilty eyes upon his angry master.

There would come the slow, measured march between the guards up to the second floor and the horror of the entry, pushing and struggling, into room 27, the empty room with the single chair and the pail, for he was no longer able of his own volition to cross that threshold of pain and terror.

Then they would push him into the chair and tie him hand and foot so that he had to sit there and could not move or budge, or even roll off, and when that was done they would pick up the big galvanized-iron pail that stood beside the chair and put it over his head so that it came down to his shoulders and blotted out all sight.

And the last thing that he would hear clearly and recognize for many an hour was the footsteps of the guard as he marched over to the corner where stood the four broomsticks they used, and he heard him return and their rustlings as they each took one, and then they began to bang with them on the sides and top of the pail.

And shortly afterward the stabbing agony of each blow, not one of which touched him or any part of him or did him external physical injury, was such that all that emerged from under the pail were inhuman bubblings and bleatings and sometimes even shrill screams torn from his lungs by the unbearable pain of the iron clangor, the hideous glockenspiel that battered against his eardrums, addled his brain, and filled his head with throbbing agony that increased in intensity each time a stick beat upon the pail.

They would extinguish the lights in the room and play their rataplan upon his being in total darkness so that in the pitch-black he would feel himself swelling against his bonds, against the pressure of the pail, against the confinement of his own skull in a rising crescendo of tension, and racking, sickening pain that must end in his bursting to pieces, and never did.

When these sessions were brought to a close and the pail lifted from his head, what remained slumped in the chair was very little of the man that Jimmy Race had once been.

17

CLASS IN ELOCUTION

WHAT THEY HAD ALL BEEN EXPECTING and fearing took place without warning late on a Wednesday afternoon toward the end of April.

It was like a tableau. Nick and Suzy and Dad Lapham came in from the outside door, just as Mark Mosher appeared on the opposite side from the news-ticker room, and there they stopped and stared across at one another. Work at the copy desk stopped, and nobody typed or spoke or did anything any more because the atmosphere and the attitudes of the people facing one another by the doors was laden with disaster.

Mark Mosher had a slip of press copy in his hands. His eyes were large and frightened, his mouth open a little, and he was pale. He looked at them as though for hope, and they to him, and all knew that it was hopeless even before Dad shook his head.

Then Mosher's eyes goggled a minute, and his voice grated before he could settle it to say what he had to say. "They've broken Jimmy!"

Nick went over and took the slip from Mosher's hand and read it.

Budapest, April 27. Minister of Affairs Andreas Ordy this afternoon announced that the trial of the American, James Race, the American spy who was arrested a month ago when he attempted to enter Hungary illegally, will take place in the People's Court on May 1. The extreme penalty will be demanded by the State.

More later—Race trial. . . .

Suzy made an odd sound in her throat and turned and went out of the room. In the ensuing silence somebody swore. Dad Lapham said quickly, "Where's Janet?" and craned his neck to look around the corner of the L into the library section.

Mitchell Connell said, "She's out getting cigarettes."

"Send her to me when she comes in. And don't let her know what's happened until I've had a chance to talk to her. It's going to be a bad moment for the kid."

Nick wondered what kind of a moment it was for Suzy. He knew what it was for himself.

Mark Mosher said doubtfully, "Are we going to use it?"

Nick said briefly, "Certainly. We're still getting out a newspaper. Page one. Let me see the later copy when it comes in."

Mark asked, "Do we still keep on trying to find—this guy?"

Before Nick could reply, Dad interjected, "You're damn right we do."

Nick dropped the piece of press copy on Mark's desk and walked out of the room. He went to his office, where he found Suzy walking up and down with a handkerchief pressed to her lips. Her eyes were red. She said, "Nick, I'm going to go to Vienna. I've already telephoned. I can get a plane out at seven o'clock. I shan't need anything but the little office overnight bag. I'm two pages ahead, except for the editorials from Chicago. Let Dad take them over while I'm away. He won't mind."

Nick said, "Very well, Suzy."

She said, "I may be able to find something. We're at a dead end here. What happened this afternoon convinced me. If we could find out his name—or something more tangible about him— Somebody in Vienna may remember him."

Nick thought to himself, *What a queer game people play with themselves when they're in love and don't know why they do things. She's going to Vienna to be nearer to him, but she still pretends to believe in that silly fiction of a secretary I dreamed up to cover my own faults and weaknesses and failures. And I can't be honest and decent and say to her, "Go to him—go to Budapest if you can and must, so that you can perhaps lay eyes on him once more, so that you can be close to him when he dies because of the mistake in judgment that I made." But I can't and I won't say it. And so I'll go along with the fiction we have brought alive between us and say to you aloud:*

"All right, Suzy. It's worth trying, but be careful. Check in with G2 when you get there. I'll wire Ed Slater that you're coming."

"Don't," said Suzy. "Let me handle this my own way and make my own contacts. I have friends there. I will keep out of trouble."

Nick nodded gloomily.

Jimmy Race was unable to keep his mind from wandering to the oddest things, and when that happened, Professor Varolyas, who had been appointed his "teacher," would have to slap him smartly across the face with his fingers to bring him back, for these were Dr. Soldessy's instructions in addition to some other methods of keeping him tractable.

Professor Varolyas had been a teacher of rhetoric and public speaking in the University of Szeged before he had come to Budapest as a party member, mouthpiece, and stooge for the Communists, and he sometimes made himself useful preparing accused prisoners for their trials. The comrades recognized that things went much better for them if the speaker or confessor at their trials spoke smoothly, without halting, and with conviction and made a good impression with his delivery.

The thought that now had occupied Jimmy's mind in spite of himself was something that had happened to him when he was a very small child, no more than three or four as he had heard it later in life, for his actual memory on the subject was not too clear. His father, when Jimmy was that age, used to dress up as Santa Claus at Christmas and would appear sitting beside the tree to distribute presents to Jimmy and his sister.

Jimmy had been enthralled and at the same time terrified by the astonishing apparition of Kris Kringle, with the result that all through the rest of the year his parents were able to control him merely by a mention of the saint. When things got badly out of hand and he had a tantrum, or refused to obey an order to clear away his toys or go to bed, the top of the red, white-tasseled hat merely pushed around the corner of the nursery door from the outside was sufficient to make him as tractable as a lamb and for days afterward.

"Come," said Professor Varolyas, and he slapped Jimmy in the face again, "pay me attention. Or do you wish me to show you the pail again?"

"You don't have to hit me," Jimmy said. "I want to do it right. I try to do it right, only sometimes I seem to forget and can't remember where I am."

Professor Varolyas actually enjoyed giving Jimmy those slaps, because Dr. Soldessy had told him it was quite safe to do so. In fact, under the influence of the new personality that had been grafted on his old, the doctor assured Varolyas that Jimmy actually wanted to be slapped and gloried in the humiliation. "We have done a good job with him," Soldessy assured the professor, "and you need not be afraid of him." Varolyas was a little, self-important, fussy, wiry mite of five feet three with a bald head and goatee, and Jimmy could have throttled him or twisted his neck or destroyed him with one hand. But he never thought of doing so, because they were right and he was wrong, and nothing that happened to him was too bad to make up for the crime of espionage he had committed against an innocent people.

"Begin again," commanded Professor Varolyas. The "lessons" were conducted in Professor Varolyas's office in one of the buildings of the Andrássy prison and always in the presence of the guard, and with Jimmy standing endlessly and never entirely out of the grip of either a scopolamine injection or another drug with which they were experimenting and which never left him completely master of the processes of his mind. Nor did they ever leave Jimmy wholly free from some kind of internal pain or approach to exhaustion.

Jimmy started slowly. "I arrived in Vienna on March 23 and immediately embarked upon my assignment to enter the Hungarian People's Republic for purposes of military spying and sabotage intended to contribute to the overthrow of the Hungarian People's Government."

"Go on," said Professor Varolyas, "and look directly at us when you are speaking, as you will be looking at me in the Marko courtroom during the trial."

"I contacted a known criminal, an Austrian, named Biosh, who led me to the Café Prater in the Czerningasse, where I paid over the sum of five hundred schillings to a Hungarian named Laszlo. I never knew his other name, but I was told that he was engaged in the trade of smuggling persons both in and out of Hungary.

"I went with Laszlo to another café called Zum Lustigen Matrosen; it was a small outdoor garden on the Vienna side of the Danube, just below the Reichsbrücke on the Handelskai. There I was introduced to a Captain Maroffy, the owner of a coal barge. The man named Laszlo went away, and I entered into an agreement with Captain Maroffy for him to conceal me in his barge when he left for Budapest the next morning. I paid Captain Maroffy one thousand schillings.

"The next morning I embarked aboard the barge *Margareten Insel* at the Franz Josefs Kai on the Donau Canal just below the Schwendenbrücke, where the barge was tied up. It was my hope thus to be conveyed down the Danube to Budapest, where I planned to go ashore, conceal myself, and proceed with my investigations.

"I was unaware that Captain Maroffy was an honest

man and a patriot and, horrified at my attempt to bribe him to sell out his country, had notified agents of the Hungarian People's Police in Vienna, who placed two men aboard the barge unbeknownst to me. When I attempted illegally to go ashore in Budapest late that same evening, they arrested me."

Here Professor Varolyas nodded his goatee, consulted a paper on his desk in front of him, and said, "Now from the prosecutor comes a question." He cleared his throat and intoned dramatically, "By whom were you sent on this mission?"

The heavily given cue started Jimmy Race off without any difficulty. "By the Intelligence Section, G2 of the U.S. Army Staff Headquarters in Washington, D.C., affiliated with the new C.I.S., the Central Intelligence Service, which works in close collaboration with the embassies of the United States. In this instance I was to report the results of my investigations to Ambassador Vannaman to furnish him with material as part of a plot in which he was involved with two Catholic bishops and a former Hungarian Minister of the Christian Socialist Party, now turned traitor, the plot being to overthrow the Hungarian Government and seize power for the Western imperialists.

"My immediate superiors in detailing my assignment and sending me to Vienna to carry it out were Nicholas Strang, the editor of the Paris Edition of the *Chicago Sentinel,* a former intelligence officer of the U.S. Army, and his—his—" Jimmy stumbled and slowed to a halt.

Professor Varolyas looked up. There were impatience and anger in his bright, beady eyes. "Yes, yes. Go on. You know it well. His—"

Jimmy hesitatingly said, "His—" once more and then stopped dead. It always seemed to be like that for some reason when he reached this point and tried to bring out Suzy's name, in spite of the fact that Dr. Soldessy had proved to him that she and Nick had conspired to trick him into going to Budapest to serve their own selfish ends. He knew that Suzy was guilty, even more so than Nick, for as the doctor had pointed out, she had led him on, by her personal appeal, to the point where even had he wished to pause he could no longer distinguish right from wrong and there was no turning back.

The professor said sharply, "Well?" and leaned over and struck Jimmy in the face with his fingers.

It hurt Jimmy, not in his physical person, but in his soul, because he wanted so much to say it right and come to the part where he really confessed his guilt and his penitence for what he had done. He always felt better after he had finished with that part. He opened his mouth and tried, but no sound emerged.

Professor Varolyas spoke to the guard in Hungarian, and the man went over to an iron slop pail that stood in the corner of the office and began to beat its side with a desk ruler, and at once Jimmy began to shout a kind of gibberish and cry and sob, with his hands over his ears, and his feet stamping up and down in one place like someone in the grip of an uncontrollable tarantella, and bubbling words would break through. "No. . . . No. . . . I can't stand it. . . . You don't have to do that. . . . I want to confess. . . . I want to be hanged. . . . Don't-don't-don't do that. . . . I can remember it now. . . ."

When the banging was stopped, he stood there, trembling and shaking as though he were afflicted with palsy, his face misshapen and his mouth twisted, his eyes glassy and his throat full of tears at their needless cruelty to him. And his mind was full of frightening phantasies and images and he saw again the red, white-tasseled Santa Claus cap being waggled around the edge of the nursery doorway and tasted the same bitterness, now full-remembered, the disillusionment that the fat man with the white beard who brought presents was also an

Argus-eyed all-knowing policeman waiting to punish him.

The professor waited until he had calmed down and then said, "Go on. From 'Intelligence officer of the U.S. Army, and his—' "

"Wife, Suzanne Vincent Strang, a former member of the French underground Resistance movement, and now a secret agent of the reactionaries plotting against the peace party of France," Jimmy continued, and then rolled on automatically and unhindered as he detailed his crimes against the Hungarian State. And as always then, his burden seemed somewhat lifted and he could look forward to the solace of being hanged, which would put an end to all that he suffered and had suffered daily, physically and mentally, since his last act.

It was literally true that Jimmy yearned toward the form of execution scheduled for him. This had been a refinement of Dr. Soldessy's, a kind of experiment in line with the whole theory of reverse psychoanalysis, or psychosuggestion, as he called it, and his theory that a subject could be led to embrace a fear and a horror, the haunting horror of death by hanging, which might be said to affect any of the civilized race, and actually come to love it and see it as his salvation.

Besides his scientific interest, Dr. Soldessy, who considered himself not at all a bad fellow, had conceived it as a kind of act of mercy. In civilized countries, he knew, the condemned man is frequently drugged before the execution in order to spare him some of the misery and terror of full knowledge of what is about to take place. The doctor had believed that he could send to the gallows this big, fair American who had proved such a wonderful subject for his theories almost like a lover who goes to an assignation mentally half drugged by the anticipation of the physical and emotional ecstasies awaiting him.

"It is," he had said during one of the rare moments when he talked at length to Jimmy while Jimmy lay resting and half dozing on the couch and was, therefore, twice as receptive to what was said to him, "one of the easier and least cruel deaths, though men do not realize this. One falls into peace, quiet, and eternal rest, swiftly, easily, and painlessly and even, as the floor slips away from beneath one's feet, with a sense of ecstasy, of having already left the earth and being airborne.

"From the moment you mount the scaffold you will begin to experience the relief of expiation and the freedom of spirit that comes with the knowledge that amendment is being made. And from there you will take the short step to the ecstasy of death, which releases you from every obligation. When you understand what I am telling you, you will be impatient of any delay that keeps you from your rendezvous with peace."

Soldessy had been right, and it was particularly after one of these sessions in which he had been reminded of the horror of the pail, and was returned to the solitude of his brightly lit cell, that Jimmy would dwell on the moments of the transition that had been promised him as something toward which he must strive with all his powers.

18

LOOK EAST TO HUNGARY

SUZY, WHO STILL HAD HER STATUS as correspondent with U.S. Army accreditation from her last visit to Vienna with Nick, went by Army car from the airport located twenty kilometers deep in the Russian zone and checked in at the Bristol Hotel, which was reserved for American brass and their guests. She got in touch by telephone with the local P.R.O. major, whom she knew, and arranged to have a wire routed through to Nick which would not have to go through the Austrian post office and hence Russian censorship, advising him of her safe arrival in the Viennese capital.

She talked with the *portier* and arranged to have Jimmy's effects that he had left behind sent to her room and also acquired the key to his car, which was still standing in the big Army parking-lot at the corner of the Kärntner Ring and the Akademiestrasse. She tested the engine, which started when she stepped on the button. She drove it to the garage inside the Ministry of the Interior behind the Mozart Platz and had the batteries, tires, and engine checked.

When she returned to her room, Jimmy's effects were there, his Valpack, his Corona portable typewriter, a small hand trunk, a raincoat, and his briefcase. There was nothing in any of his papers that could possibly be of any help to either him or them in his present predicament; nevertheless, she examined them all thoroughly in case he should have left a note. But there was nothing but a few pages of a newly started short story, a war adventure, and the outline of another. There were no notes on Vienna, from which she gathered, as she had suspected all along, that right from the first Budapest had been his destination and that he had wasted no time getting familiar with the Austrian capital.

It seemed odd to be seeing Jimmy's luggage, which she had last encountered piled up in the back of Jimmy's car parked in the rue Marbeuf the day he had driven away, more than a month ago, but it brought her a kind of comfort, too, as though by taking his personal effects from the luggage room and keeping them with her, she had perhaps started a chain of events that somehow would force matters to the point where he might at any moment be coming stomping in to claim them.

It was now past midnight, but still she did not go to bed, but made a telephone call to a girl she knew, Anna Döschl, who had married an Austrian and settled down to live in Vienna. Anna had been in the Resistance with her in Paris and Lyon during the war.

Suzy said, "Anna, darling, it's me—Suzy. Suzy Strang. I've just flown in for a little visit and to get some things. Will you go shopping with me tomorrow? And I want to go to church."

The girl at the other end of the telephone was wary at once and watched her step because there was some kind of game up, otherwise Suzy would have spoken to her in French, their native language. She was careful to do no more than acquiesce in what Suzy proposed. "Suzy, dear, how wonderful! Of course. Shall we meet at the Stefans Dom tomorrow morning at ten? It will be so good to see you."

Suzy said, "That will be just perfect, darling, and we can go on from there. See you then," and hung up.

The next morning at ten Suzy met Anna at the Stephans Platz entrance to the great bomb-shattered church that loomed above them, its stone tracery intact, but its once wondrous roof burned out and now replaced with scaffolding and temporary wooden cover. By instinct, the two, experienced in the dangerous game they had played together in France, remained outside the church chatting and renewing their acquaintance, exchanging news and greetings, while their eyes took in the people hurrying past and searched particularly for any loiterers or watchers who might indicate that their telephone conversation had been tapped and that they were under surveillance.

There appeared to be none. They went inside the church. For a while they wandered about and together examined the damage to the exquisite interior that had taken place when the Nazi SS troops had wantonly shelled the superb Gothic monument and set it on fire. Then they selected a pew well in the center of the nave and went and knelt there quite alone and whispered their prayers, and whispered, too, of other things.

And Anna said in reply to what Suzy told her, "I must be so very careful, on account of my husband. It is very bad here. Much worse than it was under the Nazis. We no longer engage in any of that kind of activity. It is far too dangerous. My husband had a brother who simply disappeared one day. We never heard from him since."

She paused and looked about her, and even in the gloom of the cathedral interior Suzy could see the expression of fear in her eyes. But there was no one near them. The church was practically deserted. Anna dropped her sibilations even lower and whispered, "In the Neuer Markt behind the Kärntnerstrasse by the Donnerbrunnen, there is a fiacre stand. The driver of number 32, his name is Anton. He used to know and do contact for people who crossed."

Suzy walked into the Neuer Markt, the wide place distinguished by the Capuchin Church and the beautiful Donner Fountain, shortly after eleven, just as a sagging and dilapidated-looking carriage drawn by a single thin brown horse turned in from the Schwangasse, circled the fountain, and took its place on the end of the line. Suzy caught sight of the number *32* painted on the side lamps and hailed him.

The driver was an old man in a lumpy Jehu's coat and battered silk hat, with red-veined cheeks, deep-set, frosty eyes, and a tobacco-stained mustache.

He tipped his hat and asked, *"Ja, wohin möcht's gnädige Fräulein fahren?"*

"Just drive around the Ring," Suzy replied in her adequate German. "I want to see Vienna again."

"Yo yo, Fräulein. But there is not much left of our

poor city."

They set out past the shell of the bombed and burned-out Opera House, which was being rebuilt, and turned into the Burg Ring and drove between the spacious rococo beauties of the Maria Theresa Platz on the left and the Helden Platz on the right. Against the clop-clop of the horse's hoofs and the rumble of the iron-rimmed wheels on the street surface, the noise of motor traffic and the shrilling of the traffic policemen's whistles Suzy talked without fear of being overheard. She talked clearly and forcefully and explicitly to the back of the driver, as they wheeled past the Palace of Justice, which was flying the Red banner, having been taken over as Russian headquarters.

The driver did not turn around at any time, and Suzy might have been talking to a stone wall until they had passed the University, the undamaged Votivkirche and turned into the Schottengasse, when he shifted his head to the right just sufficiently to let his words drift back to her.

"If Fräulein wishes to see the best view of Vienna she should visit the Hochaus for lunch on the terrace. It is Vienna's highest building. There is a waiter there named Max, an excellent fellow who can describe the view to you. His station is on the side toward the east, looking out toward Hungary and the Danube. He has the same number as this fiacre. If you mention this to him he will be pleased to serve you. If I drive you there now, you will be certain to be able to choose your table for lunch."

Suzy paid twenty heller for a ticket to ride in the elevator to the top of the Hochhaus, Vienna's only skyscraper, an eighteen-story building with a dining-terrace that ran around the four sides. It was still early, and there was hardly anyone there. Suzy went out the door to the south and was captured by a headwaiter who tried to seat her.

She said, "I want to sit over on that side in the sun." She walked the terrace. The Danube and the sun came into view. There was a waiter standing by the rail with a napkin over his arm. He was a thin man with a narrow face, bent, projecting nose, and fierce, bushy eyebrows. He was wearing a metal badge on his white coat with the number *32.* Suzy stared at it just long enough for him to catch her glance and then said, "This table will do, thank you," and sat down.

The headwaiter brought the menu and wrote down her order. *Kraftbrühe mit Leberknödel, Beinfleisch mit Meerrettigsauce und Kopfsalat,* and gave a copy of it to waiter 32 and put a duplicate beneath a plate on her table.

The sweet, scarred, ancient city lay below her, all the gray buildings and winding streets and imposing monuments; behind her rose the tall spire of the Stefans Dom, in front in the distance rose the swelling twin breasts of the Kahlenberg and the Leopoldsberg. The Donau Canal was a winding ribbon, and the blue-gray line of the Danube made a straight line and barrier to the east. Beyond the broad river stretched a green plain, and far to the east of that was a series of low blue hills.

Waiter number 32 delivered the strong consommé with the brown liver dumplings floating in it. He fussed about the table moving the bread basket, the salt and pepper, extra utensils.

"Madame is a tourist?" he asked in French.

Suzy said, "Yes. I have just been seeing the sights of Vienna in a fiacre with the same number as yours, oddly enough."

The expression on number 32 did not change. He poured water and brought another tablespoon. He said, "The view from here is superb. There is none better in Vienna."

"We are looking east, are we not?"

Number 32 said, "Do you see those hills rising there in the distance beyond the Danube? That is Hungary."

Suzy said, "It looks enticing. I should like to be able to go there. I have a–some friends there."

When he brought her main course the terrace was still quite empty and they were able to talk quite a good deal until a Russian officer and a man in civilian clothes, obviously an official or policeman of some kind, came out and sat down a few tables away.

Waiter number 32 said, "Madame desires a sweet?"

"What is good? Something Viennese. What do you recommend?"

"The Hochhaus is not noted for its pastries. If I might make a suggestion, madame might enjoy going to a *Konditorei* near by for her coffee and sweet. Konditorei Schump. It is famous for its *Sacher* and *Dobos Torte.*"

"Where is it?"

"If Madame will permit, I will write down the address for her."

He went away and returned with her bill and a small slip of folded paper on which was written: *Konditorei Schump, Wildpret-Markt Numero 2A, I.*

"It is a small place, just back of the Peters-Kirche," he said, "not far from here. Only Frau Schump and a waitress, but she does all her own baking, if you care for Viennese specialties."

The Russian and the civilian had left off discoursing in low tones and appeared to be trying to listen to what they were saying, or at least identify the language. Suzy noted that the piece of folded paper appeared to have been torn off a small scratch pad on which an addition as of items of a bill had been made, some five or six numbers. Her quick eye made a swift stab to see whether the number 32 was included in them. It was. She put the slip with the address into her purse, said, "Thank you," and paid her bill and left.

The Russian officer said to his companion, "Did you see? A damned attractive woman."

The civilian said coldly, "Too attractive." He summoned waiter 32 and asked in heavily accented German, "Who was she? What language did she speak?"

Number 32 said, "I do not know, Herr Capitaine. She is a tourist, a Frenchwoman—Parisian by her chic, no?"

The officer said, "A woman like that ought not to be alone."

The civilian grunted. Then he and the officer again resumed their conversation in Russian. Waiter 32 turned and cleared the table where Suzy had been sitting. A small bead of sweat had formed at the side of his nose. He wiped it away absent-mindedly with a corner of the napkin on which were the red marks of Suzy's lipstick, and noted that his hand was trembling.

Suzy reflected upon what children men were, as she caught a passing taxi, and how incontestably like children they played their secret-service games, a kind of solemn-faced hide-and-seek with codes and numbers and all the paraphernalia of the cloak-and-dagger spy thriller novels, but then she remembered her own days in the Resistance, where a slip meant a life, and returned to the realization that, after all, that was the *only* way to play it, and she guessed perhaps she was growing older, for it no longer carried the same appeal for her.

There had to be, she knew, a carefully linked chain that could be broken anywhere on its way to the top without endangering those two close to either side of the break. She was convinced now that Anna had started her on the right track. She wondered only how complicated was the system that led to the organization that dealt with spiriting out of the country Hungarian refugees from Communism and how many posts on the pass-along she would have to visit before she encountered someone of sufficient weight and authority to help her find what she wanted to know.

Frau Schump was only another step on the way. Suzy was directed to visit the Café Zauner and have some words with a professorial-looking old gentleman who sat there drinking *café mélange* and endlessly reading the house copy of the *Wiener Neue Freie Presse.* She went next to a Hungarian restaurant in the Russian sector of the city, a dingy, uncomfortable place where she felt afraid for the first time, but there she apparently passed her most severe test, for she was then sent to interview a perfectly preposterous man in leather shorts, a Tyroler shirt, and a big floppy hat such as Englishwomen sometimes wear when they do their gardening. By now she had acquired Jimmy's car and was driving herself. She found him, looking exactly like an owl, or the pictures she had seen of Alexander Woollcott, sitting under the wreckage of the Floridsdorfer Brücke by one of the shore piers that was still standing; he was fishing for carp with bread balls that he fashioned out of the center of a loaf of bread, kneading them out of soft dough, molding them onto his hook, and lowering them carefully into the Danube.

His name was Baron Willy von Starlem, and when Suzy came over to the bank of the river he made place for her amid his gear and said, "How do you do? Won't you sit down? I have heard about you, and of course I know about your husband. What is it that we can do for you?"

Suzy felt unaccountably like giggling, he looked so fat, funny, and owlish in his outlandish rig—the spectacle of a grown man fishing with breadballs for bait. She said, "My husband once caught a trout while lying in bed. We have a mill, you know, and the water goes right past the bedroom door."

The baron smiled and said, "I should like to try that.

Still, until one has engaged a forty-pound carp on a light bamboo rod, I should say–"

"Then you really *do* fish," Suzy said. "It isn't just–"

"Oh, no. I am most fond of the sport. Besides, it is good for my nerves. Recommended by the doctor." He looked owlishly at Suzy and then repeated, "What can I do for you?"

She told him. The baron reflected. An enormous shadow beneath the muddy surface of the river passed in the vicinity of his line, and the baron's little nostrils twitched, but the shadow failed to connect. He said, "You ought to go to the Villa Thalia. They would be certain to be able to help you there. I am very much surprised that you did not go there in the first place."

"How could I have," Suzy replied, "when I never heard of it before and don't know where it is?"

"Now, that surprises me even more," said the Baron, and tried to tease the shadow by twitching the line with the lump of dough on the end. "I thought *everybody* knew about the Villa Thalia, including the Czechs, the Hungarians, *and* the Russians. It's quite silly, you know, that all the little ones should have to hide behind drops and false names and code numbers, while everyone knows where the big fish are–like that fellow down there, and, like him, when I see him I know I shall not be able to catch him."

After this slightly ambiguous statement he sighed deeply, pulled up his line, detached the bread therefrom, and threw it into the river, where a moment later a huge swirl and splash indicated that the carp was delighted to have it without the hook. The baron said, "Very well, then I shall have to take you there. I see you have the car of that unfortunate young man who is languishing in prison in Budapest and will shortly be hanged. It is not the wisest vehicle for you to be seen around Vienna with, my dear. You have simply no idea how people talk in this city. We will park it somewhere and engage some less conspicuous conveyance."

Suzy felt like a small and not very bright child. She waited downstairs outside his flat while he changed his clothing. They got rid of the vedette at the garage and engaged a hired car at the Bristol for the evening. The baron first insisted upon taking Suzy to the Kursaal, an enormous outdoor restaurant with terraces on three levels set in a small park off the Schubert Ring, because, he explained to her, all the spies in Vienna gathered there during the cocktail hour and if he remained away it would cause comment.

At a near-by table sat a big beefy man with a pock-marked face and the build of a heavyweight wrestler. There were four dyed blondes with him. The baron leaned closer to Suzy and said, "That is Laszlo Biro. He is the one who originally betrayed your young man to the Hungarian secret police, for which he received a thousand schillings, which enabled him to add the fourth blonde to his entourage. He also does odd kidnaping jobs for the Russians."

Suzy felt a sick feeling in the vicinity of her heart. She opened her lips to reply to the possible implication in the baron's use of the possessive case to describe Jimmy, but closed them again without speaking. The baron went on and listed the spies, thugs, black-marketeers, Cominform stool pigeons, agents, spies, and counter-intelligence agents within range of them, pointed out Vienna's reigning hetaera, and gossiped about the women who were the mistresses of this fantastic hodge-podge of international intrigue.

Thereafter he took Suzy to dinner to the Balkan Grill in another part of the town, curbing her impatience with the observation that the inmates of the Villa Thalia discouraged visits before it was really dark. The food was spiced, swimming in grease, and highly indigestible, a pig and a police dog wandered amiably around the garden, the proprietor, a Bulgarian, wore knickers, and in one corner a party of American correspondents amused themselves by smashing empty bottles with which the proprietor provided them.

Shortly after ten o'clock the baron said, "Well–" and pulled his bulk together. They got into the car, and the baron gave the driver an address that lay somewhere between Grinzing and Kobenzl in the hills, though still nominally inside the city limits of Vienna and in the American zone.

It was too dark for Suzy to distinguish more than a large pillared and white-painted house with a red-tiled roof located behind an iron fence at which an American military policeman stood guard. He examined the baron's credentials by flashlight and passed them on through. At the portal of the villa the baron yanked an old-fashioned bell-pull, which disturbed the night with its jangling, and another M.P. opened the door, which the baron filled with his bulk, blotting out the lighted interior from Suzy's view. But she heard an American voice that sounded vaguely familiar say, "Hello, Baron. What's cookin'? You here on that Arvaszy deal? They won't be ready to move on that until Thursday. They haven't got that mine field located yet south of Magyaróvár. Come in, come in. Well, Suzy!"

The last exclamation was the result of the baron's unblocking the doorway and revealing Suzy behind him, and a not too happy Suzy. For she recognized the tall, uniformed man with the major's leaf at his shirt collar and the short-cropped blond hair as Ed Slater, the G2 major she and Nick both knew from previous visits to Vienna and a former associate of her husband's during the war.

He said, "Suzy, I don't get it. How did you run into the baron? Do you know him?"

Baron Starlem said, "The hard way. Through Channel 32."

Suzy said contritely, "I'm sorry. Forgive me. I didn't know. Nick told me to check in with you as soon as I got here. I thought I was being clever."

The major said with some exasperation, "Honestly, I don't know why you people don't come right to us when you want something instead of stumbling around tripping over our operatives and getting yourselves tailed by counteragents. We've always tried to give you newspaper people anything we could tell you within the security—"

Suzy said, "Please forgive me. I just didn't realize. I had to get in touch with somebody who just knew something about the underground out of Budapest."

Major Slater laughed. "Hell," he said, "we've been handling that deal for the past three years. We work with the refugee committee. They tell us who's worth having and we snag 'em out. You want to look over our little plant here. It's quite good. Come on, I'll show you around."

They went with him and saw the wireless room, the map room, the files and records where Wacs pecked away at a half-dozen typewriters, the clothing supply, the upstairs quarters where the refugees were parked until they could be sent along on the next lap through the Russian zone into Salzburg, another room where the guides stayed between shows, a dark room, laboratory, and small photoengraving plant.

"We do a couple of other jobs out here as well," Slater explained. "Now, what did you say the approximate date was when this joker whose name you don't know came through?"

Suzy said, "Sometime between the 1st and the 18th of December 1948. Because on the 18th of December there was some trouble and some shooting when the

Hungarians tried to kidnap him back again. One of the Hungarians was wounded and arrested, and the refugee escaped."

The major said without hesitation, "Oh, that guy. Little mustachy feller with scared eyes. Was supposed to have been secretary to one of the big shots. I remember him. He came through on the run made either on the 8th or the 9th. We'll just go dig him up out of the files."

Suzy followed the major into the file room. She could feel the wild beating of her heart. It was true, then. Nick had invented him out of necessity, but he was no dream. He existed.

The major went straight to one of the steel filing-cabinets and without hesitation pulled out the second drawer from the bottom.

19

NEWS FROM VIENNA

DAD LAPHAM FOUND NICK sitting in his office, his chin sunk on his chest, staring straight before him, and when Dad came in he started and involuntarily put his hand to his throat. He had been thinking of Jimmy Race—that he would soon be hanged—and his mind had dwelt horribly upon the process. He had thought of the big, vital man, full of life and energy to squander, his skin bulging with the blood and bones that filled it, his smile, his compelling gaze and voice, and then he saw him gasping and kicking like a marionette at the end of a string, the hangman crushing the cartilage of his throat and strangling the breath and life out of him, or again he saw him pendant there with his neck broken from the drop, his head over to one side like a big broken doll's and slowly revolving in the hollow of the trap.

Dad said, "Boy, you've sure got your dauber down. What do you hear from Suzy?"

"Nothing since she arrived. Dad, I'm scared to death. If she tries to go on over into Hungary–"

Dad looked at him. "What would she be wanting to go into Hungary for?"

Nick said, "To be nearer to him."

Dad said, "Are you kidding?"

Nick got up and walked up and down behind his desk. "I dunno. Maybe I wish I was. I suppose it does sound as though I'm going off my rocker. But I'm neither deaf nor blind. The whole office knew Jimmy was crazy about her."

Dad nodded. "Uh-huh. I guess that's so. But what has that go to do with Suzy?"

Nick looked out the window dispiritedly. He said, as though speaking half to himself, those things he had thought so often in the past month. "If he hangs, Suzy will never forgive me. I've seen it in her eyes. She warned me against sending him to Vienna."

Dad said softly, "Well, why did you send him, then?"

Nick had to hear himself say it. "Maybe I wanted to get him out of town."

Dad whistled. "You really believe all that baloney, don't you?"

It was Nick's turn to stare. "What's the difference? Time's run out on us. It's not only Jimmy's end, but Suzy's, and the paper's and the whole gang's. If he is executed I doubt whether the paper will survive it. That's what I get for thinking I could play God and get the guy out of the jam sitting on the editorial fat and dreaming up screwball ideas that haven't the ghost of a show of working."

Dad looked at Nick long and hard, sat down on the edge of the desk, and let his feet out in front of him. He said very earnestly, "Listen, kid. You're making silly talk and I'm not used to that from you. You've been around this racket long enough to know that it takes two kinds to run a successful newspaper, or pull stunts, and you'll find it wherever anybody comes up with a beat of from ten minutes to ten hours. There's the brain and the experience that dreams up the story or the situation because he knows, or *feels,* that that is what it ought to be like from the way things have been happening, and then there are the people who go out into the field and dig up the facts, and dammit, if they have to, make them fit the story. Maybe we haven't worked hard enough on our end of it, or been smart enough at getting more information that would lead us to this guy. I was the one who kept knocking it down when you were working it out, but I'm telling you not to write this deal off yet. Suzy might turn up stuff in Vienna we never even dreamed of. Remember, she–"

The telephone interrupted him. Nick lifted the receiver. The operator told him, "Madame Strang calling you from Vienna, M'sieu Strang."

Nick's hand holding the receiver trembled. He said, "Don't go away, Dad. This may be it. And whichever way it goes, thanks!"

Suzy came on. There was high and suppressed excitement in her voice, but she did not waste any words. She said, "Nick! You were right. The little man exists. Write this down. His name is Lajos–Gabor Lajos. You didn't go quite far enough when you invented him. You failed to give him a family. He has a wife and daughter who went to Paris through Switzerland in October 1948. The wife's name is Maria and the daughter's Ilya. She is a girl of about twenty-one or so. They had passports, but Lajos lost his when he was arrested in Budapest shortly after his family got out. The G2 boys finally got Lajos out of Hungary. I feel silly. We could have got all this if we had gone to G2 in Vienna right away. Oh,

Nick, if it's too late—"

He shouted into the telephone, "It may not be. We can't miss turning him up with that dope." He paused, hesitated a moment, and then spoke again. "You'd better stay in Vienna, Suzy. If it works we'll want you there to handle things. If it doesn't—"

"Nick! It must work. You must find him now."

"We'll try, Suzy. Keep your chin up. I'll let you know if we get a break. In the meantime maybe you can dig up someone in Vienna with whom Lajos discussed his plans, where he would go, what he would do when he got to Paris. Dad sends his love. Good-by."

Dad was studying him. He said, "The complete masochist. You sure like to make yourself suffer. If we spring Jimmy, Suzy will be the first one on hand to greet the returning hero if and when he is pushed over the border."

Nick could not get angry at Dad. He merely said, "Mebbe you're right. What difference does it make either way? Suzy deserves it. She's the only one who really showed any brains in this deal. I should have had someone in Vienna three weeks ago. I've been a flop on this from the very start—from the time that guy walked in." He thought for a moment and said, "By God, I'm going out on the street on it myself in the morning. I'll—"

Dad grinned at him. "No, you won't, Nick," he said. "You're an editor, an inside man. Never forget it. Why do they call a reporter a leg man? Because he earns his living with his calf muscles. I'd strip the office of every available guy, and you and I can handle a trick at the copy desk, or answer telephones, but sooner or later something's going to come up where they'll want somebody with a bean on him right here in the office, who can come up with something nobody else thought of, or make a decision. Kid, you'd better pull yourself together.

You used to be one hell of a good editor or you wouldn't have made this spot. You forget what an editor is. He's the captain of the ship."

To Janet Goodpenny, the news that the tragedy of Jimmy Race was drawing to a close brought a kind of numbness that was nevertheless fraught with understanding. She had neither the time nor the inclination to pity herself now that there did not any longer seem to be much chance of his surviving.

She had loved him hopelessly from the first, she had never truly had any real belief in the affair or thought that he had ever really cared for her. She knew that she had lived on the appearances of things, the one night in which they had been out together and he had kissed her with real warmth and affection. She remembered, too, the farewell that he had taken from her outside the editorial room, and knew in her heart that his kiss then and the entire little scene had been nothing but a bribe to keep her quiet so that his designs would not be spoiled.

She did not resent this or feel sorry for herself that she had been taken in. If anything, she admired Jimmy all the more for the ruthlessness with which he went after and gained his ends. He knew what he wanted and went after it, refusing to let anything stand in his way. He was a man.

But she was racked by two emotions; one, that she loved him deeply and everything in her yearned for him, the massive warmth of his embrace, in which one could lose oneself, his smile, his voice, and the tough, truculent mind that so appealed to her; and the other was that she blamed herself for having fallen victim to his line, thereby contributing to the catastrophe that had befallen him.

Even in this Janet's reaction was healthy and normal. She knew that actually she was not responsible for his predicament, but that a word from her might have prevented it. He was going to die, and she could have saved him had she been less childish and in love. Here was reproach enough.

The news told to her by Dad Lapham that Jimmy's trial was scheduled for the next day she had accepted without any outward show of emotion. She continued to do her work, but when her lunch hour came she could neither eat nor bear to remain in the office, where the talk was only of Jimmy Race and his probable chances if any.

She walked down the Champs-Elysées to the pretty little park just below the Rond-Point where the exquisitely dressed children played in the warm spring sunshine, and there she sat on a bench by herself. She tried not to think and hoped that the music of the tiny carousels, the noise of the Punch and Judy shows, the laughter and screaming of the children and the gabble of the nursemaids would bring her surcease for a little.

And, indeed, the infectious hubbub of the children's playground, the venders with their colored balloons, the tots tumbling in the sand piles, did help her, until with a start of surprise she suddenly saw Grisha, the tipster who had been booted out of the office, coming around the curve of the path and walking toward her.

He was selling assorted cookies and sweetcakes from a tray that was suspended about his neck and shoulders by two strips of leather. As always, inside the jacket collar of his suit he still wore the dreadful diamond-patterned green-red-and-yellow scarf. His small mouth and mustache were twitching nervously, as usual, and his large eyes roved from side to side, apparently in search of customers for his wares.

To see him thus was enough to awaken all the painful memories in Janet, memories momentarily stilled. She saw herself back in the office again, with Jimmy

Race looming over the little man, and she thought, too, of the dreadful afternoon when the whole roomful of men had chivvied the innocent and harmless little fellow out of the place for something that was no fault of his.

She felt ashamed all over again as she thought of this, and rather hoped that Grisha would not see her. She even started half to rise and leave when he was looking the other way, but it was too late. His glance caught her. She saw the sign of recognition on his face, and he came over to her.

They exchanged greetings. He said, "Please, you will have one of my cakes, no? A small present. They are good. They are baked at home. I think you will like."

To please him, Janet took one nibble at it. She was so sorry for him, to see him forced down to street peddling. She thought how even more ineffectual he looked because of the tray suspended about his neck.

He said, "You have not been dismissed, like me, I hope? Forgive me, but you do not look happy. You have been ill?"

Janet said, "No, Grisha, I haven't been fired. But things have not been very good at the office since you left."

And then she had a sudden impulse to tell him everything that had happened—Jimmy's trouble, Nick's discovery, the long, hopeless search, and the end that would come to Jimmy. For a moment she looked into his prominent, sorrowful eyes and felt suddenly that they were filled with depths of understanding. And the story poured out of her, and sometimes tears, too, that she could not manage to keep back. But she felt better when she had told it all to someone else.

Grisha stood looking down at her until she had finished. There was an expression that she could not fathom, and he opened his mouth to speak to her, when the look on his face was replaced by one of fear and alarm.

Then he performed something astonishing and miraculous with the tray, which appeared to have some kind of box fastened underneath into which all of the little cakes disappeared. The tray was then removed from around his neck, folded double on a hinge, and tucked under his arm. Without saying a word to her he turned swiftly away and hurried down the curving path, threading his way through the hordes of playing children, nor did he turn around again and soon he was lost to sight.

Janet thought, *What a strange little man! And why did he look at me that way? He seemed about to tell me something and then got frightened.*

She pondered upon the mystery, but only for a moment, when it solved itself for her.

From behind her, on the path, approaching with the steady, unhurried, menacing gait of the policeman on patrol, came a pair of blue-clad gendarmes. Unquestionably Grisha had spotted them and fled before them.

Janet's heart ached inside her and she thought, *The poor little man. Peddling without a license, of course. What a miserable existence!* She wished she had thought to tell him to come back to the office and try his luck again.

20

PRELUDE TO CONFESSION

IT WAS THE MORNING of the trial of the American spy in the Marko Street courtroom. In Andrássy Prison a barber and a masseur were putting the finishing touches to Jimmy Race to prepare him for the event under the ever watchful eye of Professor Varolyas. To all intents and purposes he now looked exactly like the man who had entered Andrássy six weeks before—if one did not get close enough to see the pupils of his eyes.

The preparation had been going on since two nights before when Jimmy had been permitted forty-eight hours of uninterrupted sleep. Imperceptibly, too, his prison fare had been increased and embellished so that drawn look and the starvation pallor had almost vanished from his face.

He had been kneaded, rubbed, and massaged. His hair had been trimmed and ice applied to his face and neck. He had been shaved, mud-packed, and manicured and his clothes returned to him, the linen washed and crisp, the suit cleaned and pressed, the shoes shined.

Now as he lay in the chair the barber took a small jar from the small black bag he had brought into the prison chamber, containing his tools, liquids, and pomades, dipped his fingers in it, and lightly massaged Jimmy's cheeks.

Professor Varolyas watched him curiously and then asked in Hungarian, "What is that?"

The barber replied, *"Sere Cheka,* Excellency. It is an herb. It was much used by Rumanian and Hungarian officers in"—here he coughed slightly—"the old days, to give them some color in their cheeks after a fatiguing day. You will see how it blends and that it will be impossible to distinguish—"

Professor Varolyas said, "I see. For whom did you two work in the—ah—old days?"

The masseur said, "For a certain nobleman, Excellency—like so many of us. But that is all forgotten now, is it not? Times are different today. One earns one's living the best one can. I am sure the American gentleman will make an excellent impression in the courtroom. The count used to come home in the early morning hours looking much worse, but by eleven o'clock I would always have him looking presentable for appearing to make a speech in Parliament. So now—"

He swung Jimmy upright in the chair and applied himself to massaging the colorless ointment he had taken from the jar into Jimmy's cheeks just below the eyes and over and under the cheekbones until it had quite vanished into the pores of his skin. Then he seized a piece of ice and began to work it around in widening circles over the same area, until the skin was quite chilled and white-looking. He let it rest for a little, while he skipped about from side to side and behind Jimmy and snipped a bit here and combed a bit there in the immemorial gesture of barbers the world over. He said to Varolyas, "Now you shall see the wonderful action of the *Sere Cheka*. You remember the gentleman was still quite pale and not of a too good color in spite of the packs and the massage. Well, now. And the beauty is that the results will be found to last for at least forty-eight hours."

And here he began to flick Jimmy's cheeks smartly and sharply with his finger tips. Almost immediately it seemed that blood and color began to flow into his face, healthily, beneath the surface of the skin instead of on top, where any changes in the pallor of Jimmy's face due to emotion during the trial, would have made a rouge or a cosmetic instantly noticeable.

Jimmy began to speak, clearly and without hesitation of any kind. He said, "I arrived in Vienna on March 23, and immediately embarked upon my assignment to enter the Hungarian People's Republic for purposes of military spying and sabotage intended to contribute to the overthrow—"

Professor Varolyas interrupted him with a cry of rage. He was purple in the face. "Not now, you fool! Not here! Keep quiet!"

Jimmy looked at him with a long, slow, uncomprehending stare in which there was deep hurt and bewilderment. His words came haltingly now and thick, for he was still under the influence of the drugs and was so conditioned that the only thing that would emerge from his brain and speech centers was the confession.

"But I thought—when you hit me— It's so hard to keep it in— Don't you want everyone to know—"

The barber and the masseur exchanged a quick look and busied themselves applying the finishing touches to Jimmy.

Professor Varolyas recovered himself. "Soon," he said to Jimmy. "Soon you will have your opportunity." To the attendants he said briefly, "The American is so overwhelmed with the sense of his guilt of crime against the people of Hungary that he wishes to be sure of the things he wishes to tell the court."

Jimmy repeated, "Soon it will be all over. You promised me."

The editorial room of the Paris Edition had begun to take on the aspects of a newspaper involved in a hot story rather than a dignified, semipolitical sheet ambling leisurely to press. Every available person of the staff was on the street running down leads. In the office Mark Mosher handled the rewrite, Dad Lapham was acting as news editor, reading the incoming press copy as well as working on Suzy's editorial page and the layout of the main news pages, while Nick confined himself to directing the search for three Hungarians named Lajos living in Paris somewhere under an assumed name.

Felix Victor and Art Glass had been working the police and Ministry of the Interior end in an attempt to trace the movements of the wife and daughter of Lajos, and the trail was running thin.

Both women, it appeared, had maintained the strict

legalities, entering the country by air from Switzerland. They had arrived at Orly Airport on the 13th of October in 1948, with properly valid and visaed Hungarian passports. They had filled out the small police questionnaires demanded of every foreigner entering France and had given the address of a small pension in Neuilly as the address of their intended stay in Paris. They had also completed the formalities of the *Devisen,* or currency control, and made out and presented a baggage declaration. They did not appear to have had a large amount of luggage accompanying them. Everything, Nick observed from the reports that filtered in over the telephone, was apparently intended to give the impression both in Hungary and in Paris that Mme. Lajos and her daughter had come to Paris for a brief visit or pleasure trip.

Through Nick's connections with the government, Art Glass had been able to get a look at the original police entry cards made out by the two passengers who had arrived from Zurich via Swissair. The age of Mme. Lajos was given as forty-four, and that of the daughter, Ilya, as twenty-two. They had indicated the length of their intended stay as four weeks. Under French law they were permitted three months before they were required to apply for a police registration and identity card, or an extension of their visa.

And then Felix Victor was on the telephone to Nick. He said, "Sorry. I'm a Jonah. Dead end at Neuilly. They came here and registered at this pension and stayed for a week. The landlady remembers them very well and I've got a fair description. The kid, apparently, is a pip, dark-haired and a little Oriental-looking. The mother impressed the woman here as being quite a lady, but she said she did not seem to be very happy. No, they never had any man with them, apparently went out very little and seemed to have no friends. After a week they checked out. They left a forwarding address, a small hotel on the Left Bank. I'm there now. They never came here. No evidence of them ever having arrived under that or any other name, since the proprietor has no record of two women alone registering on or about the time they left Neuilly. No mail came for them, either. What next, boss?"

Nick said, "Okay. It's all right. It figured to be that way. We're working on a list of pawnshops for you. Sooner or later women like that have to sell pieces of jewelry. In the meantime go back to Neuilly and pump the landlady of the pension. Get every possible scrap of information about the two of them, anything she can remember that may prove useful. Try to find out if the kid had any talents or could do anything—anything that might give us a lead."

Mark said, "Ferdie Hoffman's on two. He's been trying to crack the Hungarian Embassy."

Nick took the phone. "Yes Ferd."

The feature man said, "Look here—they couldn't or wouldn't give me anything but a lot of black looks and the run-around—you know how those Commie embassies are now—but I got the impression there was a hell of a lot more going on there when I sprang my sixty-four-dollar question than they wanted me to know."

Nick said, "Yes, I see. What was it?"

"That they would like to get their hooks on the Lajos family as much as we would. It was news to them that they might be in Paris, and apparently good news, from the way they looked at one another and gabbled in Hungarian. Maybe it isn't good that they know. Anyway, they started to try to pump me."

"Did you give?"

"No. But listen, Nick. When they started to gab, there was one thing I understood. It was 'Paprika Csardas.' That's a joint, a restaurant in the Place de la République section. It's real Hungarian. I went there once with a girl. Cass would know about it."

Nick said, "That's good. It's a lead. Come in." But when he hung up he swore. "Of course the Embassy wants them. Ordy would give his right eye to turn them up. If these birds can do it it'll mean decorations and promotions for them. Now we've stirred them up. But hell, we had to. Where's Cass?"

Mark said, "Dad is talking to him on 37."

"Switch it. Hello, Cass. Nick. What do you know about a Hungarian joint called Paprika Csardas?"

Cass said, "A dump. Strictly for Hungarians. Nobody else could eat there. It's on the east side of town near the Place de la Bastille. Small place and you got to order ahead of time."

"Get over there. The Hungarian Embassy mentioned the place. Looks as though they think the Lajos people might go there or have gone there, or the people running it might know where they are. But move fast, because it's a cinch there'll be people from the Embassy snooping. Dig, kid. You've got to come up with something."

Later in the day they trooped in with their reports. Felix Victor said, "I got all the landlady could remember, which isn't much. You know, it was a long time ago and they only stayed a week. They didn't seem to have much money, because they never brought any purchases home and the impression was that Mrs. Lajos had to be very careful. They didn't have any apparent means of support. The old lady—I mean, the mother—could cook. The landlady said that one day when the help was out, she went into the kitchen and baked her some kind of an Austrian or Hungarian cake, and it was good. The kid didn't seem to be able to do much of anything. She could read and speak French, but that was about all. There was a piano in the pension, but she never touched it. They both appeared to be very nervous. They paid their bill in full before they went, and didn't appear to have much money left."

At two-thirty Cass McGuire came in, his coat collar turned up, his hat at a rakish angle. He said, "Chief, I dunno. I got a kind of a lead. Maybe it's an angle. But it can't be checked—at least not right now."

Nick said, "The hell you say. Where'd you get it? The Paprika joint? What is it?"

"Well, no. They didn't seem to know anything about this pair at the restaurant, or they weren't going to give, but I got to talking to the old guy who runs the joint—he used to be a chef in Budapest—and after I promised to give him a plug in my column, he steered me to a little pastry shop in the Jewish section a half-dozen blocks away, a real tough neighborhood. It's run by a couple of Hungarians and they specialize in things like that—you know, *Kuglehupf, Linzertorte, Krapfen,* and all kinds of cakes and cookies like that. She says there is a Hungarian woman whose name she does not know who bakes for her, at home, wherever that is. She comes once every week with stuff she's baked, sells it, gets paid for it, and goes away."

"Hey!" exclaimed Felix Victor, and pointed his finger at Nick.

Nick nodded. "The cook! The woman who baked a Hungarian cake for the landlady. That would be a way to make a living, wouldn't it? And no questions asked."

Ferdie Hoffman asked, "Yes, but what about the girl, the daughter?"

Cass said, "Yeah—and I got a lead on that, too. I asked about her. The old dame in the pastry shop said the woman with the cakes always came in by herself, but that she knew she had a daughter, because sometimes during the transaction she would stop a few minutes and talk in Hungarian with her. The shopkeeper asked her how she could bake so much by herself and the woman said that she had her daughter to help her at night. She said that by day the daughter had a job as a mannequin in one of the dressmaking houses in Paris. The shopkeeper guessed that was why the daughter never came into the shop with the mother."

A copy boy came in and laid a sheet of Transoceanic Press copy on the desk. Nick glanced at it. It read: *Race Trial—Budapest, 800,* and the dateline: *Budapest—by Alan Bolos.*

In the grim, gloomy, People's courtroom in the Marko St. courthouse here today, an American reporter, James G. Race, on trial for his life on charges of espionage, joined a long list of those who have stood up at Red trials and confessed fully to having committed the crimes with which they are charged.

In his lengthy confession, which began here this afternoon and will be continued tomorrow, Race, who appeared to be fit and in excellent health, speaking in a calm, clear voice, involved not only himself but his newspaper, the Paris Edition of the Chicago Sentinel, *the editor, Nicholas Strang, of New York, former major in Army Intelligence, and his wife, as well as the American Ambassador to Hungary and many others.*

Nick felt his heart sicken within him and swore. "What did they do to the guy? They must have torn his guts out piece by piece." Then he resolutely pushed the piece of press copy over to Mitchell Connell, saying almost absent-mindedly, "Page one. Let it run," and turned back to Cass. "What dress house? Man, there's a couple of hundred in Paris."

Cass said, "She didn't know."

Nick swore again. He said, "Well, anyway, it's the mother we want. Have you got her lined up?"

Cass looked troubled. He said, "That's the catch, chief. I said it couldn't be checked immediately. The shopkeeper doesn't know where the Hungarian woman lives. And she was in yesterday to deliver. It'll be another four days before she comes again."

They all looked unhappily at Nick, but he did not swear any more. The jinx that seemed to be following them made ordinary violence seem foolish and futile. But he looked around the room, taking them all in, counting, mentally marshaling and dividing them. He said, "All right, then. It's the girl. We'll take a chance on the top houses first. If she were hiding, she might pick one of the more obscure ones, but Vic says she's good-looking so the chances are she'd make one like Dior or Balenciaga, and the pay is better. Most of the girls are well-known models in those houses so it won't take too long to check any new ones. Two questions to ask. Any girl come to work since the winter of '48 and whether she is under her right name, or was formerly known as Lajos. Everybody goes out on this except Joe Short, Mitchell Connell, Dad, and myself—Mark, Cass, Krine and Tate, Felix and Art, Ferd, Mr. Stafford, Janet, Nan, August, Lisa—"

Mitchell Connell protested. "Hey, wait a minute, Nick. You've cleaned out the whole staff. We've got to get out a paper."

Nick said, "Dad and I will read copy for you. Joe can take the desk and do any rewrite that's needed at the same time. If we want something or need to look something up, we can damn well do it ourselves. There's too much fuss made about getting out a paper, anyway. So it'll look lousy. Nobody will know the difference but us. Hey, where the deuce is Thyra? She's got most of these joints at her finger tips. She ought to know all about them. Why isn't she here?"

Mark Mosher consulted his schedule. "René Vesoul

is having an opening, the spring showing, at three this afternoon, and she's covering. We won't be able to reach her until then."

"Okay. Phone over there to have her call the office as soon as she comes in. She can start there. Janet, dig into her desk. She must have a list of all the most important houses somewhere. We'll split 'em up. There'll be a dozen of you on the street. You ought to be able to cover sixty or seventy of them. And I want you to phone in after each one, in case we've had a break in the meantime. Let's get going."

21

CONFESSION IS GOOD FOR THE SOUL

IN THE COURTROOM of the Marko-Utcza, Jimmy Race got on with his confession with the feeling of ease and confidence that comes to a good actor who has trained and rehearsed faithfully, who is up in his lines and knows that he can rely upon the grooves of his memory to supply words, sentences, inflections in the proper order.

He kept his eyes on the goatish countenance of Professor Varolyas, who was sitting in the front row next to Dr. Soldessy, nodding his head in approval at the beginning of each new paragraph, as it were. They were, in fact, something like parents at a graduation exercise, and their presence gave Jimmy a sense of comfort and the desire to outdo himself since both had worked so long and hard to help him.

The audience in the dark, gloomy courtroom sat in rows of cold, bitter hostility, hard faces bent upon him with hatred. They had been propaganda-fed to regard him with the deepest loathing, inspired by carefully instilled class-warfare propaganda. For years they had been taught to concentrate upon an abstract enemy, something called Western Imperialism, antidemocratic, warmongering, something, they were told, that wished to destroy them. Here, at last, was a tangible example of this enemy, a big, prosperous, and arrogant-looking man who had come as an emissary of these enemy nations to spy upon them and plot their downfall. The courtroom vibrated with their hatred.

Nowhere, as Jimmy gazed out across it, was there a friendly face or a soft eye, something or someone to encourage that other twisted and malformed self which had been buried so deeply within him and of which there were but the faintest of echoes from time to time. If there were foreign correspondents in the room who might have been sympathetic to him, he did not know who or where they were.

At intervals around the wall of the old-fashioned courtroom hung red-painted pails of sand for fire, with *Tuz* painted on the side in white letters. There were guards posted at intervals around the periphery of the courtroom, and their stations somehow were in front of or close to these pails so that when they stirred or moved, their Tommy guns or equipment jangled against the sides of the pails, and the metallic clank drove through Jimmy's marrow and left him no will of his own, or desire to have one. These things might have been accidental, but they were not. They were a part of the whole careful design, which left nothing to chance.

The cold lenses of newsreel cameras were on him, and there were microphones placed so that the speech of everyone connected with the trial could be both recorded and broadcast.

When Jimmy's eyes had finally fastened upon Dr. Soldessy and Professor Varolyas sitting in the front row, he felt relief as though at last he were seeing friends.

And they were friends, he knew, for they had labored long and patiently with him to help him understand the nature and the magnitude of his crime and win through to the relief that comes from genuinely expiating guilt.

The sentences came rolling forth in his sonorous, convincing voice that sometimes rattled the sensitive sounding plates of the microphones in front of him. All eyes were upon him, the steady, heavy stare of the three judges, the hot, hostile gaze of the prosecutor, the quizzical, self-satisfied look of his defense lawyer, and the inspired malevolence of the drab people, the "workers" assembled for the occasion in the courtroom.

And in front of him, the head of Professor Varolyas nodded up and down in satisfaction as his ear caught every nuance and emphasis of inflection that he had taught to his pupil, while on the lips of his good friend and second father, Dr. Soldessy, played the quiet smile of accomplishment of a difficult task.

Jimmy was so proud. He did not even hesitate, or bobble over the place where he came to incriminating Nick and Suzy Strang and all the others whose names he was blackening and selling out.

The showing of the spring collection at René Vesoul's was in full swing, with the girls about a third of the way through the suits and afternoon frocks, when the secretary, from the doorway, caught Thyra's eye and signaled to her that she was wanted on the telephone.

Thyra Addison always went into a state at the opening of a collection. She had her seat in the front row not far from the place allocated to the *Maître* himself and his friends, where she planted herself, her broad beam overflowing into the next cane chair. Here she puffed and fanned herself and waved and bowed to friends and acquaintances, smiled at the mannequins and addressed them by name as they came in for the first time for the showing, stopped them and fingered the material of their frocks or suits when she wasn't writing voluminously in her notebook or checking up with neighbors on the name and number of the creation as announced by the *vendeuse* posted at the entrance to the *salon.* She made a gesture of annoyance at the summons, smiled apologetically at the blond Vesoul, who was sitting between his wife and a reigning moving-picture queen, and waddled across the floor, skipping out of the way of Alaine, the dark-haired model with the almost Oriental cast of countenance, who was Vesoul's most photographed model at the time. Alaine was showing a panniered afternoon frock of black grosgrain with a striking peach-colored bodice and jacket and a large picture hat. Most of the models had the well-known atelier strut, the stomach thrown forward slightly, hips swiveling, but Alaine had a striking walk all her own, a half hesitation that gave an undulation to her body and a beautiful movement to the clothes she wore.

Thyra gave a little shriek. "Whoooeeee! Alaine, darling! You look simply ravishing. And what heavenly material! Let me touch it. Oh, dear, that damnable telephone. I'm coming." The model smiled at her, showing two rows of perfect teeth.

There was an extension just outside the entrance to the *salon,* and Thyra took the call from the office there with half her mind on what Dad Lapham was saying to her, and the other half, plus both eyes, on the opposite doorway, from which the models were emerging.

After Dad had finished and she had replaced the receiver, she caught the secretary standing in the entrance and said to her, "Darling, I'm *so* sorry, it's my office, and they're in some kind of a snit over some mannequin who is supposed to have come to work in one of the houses near the end of '48, under an assumed name because she is a Hungarian whose right name is supposed to be

Ilya Lajos, though why I wouldn't know, but they seem to think it's dreadfully important and want me to go chasing all over town afterward asking questions at Piguet's and Chanel and Mad Carpentier's and I don't know where all. I'm so upset about it all, I could spit. Darling, be a sweet angel and just ask your girls right away if any of them was ever known by that ridiculous name."

She went waddling back across the floor, called Vesoul *"Cher Maître"* again as she went by, blew him a kiss, and said, *"Mais cette collection, c'est superbe,"* plunked into her seat, and asked her neighbor, the wife of a millionaire miller from Milwaukee, "Oh, dear, have I missed anything important? I suppose just all of the dear *Maître's* originals—"

The parade continued. Bettina, the most famous of all the Vesoul models, showed a startling two-piece creation of lavender and bois-de-rose; Angèle, the little tow-headed model with the plump, mischievous face, came out in a zebra-striped blouse surmounted by a stiff Eton collar and flowing black artist's tie; Gisèle, who was thinner than any girl had a right to be, wore white piqué with a patent-leather belt so wide she seemed to be encased in an iron corselet; Annette, whose feline face was accentuated by eyes made up to resemble those of a lynx, glided through the *salon* sheathed in black silk cut to the lowest possible inch on the bodice and wearing, otherwise completely detached, around her neck a man's dress wing collar and white tie, with a black hat as big as a cart wheel.

Alaine reappeared again. This time she was modeling a *bouffant* evening gown shaded like the end of a spectrum from white-gray through to black, with one silver sleeve and other arm daringly bare. A diamond-and-platinum necklace sparkled at her neck. There were diamond star clips scattered through her blue-black hair. The effect was celestial and—Oriental. The dress was called "Moonlight."

There was a burst of applause as she entered. This was one of Vesoul's sensations, and the hit of the show so far. The girl moved forward with her beautiful, enticing, half-hesitating step, but there was something wrong with the rhythm of it. It was as though she were pushing some great weight with her limbs, something that suddenly appeared to be too much for her, for she faltered, her hands went to her temples, and she collapsed slowly to the floor almost at the feet of Vesoul and the movie queen.

There were cries of pity and dismay from the audience and that beginning panic movement where people in the back rows get up to see better and scrape and shuffle their chairs. Vesoul was on his feet—

But the organization worked smoothly. Two men and several women came out from somewhere behind the scenes and knelt by the girl for a moment. The secretary said, "It is nothing. She has just fainted. She will be all right." They picked her up, as the audience subsided into murmurs of sympathy, and carried her out. Vesoul followed. So did Thyra Addison. She was a fashion writer first, but she was also enough of a newspaperwoman to pursue to its conclusion, whatever it might be, something so unusual as a model fainting on the floor of the *salon* at an opening.

In an anteroom they placed the girl on a couch, expertly elevated her feet, bathed her temples with Eau de Cologne, and held smelling-salts under her nose. Color returned to her drained face. She sighed and opened her eyes.

The head saleswoman bent over her sympathetically. "That's better. Now then, my little one, what was it came over you? Are you ill?"

The girl looked up at them standing over her, blinked

her eyes, gasped, and cried, *"Oh, c'est ma guépière."*

Vesoul shouted, *"Oh là là! Alors! Enlevez sa guépière! Vite!"*

The women were at her already, opening her dress and loosening the bindings of the small corset beneath.

The distressed *couturier* watched the operation with a look of distaste on his face. *"Ces sacrées guépières,"* he said to no one in particular. *"J'ai dit toujours que ça ne vaut rien. Pauvre petite. Fini avec les guépières."*

Thyra drew in her breath as though she had been stabbed. She looked quickly about her. On her face was the expression of one who has just been privileged to hear a genuine pronouncement from on high. There were no other reporters or fashion writers in the room. She felt dizzy, and her mind rocked with the import of what had happened. No one but she had been present to hear the remark made by the Master which would rock the world of fashion from Paris to San Francisco as it had not been shaken since Dior dropped the hem line.

She fled the anteroom and waddled down the stairs. Once she was in the street, she began to run as fast as her fat little legs and stumpy heels would permit her until she could flag a taxi and breathlessly command the driver to rush her to the rue Marbeuf for both their lives.

She burst into the editorial room like an elephant gone must, in a state of near collapse from breathlessness, her little eyes starting from her head, her small mouth working. Gaining her desk, she fell into the chair and took a moment to fan herself and catch her wind, in the meantime uttering delighted little shrieks.

Nick, Dad, and Mitchell Connell were on her like hawks.

Nick said, "Thyra–kid! You've got it! Give!"

Thyra fanned, wheezed, and puffed. "Got it, darling?

Whoeeeeee!" she shrieked. "I should say I have. It's the biggest thing since V.E. day. And it's exclusive. I was right there in the same room. Nobody's got it but me, darlings. I'm so excited I'm afraid I'll bust before I can get to writing it. This will make me famous."

Nick looked completely baffled by the outburst, but Mitchell Connell had that expression on his face reserved for Thyra's outbursts. He was afraid he knew what was coming. Dad Lapham took the practical line. "Thyra, what the hell are you talking about?"

She let out another shriek. "Whoeeee! What am I talking about? *Guépières* are out. You won't believe it, but it's true. Absolutely and positively out. Done and finished with. I heard the *Maître* say so with my own ears. *'Fini avec ces sacrées guépières,'* was the way he put it. It will revolutionize *couture* in America—all over the world. And I was the only one there when it happened—I mean right there on the spot when the girl who fainted was brought in—"

Nick said, "Oh, my sanity! What girl who fainted? For heaven's sake, Thyra, make sense."

"But, my dearest, I *am* making sense, the greatest sense you ever knew on this paper. Wait until America hears about this. It was the model Alaine. She passed out right on the floor because her *guépière* was too tight. When they carried her into the anteroom, I followed, naturally. And René Vesoul himself came in and right then and there said, *'Ces sacrées guépières!* I have always said they were worthless.' Do you know what that means, darlings?"

Dad said to Nick, "Don't kill her now. There'll be plenty of time later." He then turned to Thyra and said heavily, "And that little detail about which we phoned you? What about the girl, the Hungarian whose right name is Ilya Lajos? Did you do what we asked you to and inquire whether—"

Thyra gave a piercing shriek. "Whoooeeeeee! Darlings! How awful of me! I asked, but of course I forgot all about it in the real excitement of the poor girl passing out. Really, dears, with such an important exclusive, I didn't think you'd care about some foreign model. Whoooooo! Look at the time! I must rush this out for New York and the syndicate. They'll be simply aghast, darlings."

Dad insisted. "Okay, okay, but you did ask, didn't you?"

"Oh, but certainly, my pet, as soon as ever I finished talking to you and hung up the telephone."

"Whom did you ask?"

"Why, the secretary, of course. She was standing right next to me. She went right in to try to find out. Now I really must get on with it, dears, or—"

Nick said wearily, "Yes, do, Thyra, but you might just tell me one thing more. What the devil is a *guépière?*"

"Whoooooo! But, darling, I thought you knew. I thought everybody knew. Why, it's a corset, of course. They had come back, you know. But after this they're absolutely and positively finished. No self-respecting woman will want to be found dead in one."

Something was gnawing at the back of Nick's consciousness, something that wanted explanation. He got up from the copy desk and went out of the editorial room and back to his own office, where his secretary, Mme. Visson, was typing in the anteroom where she had her desk.

He said, "Madame Visson, I want to know something about *guépières.* If Suzy were here, she could tell me, but since she isn't— It's a kind of a corset, isn't it?"

"That's right. They 'ave come back into fashion just recently."

"Well, would a girl, or anybody be likely to faint because one was too tight?"

Mme. Visson laughed. *"Oh, mais non!* Who 'ave been telling you such story? Not any more. That is from the olden times, no? When the woman lace themselves too tight in their big corsets. The *guépières* are just leetle ones that hold in her waist and make her heeps to be round so she can wear the latest modes. It just hold her in comfortably, but nobody faint from thees."

Nick went back into the city room. He moved quickly. His gorge was close to his throat. Dad was talking on the telephone. Nick said, "Who is it, Dad?"

Dad said, "Felix Victor. He's calling from Marcel Rochas's. Blank."

Nick grunted. "That's in the avenue Matignon. Tell him to get in here fast. But fast. I want him here in five minutes."

Nick turned to Thyra. His face was red and his eyes hard. He said, "Stop that damned typing. That story can wait. You're fooling around with a man's life. I want some questions answered."

Thyra looked frightened. Her stubby fingers moved futilely over the keys, but no longer tapped them.

"But, Nick, dear, I only–"

"Shut up, Thyra. You talk too much. You may have cost us Jimmy Race. Now, pay attention. What was the name of the girl who fainted?"

"Alaine." Thyra's voice was small, but her eyes showed that she understood and was concentrating.

"What is her last name?"

"Why, I don't know. I don't suppose anyone really knows. She's just known as Alaine, just as Bettina is known as Bettina. I suppose they have last names, but nobody ever thinks of that. When you see them you just say, 'Oh, there goes Alaine from René Vesoul's.' "

"What does she look like?"

"Oh, but she's a beauty. A famous beauty. She's dark and glowing, in a sort of a Chinese way. Well–

Whoooeeee!" she gave her little shriek. "But how silly of me! The simplest way would be to show you her picture."

Thyra reached onto a shelf by her desk and pulled down a copy of *Paris Vogue* and leafed through the advertisements in the front section. "There she is," she said, at a full page of the model pictured wearing one of the Vesoul afternoon creations of the past winter. "That's Alaine. And this one and this one, too. He uses her for all his sophisticated clothes."

Nick stared hard at the picture of the girl with the raven hair, the full hips, round face, and slightly slanted eyes. He said, "Where the hell is Felix?"

Dad volunteered, "Ought to be here any second. He was only down the street. I told him there was some heat on."

Nick addressed Thyra again. "How long has this girl been famous—as a model?"

"Oh?" Thyra thought. "For over a year, I guess. She was quite a sensation in last year's shows."

"But not before that? Not in 1948?"

"I don't think so. I suppose I could check the back numbers of the fashion maga—"

"Never mind. Now tell me exactly what happened there this afternoon and don't leave out anything. From the time you got Dad's call on the telephone."

"Well, I told the secretary—just what Dad had said about inquiring whether any girl who had been with them since the winter of '48 might have been known as Ilya Lajos. I *said* it was important."

"Yes, and then what?"

"Well, the secretary went inside into the rooms where the girls dress—I suppose to ask."

"Where did you go?"

"I went back to my seat in the *salon*. I apologized to the *Maître* for disturbing—"

"What girls were on the floor at the time?"

"Bettina was showing in the main *salon*. Gisèle had just left the big room and was modeling in the *petit salon*."

"Where was Alaine?"

"I don't know. I mean I'm not sure. I suppose she was changing."

"How long was it before she appeared again?"

"About five minutes, Nick."

"Long enough for her to have been in the dressing-room when the secretary inquired about anyone ever having been known as Ilya Lajos?"

Thyra looked miserable. "I suppose so. Oh, Nick, dear, I've done something awfully stupid, haven't I?"

"My darling," Nick said without smiling, "I could quite cheerfully kill you."

Felix Victor slammed into the office. "Yeah," he said. "What gives? I had to come around by the Champs-Elysées. The rue de Ponthieu was jammed up with traffic. Is there a break?"

Nick took the copy of the magazine with the picture of Alaine and said, "Take a look at this babe. Would she tally with the description the landlady gave you of the Lajos girl?"

Victor whistled. "Hell, yes," he said. "She remarked that the kid had a kind of a Chinese look about her. Have we got her?"

Nick said bitterly, for he had been sorely tried, "We *had* her until bird brain over there let her slip through her fingers. Had her cold."

Thyra began to cry. She sniffed. "Nick, I think you are being cruel."

He said, "Yes, I know. Sometimes there's a time for that, too. What is happening to Jimmy Race in Budapest is a lot crueler. Come on, Thyra. This is no time to howl. Pull yourself together and get on over to René

Vesoul's and be quick about it. Take Felix Victor with you. He's got brains and knows what to do in a pinch. Latch onto that girl. If she's still there, bring her here. If she's gone home, find out where she lives. Somebody there will know. Somebody's got to know. She can't work at a place like Vesoul's without giving some name and address where they can reach her in case of some kind of emergency like a special show. If she's gone already, get on out there as quickly as you can and get hold of her father. Because if she gets the wind up on account of what happened there this afternoon, the whole family may blow and we'll never find them. Keep in touch."

When they had gone, Dad Lapham said softly to Nick, "That will just give you a general idea why I wanted you on the inside."

22

MATERIALIZATION OF A STOOL PIGEON

IN BUDAPEST in the Markó courtroom, Jimmy Race came to the end of his confession. There were "spontaneous" demonstrations demanding death for the American spy, which were quelled only after the chief judge pounded the bench with his gavel, and the guards at the side of the courtroom stirred in the direction of the disturbance.

Jimmy Race was conscious of nothing but pride and relief. It had gone off well. He had not fumbled once or made a mistake in the narration. Down in front of him, Dr. Soldessy and Professor Varolyas were engaged in a whispered conversation. He tried to catch their eye for a final glance of approval from them, but they refused to look at him any more.

Jimmy stood there in the prisoner's dock before the

microphones, uncertain what he should do next, for this was the one thing they had forgotten—to tell him what he should do after he had finished his confession. He felt drained, glad that he was unburdened at last, and a little sad that it was all over and that he could be of no further use to anyone.

His own lawyer came, tapped him on the shoulder, and beckoned to him, and he followed him over to the table and sat down. It was only then that the Hungarian correspondent for the Transoceanic Press noted that he stumbled a little as though he was not sure of where he was going.

The Hungarian prosecutor rose and made a speech in Hungarian, resting his case on the full confession of the prisoner and asking for the death penalty for the American spy.

The defense lawyer spoke briefly, likewise closing his case, confirming the confession and indicating that the prisoner threw himself on the mercy of the court with a plea for clemency.

The Chief Justice acknowledged the two speeches, announced that sentence would be pronounced the following morning at ten o'clock, and adjourned the court.

Shortly before ten the next morning the little group sat tense and nervous, fidgety and short-tempered in Nick's office and awaited the coming of a Hungarian refugee by the name of Gabor Lajos who once had been the assistant and private secretary to Andreas Ordy, Minister of Affairs in the Communist Government of Hungary.

Unless this man Lajos appeared as had been promised, this Minister Ordy would within twenty-four hours carry out the sentence of death by hanging which the court in Budapest was to pronounce upon Jimmy Race that same morning.

Besides Nick, there was Dad Lapham, Mark Mosher, Felix Victor, and Janet Goodpenny. Janet had begged to be allowed to be present in case a ray of hope appeared for Jimmy. Nick hadn't the heart to deny her.

And in Vienna, Suzy sat in her bedroom on the third floor of the Bristol, a prey to her own thoughts and broodings, and waited for the telephone to ring.

Strangely, of them all, only Nick had a certain calmness and the ability still to think objectively. Things had gone badly all along, but at least now they were nearing the end of the trail and the horrid suspense. They had done what they could up to that point, and within twenty-four hours it would be over, one way or the other. He did not know whether Lajos would come or not. He had no hunch or feeling about the matter whatsoever. The man had been contacted, by Felix Victor, though indirectly. He would appear or he wouldn't.

But Dad and Mark Mosher were less controlled, and the latter was inclined to take it out on Felix Victor.

Dad said, "What really makes you think the guy will show up, Felix?"

"Well, only what the woman, Mrs. Lajos said. She was a lady. It was the way she said it, that she'd *try* to get him to come—"

Mark Mosher snapped irritably, "And you walked out and left 'em on that? Honestly, if that isn't the dumbest thing I ever heard of for a reporter to do—"

Victor said with a kind of desperation, "But I told you they were scared to death of the police, both the daughter and the mother. If I'd tried to use any pressure or threatened 'em, or even hung around, they would have managed to warn off the man we were after. He was out and wasn't expected home, and they said they would try to reach him later. Don't you see, they'd been living a life of fear, all of them."

Dad asked, "Why didn't you leave Thyra with them

while you kept a lookout for the man?"

"Look, I was there. I know what it was like, and Thyra knows, too. We got there about five minutes after the girl got home. She'd put the panic into her mother. You could tell from the way they looked and acted. And they'd got bags out, ready to pack. The girl must have told her that the police were making inquiries after them at René Vesoul's and that it was all up with them. The only thing that calmed them down was when I proved to them that we were not from the police but from the *Sentinel.* But don't you see, if I'd acted funny by hanging around, or posting Thyra there, they'd have been suspicious that something bad was in the wind. We were only saved by the fact that Thyra was along with me. The girl knew her, of course. So we had to take their word. You sent me out on this thing. I had to handle it the way it looked to me."

Mark Mosher said viciously, "Well, you sure gummed up the deal. Why isn't the guy here?"

Janet Goodpenny gave a little hurt cry and said, "Oh, Mark, leave him alone. Vic's done the best he can. He's *got* to come."

Nick was biting at his lower lip. He said, "You said they seemed to calm down when they found out it was the *Sentinel?* Isn't that a little odd? Tell me again exactly what happened."

Felix looked nervously up at the clock. It stood at five minutes to ten. "Well, I knocked and went in first. The girl Ilya and her mother were standing in front of a table with their arms around each other. There were some empty suitcases. I said, 'Mrs. Lajos–' The kid just stared at me and started to cry, but the mother had a wonderful kind of dignity. She said, 'Very well. Yes. I will not run any more. But we have not done anything except try to live in peace. Must you persecute us?'

"I said we didn't want to persecute anyone, that we

were from the Paris Edition of the *Sentinel* and wanted only to have a word with her husband. Well, it was a kind of new hope came into the woman's face and she said, 'The *Sentinel*? Is this true?' Thyra came in then and talked to Ilya, who confirmed it, and they both started to laugh and cry a little and the mother said to the daughter, 'There, you see, you were needlessly alarmed. You thought it was the police and it was only the newspaper that wishes to speak with your father.' "

Nick said, "I still don't get it."

Dad said, "Don't get what?"

"Why the relief? Why the woman ever should have heard of the *Sentinel*."

Mark interjected, "The whole thing could have been a gag, just to get rid of Felix and Thyra, so they could blow."

"Yes, it could," Nick agreed, "but it still doesn't add. Then you asked about Lajos, her husband," he said to Felix.

"Uhuh. I said the editor of the *Sentinel* wanted to speak with him and that it was very important. She said that he was not at home but that he would communicate with them before he came home and that she would then convey the message. She said that it was no use our staying there, because then he would not come home. She said finally that she would ask him to come to the office to see you at ten o'clock. Well, the way things were, I believed her."

Mark Mosher shook his head pityingly and said, "Oh, boy!" and then directed his gaze up to the clock. The hand had gone past ten.

Nick said, "Well, don't forget they had to be careful. There was one attempt on him in Vienna. And if the Hungarians found out where he was living here in Paris – They never hesitated anywhere in the world to knock guys off. Damn, and they *will* find out. At least you got there ahead of them, Vic."

Dad said, "They probably had some kind of an agreed signal to keep him away from their rooms if something was wrong. Still, I think you ought to have stayed there."

Mark Mosher said, "If I had my way, I'd grab a couple of guys and beat it on out to the house right now. It's a cinch the guy isn't going to come here. Why the hell should he?"

Nick said curtly, "Forget it. You were right the first time. You wouldn't find anybody there. If they blew, they were out of there fifteen minutes after Vic and Thyra left and we'll never see them again. At least not in time."

Vic suddenly sat down at the glass-topped table and put his face in his hands. He was very young. Janet Goodpenny gave Mark a look of contempt and said, "Oh, how I despise you men!" She went to Felix Victor and put her arm about his shoulder and said, "Felix, don't let them. You did right."

Nick put his hand on the boy's shoulder and said, "I think so, too. I don't think they've blown. I don't understand what is going on with them, or what they are up to, but it doesn't sound like a getaway." Mark's eyes were on the clock again. It was now twenty minutes past ten. Nick said, "I know. But she didn't say positively. There's nothing we can do but wait. If we go out there now and they're watching, it will put the wind up for fair."

They all fell silent and waited. Dad doodled on a pad, Nick smoked. Janet talked to Vic in a low voice. Mothering him took her mind from the terrible strain. Mark Mosher dragged at a cigarette and stared at the clock.

At half past ten the city editor exploded. "Dammit, you guys can do what you like. But I've carried responsibility in this thing for the past month as well as you.

I'm not going to see it thrown away. I'm going on out to that address and–"

They were all galvanized by the knock on the outer door which interrupted him. Mark Mosher reached it first, for he had already started to leave the room. He turned the knob and yanked it open and the next moment emitted a bellow of rage.

"You! My God, of all people to turn up here at this moment! Didn't I tell you to keep the hell out of this office?"

Standing in the doorway was Grisha, the little Central European stooge and tipster, hatless as usual, his drab raincoat over his arm, and around his neck under the collar of his coat the dreadful green-yellow-and-red diamond-patterned scarf. In his fingers, impaled on a pin, was the near-burned-out stub of a cigarette, his mouth twitched nervously, and his large, prominent eyes were more deeply haunted than ever.

He went white at Mark's aggressiveness, but stood his ground, his eyes looking beyond at Janet, Felix, Dad, and Nick sitting behind his desk. He seemed to be trying to say something, but no words came.

Mark Mosher yelled at him. "I guess you can't understand plain English about keeping the hell out of here. Maybe a good kick in the pants will give you the idea."

Janet's cry distracted him for a moment even as he was reaching for the slack at the breast of Grisha's coat to manhandle him out. "Mark, don't. He hasn't done anything to anyone. He's good."

But an even stronger deterrent was Nick's commanding cry. "Mark! Dammit! Leave him alone. Get away from that door and shut up. I understand it now. We could have saved a hell of a lot of time if anybody in this office, including myself, had had any brains. Come in, Mr. Lajos."

The man who used to be known as Grisha was still

standing in the doorway. He had not moved or cringed. He said now, "You did send for me, Mr. Strang?"

Nick said, "Yes, I did, Mr. Lajos. Come in. We are very badly in need of your help."

They could all see the effects of the phrase "in need of your help" on the little man, the thing it did to his carriage, his color, the sudden firmness that appeared in his mouth and the expression of his eyes as well as his body. He came across the threshold with a new kind of dignity, pausing only to smile with almost a tenderness at Janet as he passed her, saying, "It is you who are good, mademoiselle." Then he dropped his raincoat over the back of the chair and said to Nick, "I am at your service, Excellency."

23

ONE-WAY TICKET TO BUDAPEST

A LITTLE LATER the two men were alone in Nick's office and got down to business.

Nick said, "Do you know why I sent for you, Mr. Lajos?"

Lajos nodded. "I do. I encountered the good mademoiselle in the park, Mademoiselle Janet, and heard something from her. Otherwise, perhaps, I should not have come at all. It is because of the reporter, Mr. Race, who—is in difficulties in Budapest."

Nick said, "It is fortunate for us all that she encountered you, then. You have been very badly treated by us, and this I regret. Still that is all in the past. Is it true, Mr. Lajos, that you are in possession of information and proof which, if properly presented, might exert the strongest kind of pressure upon Minister of Affairs Andreas Ordy?"

The little man was silent for a moment and glanced down at the cigarette burning in his fingers, a new one from Nick's pack of American brand. When he looked up again, it was almost in an embarrassed and strangely self-conscious manner. He said, "Excellency, I was saving it for my family and my old age."

Nick said, "Then it is true?"

"Yes, it is true."

"You have it with you?"

"No."

"Where is it?"

"It is in Hungary."

Nick said, "Damn!"

But Lajos made a quick gesture. He said, "It is better this way. It is well hidden. Nobody but myself knows where it is. In this manner it is impossible to take it from my person, whether I am alive or dead."

"I understand. Still, if you were dead it would then hardly be of much value to your family. Or if, let us say, something were to happen to Ordy."

Lajos nodded. "That is true."

"Which makes your remark about saving this for your old age rather a comparative matter."

Lajos merely smiled this time and nodded again.

Nick said, "You understand, of course, why I have tried to find you and why I have sent for you. I believe the information you possess is sufficiently dangerous to Ordy to cause him to release our man Race in exchange for it. I want to buy that information from you."

"I understand."

"You must have, yourself, come to a decision as to the value of your information and its negotiability, or you would not have come here at this time—after the way you were treated by us."

Lajos said, "That is so."

Nick thought, *I am on the right track. He wants the*

bargaining to begin. He said, "Very well, then. You know the circumstances and that the life of one of our men is at stake. I am certain that, using your information and proof as a wedge, we can still save him, though the time is very short. What is your price for this service?"

Lajos considered a moment and then replied slowly and softly with the conviction of one who has made up his mind. "Freedom and security for my family so that my wife and daughter need not run away or to hide any more; that they will not have to be afraid when comes a knock on the door, or goes by a policeman. I would wish them to be in America with the right to live under our own name of Lajos and some day to become the citizen."

He paused and appeared to reflect earnestly. Then he continued. "There must be moneys for them to live on until they are secure of themselves. One hundred thousand dollars, deposit in United States, New York, in their name." And now he looked up in Nick's face with an anxious expression as though to see whether he had asked for too much. There was some undercurrent that Nick did not understand.

He said, "All of this might well be done. I will telephone our Ambassador here, who will get in touch with Washington by telephone. Your wife and daughter can be on an airplane for the U.S. within eight hours. Until that time we will conceal them either here or in a hotel we know is safe. I do not know whether you are aware of it, but the Hungarian Embassay knows you are in Paris and is looking for you. It is later than you think."

Lajos nodded and sighed. "And the moneys?"

"Will be deposited in their name in the Guaranty Trust Company, at the start of banking-day in New York. That is one o'clock Paris time. By two o'clock you should have a cable here from the bank confirming the deposit. I will telephone to New York and order it set up as a trust fund with annuity payments. You will have your visas or necessary entry documents and the bank confirmation by three o'clock this afternoon. Will that satisfy you? You see, Mr. Lajos, I do not bargain for the life of our colleague."

A ghost of a Chaplinesque smile showed at the mouth of the little man. He said, "Yes, when that is so, I am satisfy."

Nick then asked, "We will consider that settled. How do I know that you will keep to your end of the deal?"

The smile was more pronounced at Lajos's mouth and Nick was aware that it had a strange sort of sweetness. He replied softly, "Oh, you will know. For to keep my end I must go to Hungary and speak directly with Ordy. I told you my proofs are there. He will never release Mr. Race unless he is certain that the documents will be in his hands immediately after the American has crossed the border. You understand? I do not bargain, either, Mr. Strang."

Nick drew a deep breath and exhaled it in a sigh somewhat in the manner of Lajos, for he understood quite well now the kind of deal the little man was proposing. He was offering to exchange his own life for that of Jimmy Race for the price of the safety and security of his family. For Nick knew that, win or lose, once Lajos returned to Budapest, his chances of leaving the city alive were slim.

This, then, was the decision that Nick had to face. For Lajos it was already over and done with and the once timorous and cringing tipster and stool pigeon who sat on the opposite side of the desk from him had suddenly taken on the aspect and glamour of a brave and gallant gentleman with only the dreadful scarf contributing a touch of pathos.

Yes, Nick thought, as always with his work, it came down to a question of making a decision, one that was irrevocable for right or wrong and, once it had been made, would start trains of action that could not be halted and would shape their consequences beyond his power to alter them. It had been like that when he had decided to send Jimmy Race to Vienna, and in the end it was to be a date with the hangman. Now he could make the decision whereby he could have him back alive, and to gain this end he must send another to his death, a brave man who had the courage to die for the ones he loved.

Nick wondered whether Jimmy Race had that kind of courage, or, for that matter, he himself. And he thought of the love that Race had for Suzy and that in a way he might be buying him back for her with the life of this other man who sat so calmly and expectantly in front of him. For a fleeting instant he tried to evaluate who was the better man, Race, who was so wrapped in his desires and his own imagination that he overwhelmed anyone who stood in his way, with never a thought or a care of the consequences to others, or this not too appetizing little fellow who the first time the going had got rough had ratted on his employer, had stolen material that endangered this man's life, and had thought only of his own skin.

In spite of their seeming strength, they each had fatal weaknesses which were dangerous not only to themselves but to the society that surrounded them, but when the showdown came, they could recognize the inevitable and die like men. What both angered and sickened Nick was that fate should have made him the arbiter of their destinies. It was too much. And he thought of Suzy sitting alone by the telephone in the dismal hotel room in Vienna waiting to hear from him whether he had succeeded and whether Jimmy Race was to live or die.

He wished that he had more time to think, that he could have a chance to talk to Dad Lapham about it and hear what he had to say; and even as he wished this he realized that there was nothing to discuss with Dad or anyone else, that all his other thoughts and worries had been nothing but his own human weakness and that there was now no time for any of this.

And a great clarity replaced all of his doubts, for the decision was essentially a simple one which from time to time faced every man who directed the work or the play or the combat of other men, and could be reduced to one sentence, our side or theirs; one of your own, or one of theirs. You stood by your own, of your land, your kind, your speech, your town, city, or village, and there was an end to it. If blood was thicker than water, so were other things.

He knew, too, that one never wholly escaped from the consequences of one's own acts. One might repair some of the damage, or ameliorate the punishment, but there was no wiping clean of the slate. He would have the death of one or the other of the two men on his conscience as long as he lived. Without any further hesitation, he chose Lajos.

Nick said, "Yes, I see. I understand. Well, we'll have to work it out so that we get you out of there along with Mr. Race, naturally."

Gabor Lajos no longer smiled; he said gravely, "Yes, naturally," and the two men exchanged a look of mutual understanding the way men do when the truth is too terrible to contemplate. Nick picked up the telephone and said to Mme. Visson, "Get me the American Ambassador. Wherever he is, I must speak with him at once."

Later Nick and Lajos went over the plan of action they had worked out between them for the release of Jimmy Race. A story had come through from Budapest that sentence of death had been pronounced on the American spy and would be carried out within twenty-four hours, unless the appeal for clemency and review automatically entered by the stooge lawyer assigned to defend Race was accepted, which appeared unlikely. Lajos said that, according to the custom in Hungary, Jimmy would probably be executed at dawn of the next day unless Ordy or someone else intervened. This gave them some twenty hours.

Nick said, "Let me see now if there are any loopholes. It is a direct deal between you and Ordy. If the documents are of more value to Ordy than hanging an American, he will have to make it."

Lajos said gravely, "I believe that they are more dangerous to him now than they were then. Then he might have only been purged or dismissed from the party. Now he could be executed as a traitor as an example."

Nick nodded. "Let us hope so. All right. Let's say he has agreed. He is to send Race to Vienna by car to the outskirts and deliver him to Suzy. Suzy will notify you in Vienna that this has been done. You will then deliver the documents to Ordy. How do we convince Ordy that this will be done? He has to make the first move by delivering Jimmy."

Lajos said, "I am there as a guarantee. He holds me as hostage. At that moment I am more important to him than the American."

"Hmmm. And what is to prevent him from grabbing you as soon as you get to Budapest and have you tortured to reveal where the stuff is hidden?"

Lajos's lips twitched. He said, "I have been tortured before. You may count that I will last twenty-four hours, possibly longer. If by that time there has been no positive reaction either from Ordy or myself, you may take steps to inform the Hungarian Government of the onetime Titoist activities of their Minister of Affairs. Your counterintelligence will be the best means of passing this information. *With* the whereabouts of the documents. They are concealed in a space beneath a ventilator grating in Ordy's office. I will draw you an exact plan of their whereabouts."

Nick whistled. "Right under his nose all the time. The classic concealment. But why wouldn't they have thought of that?"

"The Hungarian mentality is much more complicated."

"How do you know they are still there?"

Lajos gave Nick a look. "The attempts upon my person have not ended. You said yourself you stirred up great excitement at the Hungarian Embassy." He fell moodily silent for a moment and then said, "No. I do not think that Ordy will try to do anything to me—until the danger is past for him and the incriminating evidence is in his hands and destroyed."

"And after that?"

Lajos drew a deep breath. "You may leave that to me. I will work it out to make it a part of my bargain with Ordy. And besides, that is not the way the game is played. They have no time for something so childish as revenge."

It was Nick's turn to stare silently at the little Hungarian. Was he trying to comfort him and ease the load on his conscience? Or was there some grain of truth in what he had said? After all, the Communists were conducting a living revolutionary conspiracy and not a maffia. He thought then of Trotsky's end in Mexico and the hounding of the Titoists all over Europe. The party leaders were vicious, small-minded, vindictive, unrelenting.

Nick said, "It is Ordy who has been the instigator and the prime mover in the death sentence of Jimmy Race. Ever since the Frobisher case he has been moving toward the goal of hanging an American as a blow to American prestige on the Continent. Granted that your evidence is his own death warrant and powerful enough to make him *want* to release Race in exchange, *can* he?

Would not such a right-about-face bring him equally under suspicion? How will you convince him otherwise?"

Lajos smiled faintly. He said, "When there is any choice between the lesser of two evils, do we hesitate? Once you set in motion the machinery that will result in turning up Ordy's Titoist activities—with proof—he is a dead man. On the other hand, he has a chance to explain and justify his release of Race after sentence of death had been passed on him. The Americans tried and sentenced the Russian spy Gubitchev and then suspended sentence and sent him home." Lajos smiled again as though there was a thought he relished. "After all, the Communist is a master at propagandizing to prove that black is white, if necessary. Ordy will have the opportunity to exercise some of his Moscow training to convince his superiors and the people of the wisdom of releasing Race once his guilt had been established in court."

Mme. Visson appeared at the door. She said, "There is a plane leaving Paris for Munich and Vienna with a connection for Budapest at 16:30 hours. It arrives in Vienna at 19:00 and Budapest at 20:45. I have taken a ticket. The confirmation from the Guaranty Trust Company has arrived. Mr. Victor and Mr. Hoffman have taken Madame Lajos and her daughter to the George V and are remaining there with them. The American Embassy has telephoned that permission from Washington has come through and their papers are ready. They will be leaving at 21:30 tonight from Orly for New York. Ann McAlenny of the Chicago office will meet them. That has all been arranged."

Nick exchanged a look and nodded. He looked at his watch and said, "We'd better be getting on out to Orly ourselves. You can look at the confirmations on the way out."

Lajos nodded. Nick had one more thought. He asked,

"What about your entry into Budapest? Your papers can no longer be valid. You may never get by the immigration at the field. Ought I not send Ordy a telegram indicating—"

Lajos shook his head. "It would not be wise. It would leave a trail to be followed from Ordy to me to you. Our only chance of success is to give Ordy utmost latitude of operation in this matter. You understand? And besides," Lajos concluded with another of his gentle, introspective smiles, "I shall not be needing any papers. I have only to say to the first policeman I encounter on the field, 'I am Gabor Lajos. I wish to be taken into the presence of Minister of Affairs Andreas Ordy.' A telephone call will be made. And less than an hour later—I will be with him."

Nick nodded and remained seated and in thought for a moment longer. He rose finally with a sigh and said, "We'll manage to get you out somehow. After all, I know what Ordy was up to in Yugoslavia."

Lajos smiled enigmatically and agreed lightly. "Oh, yes. I shall indeed get out somehow."

A little over an hour later Nick stood with Lajos on the concrete apron of the Orly airport a little distance from the big four-motored twin-tailed Air France ship that was loading passengers for the east—Munich, Vienna, Istanbul.

Farther down, a giant TWA Convair was being gassed and primed for flight. The metallic voice of the airport public address announced: "Flight 605, TWA, Rome, Paris, Shannon, and New York, is now ready. Passengers for Shannon and New York will please have their tickets ready at gate 3."

Nick followed the little man's glance as it went to the waiting transatlantic plane. He said to Lajos, reading his thoughts, "In about five hours from now your wife and daughter are going on Flight 608. It originates from here and leaves at 9:30."

"In a machine like that?" Lajos asked.

Nick nodded. Lajos seemed to devour the plane with his eyes. He said, "And they have not been told that I am returning to Budapest?"

"No. We did as you requested. Your letter to them was delivered, and they were assured that you would be joining them in New York within a week."

Lajos echoed, "Within a week. Who can tell, perhaps I shall be free even sooner?"

The use of the word "free" fell strangely on Nick's ears and at once shocked him to the realities of his position. He was an executioner. In a moment Lajos would be mounting the tall flight of movable steps that led to the interior of the airplane. They might as well be steps leading to the block or the gallows. When the door closed behind the little man, it would be as inevitable as the fall of the headsman's ax, or the springing of the trap. Nor was there any guarantee that his life would not be sacrificed in vain.

"Well," Lajos said, "I believe I must go. Thank you for all you have done for—for us. I thank you particularly for being the kind of person that one can trust."

They shook hands, and their glance into each other's eyes was direct and unwavering. In each was the complete conviction that they would never see each other again. It was astonishing, Nick thought at that moment how Lajos had changed. There was no longer anything furtive or sly about him. His head sat so differently on the chicken-thin column of his neck. He seemed to have added inches to his stature.

Nick said, "Good luck!"

Lajos said, "Thank you," again, turned away, and then, looking back, added, "I am very, very happy that my wife and daughter will again live in dignity. Be assured."

It was a last kindness on his part, Nick knew, an attempt to bring comfort to his conscience, a genuine sweetness.

Nick watched Lajos climb the steps, pause a moment at the entrance to the door of the ship, and then vanish within. He waited until he saw the aircraft lift itself from the airport and retract its wheels into its belly. Then he went and got into his car and headed back to Paris and the vigil that awaited him. He felt drained and sad. He did not even speculate upon the result of Lajos's trip and whether it would result in the freeing of Jimmy Race. He had done what he could. What happened now, outside last-minute preparations and liaison with Suzy and the G2 boys in Vienna, was beyond his control.

24

A PIGEON FLIES HOME

In Budapest, Professor Varolyas dropped into the condemned cell of Jimmy Race back in the Andrássy, where he had been taken after the trial. The old man came inside the small dungeon, similar to the one Jimmy had first occupied after his arrest, and in which there was nothing but a kind of stone couch that was a part of the wall. He seemed to be moved by genuine pity as well as gratitude. Jimmy's courtroom performance would have done much to consolidate his own position with the party and convince them of his loyalty.

He said, "Well, I came to say good-by. You did very well. I was quite proud of you. You left out nothing. It is a pity that it has to end this way. I just wanted you to know that I was sorry."

"What is a pity?" asked Jimmy Race, and stared at the goatish man as though he had not the faintest idea of what he was talking about.

Professor Varolyas cleared his throat. "Of course a clemency appeal has been made. It has yet to be heard. I shall naturally add my recommendation for mercy."

This was a lie, since he had no intention of endangering his own position by doing so, but the big, handsome, healthy-looking man who sat beside him on the stone bench seemed to have no concern with that. He merely asked, "Why do you say that? You know I deserve to die."

Varolyas grimaced. He rose, and the guard unlocked the door. "Well," he said, "I just wanted you to know." He went away.

Later Dr. Soldessy also came to see him. The psychiatrist sat down alongside him without speaking. After a few minutes he said, "Well?"

Jimmy said nothing and stared before him.

Dr. Soldessy asked, "Do you know me?"

"Yes, I know you."

"What are you thinking?"

"I was wondering whether you were satisfied or came to scold me."

Soldessy smiled inwardly. The infantile application of the word *scold* delighted him. He asked, "Do you feel that you merit a scolding?"

Jimmy said, "I don't know. I never know what you are going to say. I suppose I could have tried harder—to make them understand how sorry I felt. Do you think they understood?"

Dr. Soldessy said, "Yes. I think everyone understood." Then he asked, "How do you feel?"

"All right." This man always confused him. When he was not with him he sometimes hated him desperately, and at other times loved him. In his presence he had but one desire, and that was to please him.

"Are you being well treated?"

"Better than I deserve."

"Is there anything you wish? Anything I can do for you?"

"Ask them to hurry. Get it over with. Why do they keep me waiting?"

"You want to be hanged, don't you?"

"Yes."

Dr. Soldessy rose. "It will be not very much longer," he said. "Try to get some sleep." He went out without saying anything further or another glance at the American. He walked down the corridor feeling excited and well satisfied with himself. He did not give a hoot for the Communists, or their doctrines. But he was interested in his work. Mentally he began to organize and arrange his proposed monograph on *The Use of Drugs and Self-Hypnosis Induced by Fatigue in the Inculcation of False Guilt Feelings Manufactured Post Facto to Meet Any Set of Given Circumstances.* He had been trained in Germany and liked long and imposing titles.

He had destroyed Mindszenty's mind. But then Mindszenty was a Hungarian and a prelate. The wrecking of this hard-boiled, tough, cocksure American had been indeed a triumph for some of the less appetizing theories held by the doctor with regard to the human mind. He had short-cut every known psychiatric method and produced almost complete infantilism in a grown man within a period of six weeks. Naturally, he conceded as he pattered down the corridor, it had to be there for him to bring it out. But it had taken him to produce it so convincingly and in so short a time. He had a right to feel pleased.

The twin-engined Hodka plane that made the connection between Vienna and Budapest slipped over the rim of the low hills that formed the western edge of the Danube Valley, and below in the dusky distance glittered the lights of Buda and Pest on the opposite sides of the gray, winding river. A dash of light remaining in the sky reflected a glassy pink, blue, and lavender from the surface of the water between the massive stone piles of the twin cities.

Gabor Lajos looked down from his porthole and with practiced eye picked out the familiar landmarks—palaces, government buildings, castles, barracks, and even squares.

Below, he thought, was his youth, his ambition, his career, his middle life, the memories of his love and marriage, the recollection of houses and flats in which he had lived, the faces of friends, the recalling of the mixed pleasure and bitternesses of living.

Like a slowly spreading, ineradicable stain, the wave of political poison from the East, the Oriental philosophy of blind obedience to the satraps in power, the Eastern product of rule by terror, had spread out over the beautiful city, engulfing and stifling it.

Down there somewhere in that gray mass toward which the ship was now dipping its wing was his end, too. Beneath him Lajos saw the airport beacon flashing and the red boundary lights. A long sigh escaped him. In spite of his thoughts it was one of satisfaction. Whatever awaited him down there, he knew that he was glad to be home.

25

THE EMPTY BOTTLE

SUZY SAT IN THE LEAD CAR, a chauffeur-driven limousine supplied by the hotel, and waited the dark, fragrant predawn gloom on the outskirts of Vienna. A dozen or so yards behind her, in the rear-vision mirror, she could make out the shape of the military car containing Major Slater and four military policemen.

They were drawn up at the side of an empty and deserted stretch of road leading to the east, but still within the city limits of Vienna and therefore reasonably safe from challenge by the Russians. Off the side of the road and about twenty yards from where the cars were parked, there was a small villa. The door was ajar, and there was a light burning in the vestibule and another in a downstairs window.

The time was shortly after five o'clock in the morning and the first grayness that heralds the end of night had begun, though the few cars that passed them by were still burning their bright lights.

It was chilly, and Suzy sat bundled in her camel's-hair greatcoat, nervously smoking cigarettes and wondering what it would be like now that it was almost over and how she would think and feel when she first saw Jimmy Race again after all that had happened and what he had been through. And she thought, too, of the last-minute possibilities of slip-up in negotiations so delicate and a timetable so precise, and that it might be that Jimmy Race would never appear out of that damp early-morning mist which was blowing toward them from the east. Until the last second it would be touch and go.

She recalled the weariness and sense almost of defeat in Nick's voice when he had called her from Paris to tell her that Lajos was on his way to Budapest and would telephone her in Vienna if he was successful in his mission, the endless, nerve-racking waiting as she lay on the bed by the telephone in her room at the Bristol, and then the shock when at two o'clock in the morning it rang and she heard the concierge say, "Madame, there is a call from Budapest coming in for you. Will you remain on the line, please?"

She had talked thereafter, and the whole thing had

imparted to Suzy such a feeling of imminent precariousness that she found herself trying to hold together the situation, the distant voice, the tenuous connection, with the muscles of her stomach, as though if she relaxed for an instant, said one wrong word or so much as disturbed the way she was holding the telephone instrument, connection, plan, voice, and the rescue of Jimmy Race would forever vanish.

"Madame Strang?"

"Yes, this is Suzy Strang."

"This is Gabor Lajos. I am calling from Budapest. I am calling you with authority. Do you understand?"

"I understand."

"Very well. Everything depends upon your following instructions in exact detail. Take down this telephone number. It is Budapest 37-555. The second number that you will give to the operator who replies is 100."

And then he had given her the exact location of the meeting-place and the plan, the intricate, complicated timetable that had to be observed. And never a word or mention of Jimmy Race.

"Will you be so good now, Madame Strang, and repeat it exactly?"

Suzy did so. The voice said, "Very good, Madame Strang. That is all for now."

"Wait!" Suzy had said. "Am I permitted an escort?" She asked it not out of fear for herself, but she was an old hand at underground rendezvous and no fool. If Jimmy had chosen to walk blindly into a trap, she had no desire to do the same. Lajos, for all she knew, could be speaking under pressure. Alone, on a deserted road, she could be swept up into the same net that had caught Race. It was not for that Nick had let her stay in Vienna and entrusted her with the climax of the adventure.

There was a long silence from the other end of the line—as though Lajos were consulting with someone, or as though he were gone, the connection broken. She had felt sick. Then his voice had returned.

"Yes. You may have one car containing no more than five men. If there should be more than two cars at the appointed place, there will be no contact made. That is clear? Good-by, Madame Strang. We will speak again, I hope, later."

She had hung up, too, and had sat there for a moment, weakly looking at the penciled notes she had made. Into her mind had come a vision of the weak, pathetic little creature she remembered Lajos to have been when he was seen around the office as Grisha, the tipster. Now he was trapped in Budapest in the hands of his enemies. Nothing was positive, nothing was certain. All he had been able to offer her was hope.

And hope of what, Suzy thought as she strained her eyes through the grayness and the wisps of whitish ground fog for oncoming headlights and drew on her cigarette so that the end glowed redly and reflected from the windshield of the car. Hope that out of this void into which she was staring would come Jimmy Race back to them, big, lusty, booming, possessive, overwhelming, contemptuous of everyone weaker than he, to take up where he had left off—all of them to pick up the loose threads of what they had been doing just as it was before the shock and tragedy of his arrest, trial, and condemnation?

She could not go beyond her desire to see his great figure standing once more beside her, hovering over her, mountainlike, to hear his rich, vital, aggressive voice and to know that the agony of uncertainty, worry, and trial was over and that they had been successful in the desperate measures they had undertaken to save the life of one of their own. And thus she projected his figure on the screen of the gray void all about her, and in anticipation his voice was in her ears.

And part of the time, too, she wondered what their meeting would be like—this possessive man and she, Suzy Strang, wife of Nicholas Strang. And she thought back upon the last time they had been together and he had kissed her as though she already belonged to him and said words of possession to her. She thought of it without emotion now, as a picture of something that had once happened to two people she had known.

It was strange that she could not catch any of her emotions, but only be conscious of the quivering of her nerves and the overwhelming desire once more to set her eyes on Jimmy Race.

Several cars had come from the east and passed without stopping, giving Suzy the uncomfortable feeling that one of them might have been the one containing Jimmy, and she had always looked back uneasily to make sure that there had been no extra-security double cross on the part of the American Intelligence in the shape of another car added to their limit of two.

But at twenty minutes past five the gloom and the thinning mist were lightened by the slow approach in the distance of a pair of extraordinarily bright headlights denoting a large and powerful oncoming car.

Nerves tingling, Suzy sat up in the front seat next to the driver and extinguished her cigarette. The car, a big limousine, came around the bend in the road and poked along as though reconnoitering. Then it dimmed its lights and stopped some fifty yards away. Its headlamps came on swiftly three times in succession, and then after a short pause twice more.

Suzy exhaled a long sigh and knew that her heart was pounding so that it seemed to shake her entire frame. "Quick!" she said to the driver, who reached forward to his light switch and with his own lights sent back the same signal.

The strange car, its lights dimmed now, crawled forward again and came to a halt about fifty feet away, where it then deliberately turned around and pulled up at the side of the road facing back toward the east and Hungary. After a short wait three men piled out and stood in the road. Jimmy was not among them, Suzy noted with a sinking heart. He would have loomed over all of them. She got out of her car and saw as she did so that Major Slater and the three military policemen had climbed out of theirs and were standing on the road behind her and talking in low whispers. The fourth M.P., a sergeant, she knew was in the villa, monitoring the open line to Budapest.

A man separated himself from the group of three and walked forward alone. Like the others he was in civilian clothes, wearing a belted, tan raincoat turned up about the ears, and a well-pulled-down slouch hat.

He paused in front of Suzy. He did not bother to raise his hat. "Madame Strang?" he asked.

"Yes. I am Suzanne Strang."

"We have Mr. Race with us as agreed. You have arranged for the telephone call to Budapest?"

"Yes. The telephone is in this house here."

"What is this house?"

"It is a private villa as agreed. We made the arrangements an hour ago. The line is open."

He looked at Suzy and then at the house suspiciously for a moment. "Very well. Then make the call, please."

"When you have delivered Mr. Race in accordance with the understanding."

The Hungarian stared at her for a moment, turned on his heel, and walked back to his car.

Oh, God, Suzy thought, *what have I done? If they take him back now, or if it was all just a bluff and they never had him with them! But if I give in and make the call first, it will be the end. They can get away and we'll never see him.*

She heard Major Slater call from behind her. "What's up, Suzy? Is it a cross? Do you want us to go and take them?"

"Oh, no, no, please," she said. She felt that if the Americans so much as made a move, the car, whose engine was turning over audibly, would be off and lost down the road. They could never chase them into and through the Russian zone. It remained to be seen how much they needed the one trump card she held, the sound of her voice over the thin strand that connected them to Budapest. There was nothing to do but wait and see what their orders were, in case she did not fall into the trap that had been set for her in typical Communist disregard for an agreement.

There was a consultation over by the Hungarian car. Then the door was opened, and three more men got out from the rear. One of them rose like a giant, dwarfing the two on either side of him.

Suzy's heart gave a leap and she came close to crying out. In size, shape, and form it looked like the Jimmy Race that she had known. But she held herself under control. She could not trust them. It was too distant and too dark for her to see his face.

Now the six came slowly forward with the tall man in their midst. Suzy said in a low voice to those behind her, "All right, Major. Now, if you will."

Major Slater and the three military policemen moved slowly forward and ranged themselves next to Suzy. The two Hungarians alongside the tall man were carrying submachine guns cradled in their arms. Neither the major nor his three men showed any interest in their weapons. They wore only their sidearms.

The two groups were facing each other now, a few yards apart. The two men with the machine guns and the big man in the middle of them now stepped forward. Then the guards moved two paces back, leaving him standing there by himself.

Suzy said something to Major Slater, who raised a flash lamp, which he had already turned on to prove the nature of what he held in his hand. He beamed it directly into the face of the big man.

All the familiar, handsome features of Jimmy Race leaped out of the darkness, the huge head with the gleaming, forceful eyes, the light-colored hair crammed beneath the battered slouch hat, the long, possessive nose, the careless mouth turned up at the corners, and the forward-thrust, rounded, stubborn chin.

Why, he isn't changed at all, Suzy found herself thinkin this weird, tense moment. *He looks exactly the way he did the first day he walked into the office.*

He appeared so natural, healthy, and unharmed that for a moment Suzy entertained the thought that somehow they might have found an actor to impersonate him, that in this what seemed her hour of triumph, it might yet turn out somehow to be a sell. She let the light held in the steady hand of Major Slater linger on his face while she studied each feature. He could not see her behind the light shining in his eyes. Suzy suddenly found herself thinking with an odd little shudder of distaste, *I could never mistake that mouth. No, never.*

The tall man spoke now. He said only, "Please don't do that any more."

Suzy nodded to Major Slater, and the light snapped off. She said, "Yes, that is Mr. Race." Then she said to Jimmy, "Go into that first car there and wait for me."

Without another word Jimmy started to amble over to the car, but the two armed men checked him. The Hungarian who had first parleyed with Suzy stepped forward. "First I must ask you to come forward and join our group, Madame Strang. We cannot afford to take chances."

Without a moment's hesitation Suzy crossed the line

and mingled with the Hungarians. The trump card, the telephone call, was still high. She waited until she saw that Jimmy, now unmolested, had obeyed her. He ducked his big head and got into the back seat of the limousine. Two of the M.P.'s ranged themselves on either side of the door.

"Very well," Suzy said. "I am prepared to complete the call now."

She and the Hungarian walked down the path and into the villa together. There was a telephone in the vestibule, with an M.P. sitting at it. In the background at the end of the hall, several people in dishabille stared curiously out of a doorway.

The Hungarian started when he saw the sergeant at the telephone and looked about him in alarm as though about to take flight. Suzy said evenly, "You need not be afraid. He won't hurt you. He has been monitoring the line and keeping the connection clear."

The man's face darkened for a moment and then as suddenly cleared and he turned an appreciative grin on Suzy. "Forgive me," he said. "Madame is obviously not an amateur at this sort of thing. It is only the amateurs who are really dangerous."

He went to the telephone and picked it up. He spoke in Hungarian, but Suzy heard him mention his own name, Gottschalk, then that of Lajos, and lastly her own. After a brief wait he handed the combination speaker-receiver telephone to Suzy and hovered close by, listening.

Suzy spoke into it, asking, "Mr. Lajos?"

"Yes. This is Gabor Lajos in Budapest."

Suzy hesitated a moment, not certain of the identification of the voice. But then she realized that it was just that the strain seemed to have gone out of it and it had about it a kind of calmness that communicated itself to her.

"This is Suzanne Strang, speaking from Vienna. Mr.

Race has been delivered to us a few minutes ago. He appears to be uninjured. He is now in the hands of our military police. . . . Yes, I am perfectly safe. Yes. . . . Thank you very much. We are leaving now. Good-by, Mr. Lajos."

She offered the telephone to the Hungarian, but he shook his head, and she replaced it in its cradle and drew a long breath. The sergeant of military police had produced his .45-caliber pistol and held it nakedly in his hand while he ranged himself alongside Suzy and prepared to escort her from the villa. The Hungarian did not appear to be at all disturbed by this. He did not give the gun a second glance, but instead smiled at Suzy and said, "Madame's arrangements are excellent. I could not have done better myself."

But there was one surprise awaiting both of them when they emerged from the villa. The Hungarians were standing some distance away in a little knot with the two machine-gunners facing the car where the four Americans had suddenly and in some manner become seven. Two of them had joined the two guards at the door of the limousine and carried Tommy guns. The third was standing straddle-legged in the middle of the road with a queer-looking tube that looked something like a contrabassoon on his shoulder.

The Hungarian noted everything at a glance, but made no remark. He went over to his group and spoke to them in low tones in Hungarian for a few moments. Thereafter they all turned and without another glance at the Americans made their way back to their own car, climbed in, and drove away.

Major Slater noted Suzy staring at the weird-looking M.P. in the road. "Bazooka man," he said. "He came along for the ride."

"But the others," Suzy said; "I don't understand. We agreed— How did they get here?"

"Bottom of the car," the major explained succinctly. "Why be suckers? They had more than they said they would, and they came armed. We rather thought they might have a try at getting Race back after you had telephoned. So we brought artillery. They didn't. Hence peace. Sorry, but we couldn't take a chance."

Now that it was over, Suzy felt weak and realized that she suddenly had a ridiculous desire to put her head on Major Slater's shoulder and cry, simply because he had been no fool, but a man who had known what to do, when to do it, and, above all, how.

The thought of how he would probably react to such a show of emotion helped her to pull herself together and even brought a faint smile to her lips. She said, "Thank you, Major. Will you follow us back to the Bristol?"

She went and got into the back seat of the limousine next to Jimmy Race, nodding to the chauffeur, who started the engine, turned the car around, and headed back into the city. The military car trailed them close behind.

They rode thus several blocks in silence, Jimmy staring straight in front of him. Suzy was aware that she was no longer without emotion, that she never had been all through the long, horrid nightmare of the affair, but that always, and particularly as it neared its climax, she had suppressed it, held it in check so that it would not interfere in the doing of those things that needed to be done. But now that the object of it was sitting beside her she no longer needed to control it. She could give way to it at last.

She turned and looked at him and said, "Well, Jimmy?"

He returned her look, but did not reply to her invitation to speak.

Suzy's brain seemed to go aflame. *Dieu,* she thought,

is this man sulking? Is he sitting there pouting like a child because a woman was witness to the stupid mess into which he got himself and helped to get him out?

Her gorge rising so that she could barely control herself, Suzy said, "I suppose you aren't even going to have the decency and politeness to say, 'Thank you.'"

Jimmy Race repeated, "Thank you?" And then as if something was puzzling him added: "For what?" Then nodding his head slowly, he said, "Yes. I will say, 'Thank you,' if you want me to."

Coming from him, and the way he looked, it sounded both arrogant and sarcastic, and it burst the last barriers of self-control that were holding back the anger that had been pent up in Suzy for so long.

"How dared you?" she cried, her voice shaken with anger and bitterness. "How dared you do that to my husband, to the paper that was providing you with your living, to us all? By what right did you play with all our lives to satisfy your puffed-up, ridiculous, adolescent vanity? You are not a man. You have never been one, for all your medals, your rank, your exploits, your boasting, or for all of that big, overbearing body. You are worse than a willful, heedless, irresponsible, disgusting little boy. Do you hear what I have said? In mind and body you are disgusting, and to look at you makes me want to be sick to my stomach."

Suzy's mouth twisted and she actually fought back the nausea engendered by this big, silent pudding of a man. She continued. "And you dared ever to look at me, and touch me? And go about sneering at and cheapening Nick? If my husband were not the man he was, with the courage and brains he had, if he weren't all man, from his head to his foot, you would be dead now, hanged by the neck like a dog. I loathe and despise you, and what I am about to do is a measure of my contempt for you and what you have done."

She reached over and with her right hand slapped him hard across the face so that it stung her, and again with the back of her hand, and once more with the full palm.

The three blows sounded sharply in the still morning air, crisp, almost like pistol shots and over the sound of the motor, causing the chauffeur to turn his head around quickly and look back for a moment before he returned his eyes to the road and the built-up but drab gray district through which they were now riding.

Jimmy Race neither flinched nor moved. He did not raise so much as a finger to protect himself, or twitch a muscle. He continued to sit upright, staring straight ahead of him. Only two large, glistening tears began to roll down his cheeks, and his full lips commenced to quiver like a child's.

He said, "You don't have to hit me any more. I've learned it the best I could. I'll say it for you." And he commenced his confession, speaking once more in the full, rich, booming tones that were intended to convey so forcefully what he had to say.

"I arrived in Vienna on March 23 and immediately embarked upon my assignment to enter the Hungarian People's Republic for purposes of military spying and sabotage, intended to contribute to the overthrow of the Hungarian People's Government. My immediate superiors in detailing my assignment and sending me to Vienna to carry it out were Nicholas Strang, the editor of the Paris Edition of the *Chicago Sentinel,* a former intelligence officer in the United States Army, and his wife, Suzanne Vincent Strang, a former member of the French underground Resistance movement, and now a secret agent of the reactionaries and imperialists, plotting against the Cominform and the peace party of France."

He paused here, and a slow frown gathered on his brow. He shook his head once. "No—that isn't right," he said. "That part doesn't come yet. That's much, much later. Now I suppose you'll hit me again, or give me the pail. Please don't give me the pail— I'll try to remember— I'll try again."

And he turned moist and stricken eyes upon her, eyes in which there was not the faintest sign of recognition, and for the first time Suzy saw how the pupils were dilated, giving them a peculiar look as though life had gone out of them.

"Jimmy!" Her scream of horror rang out so loudly that the chauffeur tramped on the brakes and brought the car to a halt, and the military car swerved quickly and dashed up alongside. "Jimmy! In the name of good God, stop. I didn't know—I didn't realize—"

Jimmy Race pleaded, "You won't give me the pail, will you? I couldn't bear it another time. I do try so hard to remember. Don't you think I know how guilty I am? Don't you think I *want* to be hanged?" And here he put his hands to his face and began to sob.

Major Slater and two of his men were out of their car, and the major yanked open the door of the limousine and stared at the sobbing man and the white-faced girl.

"Suzy—what's happened? What's wrong?"

She stared at him for a moment, shaking her head and licking her dry lips.

"It's Jimmy," she whispered. "They sent his body back. But there isn't anything in it. He's not there any more. I—I didn't realize. His mind is gone."

They all stood there staring helplessly at the empty shell of what had once been a man.

26

ENDING ON A NOTE OF TEMPERED TRIUMPH

EVEN AFTER THE DISCOVERY of the horrifying thing that had been done to Jimmy Race, Suzy did not give way or break down. With Major Slater sitting in the car beside them she accompanied him back to Vienna and remained with him until he was taken over by an Army doctor and a nurse.

She got through to Nick on the telephone, told him of the return of Race, his condition, and their immediate plan. The Army would supply a C-47 and fly Jimmy to Paris that day and she would fly with them. They would be arriving in the early afternoon. The press in Vienna had not yet caught on to what had happened. They would land at the U.S. Air Force's section of Orly, which was private, and there the Army would then step out of the picture. She suggested that Nick meet them at the airport with civilian doctors and a closed car. Thus they might be able to keep secret, not only Jimmy's return, but likewise his condition until they had a chance to find out what hope there was for him.

"Is he very bad?" Nick asked.

Suzy thought a moment and then answered, "He is a zombie."

Nick groaned. "Oh, Lord! Suzy, you poor kid. I shouldn't have left you to handle that alone."

Suzy asked, "Why not?" and when Nick did not reply, continued. "Is the paper all right? It is rolling again?"

Nick said, "Yes."

Suzy said, "Then that's good. I will see you at Orly at

two," and hung up.

It had all worked out exactly as scheduled even to the time the big plane settled on the field and Jimmy Race, still walking in a daze, was delivered into the hands of a physician, a psychiatrist, and a male nurse. Except that, once Suzy was again alone with Nick in his office, her strength and resistance came to an end.

After Nick had seen Race in an ambulance in the doctor's care, he drove Suzy to Paris from the field in the Citroen. She spoke hardly at all. She was white from fatigue, and there were lines of strain and exhaustion in her face. But she refused to go home and rest and insisted upon returning to the office, at least until there had been a report of some kind from the doctors on Jimmy's condition.

And sometimes on the ride back Nick stole a sideways glance at her, and even as his heart was sickened he marveled at the strength and determination that can be shown by a woman who is in love and is concerned and fighting for the object thereof. And he thought, too, that nothing ever turned out the way one thought it would, or the way one had planned. He had kept Suzy in Vienna to give them their chance, to let them be together, to let her be the first to greet him and speak to him when he returned to life and freedom after his bitter captivity, for surely none had fought harder for him than she.

And instead he had exposed her to the shock of having the enemy dump the empty shell of her man at her feet. And he blamed himself for this and wondered when he would bring to an end his series of catastrophic blunders. Since Race had come to Paris, nothing he, Nick, had touched had gone right except that in spite of hell and high water, where the Government of the United States and everything else had failed, they had rescued at least what was left of Jimmy Race out of the clutches of the Communists.

But Suzy, he was certain, he had lost, whatever happened.

They had hardly crossed the threshold of his office and closed the door behind them when Suzy went over to the big glass-topped table, put her head down on her arms, and began to cry.

Her crying was a dreadful thing, compounded of strain, fatigue, relief that it was over, and the awful crosscurrents of the emotions and feelings that had for so long been pent up within her. Sometimes it was strangled and choking as though there were still things that would not come out, and at others the free, torrential sobbed-out misery of a child.

Nick stood near his desk and watched her helplessly and with that waxen stupidity which comes over men in the face of their women crying.

He was shouldering all his own guilt and shortcomings now and was of a mind to confess them once and for all if it would only bring an end to Suzy's unhappiness, assure her of Jimmy's eventual recovery, offer her her freedom, convince her that he understood the call of youth to youth.

Nick came over and sat down opposite and dropped his hand onto her head. He said, "Suzy, dear—I'm sorry."

His voice penetrated through to her quite wholly normal case of post-crisis hysteria, and as suddenly as she had begun, she ceased to cry and raised her tear-stained face.

"Nick! You're sorry! It is I who am sorry. But I couldn't help it. I've acted like a fool now that it's all over, but I've also acted like a woman. Oh, God, it's so good to be with you again, Nick—so very, very good." And she took his hands in both of hers and rubbed the knuckles against her forehead, hard, as though by the pressure of them she could eradicate forever the memories of the days past.

He yielded his hands and stared at her with a kind of hopeful bewilderment.

Suzy sniffed and went for a handkerchief to attend to her nose. She said, "It's been such a strain, and I've been so angry, Nick, so terribly angry for what he did to you and to the paper. But I had to hold it back, because if I let it out it would have seemed that I was criticizing you for what you had done in sending him to Vienna.

"And when I think, that that half-witted, muscle-bound creature could have cost you everything for which you've worked so hard! You've been the paper, ever since the war, a new kind of paper, wiser and more responsible to its times than it had ever been, and he could have and would have wrecked it and you, for the sake of his own swollen head and miserable vanity. It was for that I despised him so from the moment it was evident that he had sold you out after you trusted him. He would be dead now, but for you."

She paused and looked up at him with her earnest, direct gaze. "Do you know, Nick, that you are very wonderful, and that I am proud to be your wife—so proud?"

Nick drew a deep breath and shut his eyes for a moment for fear that he would give himself away. All his nerves were tingling as they did when some terrible suspense was lifted and one yet barely realized that a danger, real or fancied, was over. He felt suddenly weak with relief.

Nick said, "They must have put him through hell."

Suzy looked up sharply. "He was a weakling. You never would have broken as he did. They could never have done it to you. Only an immature and adolescent mind such as his could have reacted to their attack and become that of a badgered and beaten child. It must always have been there, only he hid it beneath his aggressive exterior and by pushing people about."

It seemed strange, Nick thought, that he should be defending Jimmy Race, and yet, after all, not so strange. He said, "They are cruel, subtle, and, I understand, selective in their methods. And every man has his weakness when probed long enough."

Suzy said, "Every man?" She gave her husband a long and searching look. "In the sense that we are all human, I suppose. There are weaknesses in men that women can understand, and others that they cannot bear."

"Such as?" It was hard for Nick to ask the question, but he felt he must.

"Vanity, self-esteem, irresponsibility." Then she added, "Nick, this has been a bad time for us both. Remember what I am about to say. It is I who have been weak. You have played the part of a man throughout. You are everything I love, Nick. You are everything a woman could want. Never forget this."

Nick picked up her hand from the table, held it to his cheek for a moment, and then kissed the ends of her fingers.

And all the time he was thinking—was it possible that she was not aware of his greatest weakness, the soft link in the chain, the chink in the armor of his person, the one that had surely contributed to the catastrophe that had faced them all and had come close to costing the life of an employee and a colleague?

He now saw so clearly that out of his love for her and the difference in their ages had come jealousy and self-depreciation, and the latter was by far the more dangerous. She was a woman who wanted an adult man and he had been prepared to relinquish her to an adolescent in whom she had had no more than a passing interest. He realized that he had not been flattering to his wife. If she were to guess at what had been passing through his mind during those dreadful days, she would have the right to be very angry with him.

Or did she know? Had she perhaps not known all along and forgiven him? Was she not, after all, so wise that never, as long as their time together, would he ever really know how much of his jealousy she had been aware of, or to what extent she had guessed the phantasies that had caused him so much needless misery?

He thought that this last was probably true and that in her own way she had done what she could to help him. She had given him the spiritual wherewithal to stop the leakage that might have wrecked their marriage. In her own way she had announced herself an adult as well as a woman and challenged him to meet her on this plane. If he failed again, it would be through no fault but his own. He felt tried and older at that moment, but he thought with a kind of desperate gratitude that there were quite definite compensations for being no longer a youth. One need have no fear of growing old with a woman like Suzy.

It was as though she read his thoughts. The look on her face as they smiled across the table was one of infinite tenderness.

Late that afternoon there was another meeting in Nick's office, when Dr. Beltrane, the physician, and Dr. Lessing, the psychiatrist, came over from the American hospital in Passy to report.

Present, in addition to Nick, Suzy, and the two doctors, were Janet Goodpenny, thin, pale, and hollow-eyed behind her spectacles, Mark Mosher, Felix Victor, and Dad Lapham. Nick was behind his desk with Dad at his side. Suzy and Janet occupied the couch. Mark and Felix and the medical men were at the table.

Dr. Beltrane said, "It's really more in Doctor Lessing's line, and he will speak to you of his early diagnosis. My own examination indicates that, in spite of the shock strain, fatigue, and nervous exhaustion, Mr. Race is in fair physical condition. There is no mark or injury of any kind on him. I have made a note, however, that he appears to be highly sensitive to any kind of loud noise, particularly anything metallic, and I intend to have his ears examined more thoroughly by one of our own specialists. But for the rest–" he paused and looked at his colleague.

Dr. Lessing was a short, businesslike man in a blue suit, young, brisk, and looking more like a stockbroker or a lawyer than a psychiatrist. Only his eyes were extraordinary, filled with a mixture of great intelligence and deep humanity. He looked at each one of them keenly before he commenced to speak.

He said, "I gather I am in the presence of those who are intimate with or have a strong interest in the case of Mr. Race and whose discretion can be relied on. Very well. The narcosis is passing. You may or may not know that he has been under the influence of a drug, or drugs –scopolamine, or derivatives thereof, was surely one of them, for days, probably weeks. However, there must be continued administration to achieve the full effects. He has probably had none for the last twenty-four or thirty-six hours. He is therefore now aware of who he is, also where he is, and certain circumstances connected therewith. The bewilderment, confusion, and semihysteria caused by narcosis is disappearing, and he is in the grip of a deep mental depression."

Nick leaned forward and asked, "Is this serious?"

"Very. I have had only a few hours with him, but it is evident that under the influence of the drug, as well as due to the torture of exhaustion, strain, and fear induced by fatigue and the sense of abandonment, he has entertained thoughts and committed acts that under normal conditions would be completely foreign to him."

"Such as–" Dad Lapham asked.

"Betrayal of country, betrayal of friends nearest and

dearest to him, and, above all, betrayal of himself, for he accepted as fact many ideas and suggestions that were wholly false and that at all other times he violently rejected."

"Such as the Communist cause?" questioned Felix Victor.

"Such as the Communist cause, among other things," Dr. Lessing replied.

Janet Goodpenny said with absolute conviction in her voice, "But he would never! Never in a million years–"

It was Suzy who took up the interrogation. She said, "But I would think that if he was aware of all this now, that he had been tortured and drugged into doing and saying things in which he did not believe, he would realize–"

Dr. Lessing shook his head. "No. That is not the way it operates in such cases. It is fairly obvious that he has been through a long process during which time his mind and his personality were taken away from him and another substituted. He was made to feel guilty and highly culpable for something based upon a palpable lie–namely, that he was a spy sent into Hungary by the U.S. Government."

"But now that he knows he wasn't–" Dad Lapham said.

"He has substituted one guilt feeling for another, the guilt of his own weakness, failure, and betrayal of his friends. There is no blacker despondency that can come to the human soul. He cannot hold up his head, you see. And he is a big man who was once full of pride."

Bluntly and with his usual tactlessness Mark Mosher asked, "Has he suicidal tendencies? Does he want to die?"

"Yes," replied Dr. Lessing.

An uncomfortable silence fell upon the group, and for a moment nothing was heard but their breathing. Finally

Nick asked, "Is there any hope for him? Can he be helped, I mean."

"Yes," said Dr. Lessing again. "I think so. But only time will tell. For the present he cannot be left alone for a moment, and perhaps not for a long time to come. What he needs more than anything is someone who would be with him night and day and help to rebuild his ego. When a man has been untrue to everything he ever cared for, or believed in, it is a long and difficult climb back out of a deep and very dark pit. There is scar tissue that results from mental degradation as well as physical injury. For the present," he concluded, "he must have a full-time nurse or companion, someone who will never let him out of sight. It would be better for the sake of his recovery if he could be away from the hospital—anything institutional is a handicap to his present condition—he ought to be in comfortable, normal surroundings in a home of some kind. I will see him every day. When, through association with him, I am better able to judge the nature of the attack upon his mind, I will then tell you more as to the length of time needed to effect a cure and restore his soul, because it has been taken away from him."

The meeting broke up. Dr. Beltrane left. Dad stopped to drop his hand on Janet's shoulder for just an instant and give it a half pat, half affectionate and fatherly squeeze, but she did not seem to be aware of him. Mark Mosher and Felix Victor drifted back to the city room. Dr. Lessing remained behind for a moment to talk to Suzy and Nick. None of the three were aware of Janet Goodpenny sitting bolt-upright on the couch until she suddenly spoke to them.

She said, "Please! Mr. Strang—Suzy—Doctor Lessing—may I say something?"

They all turned to her. Nick thought to himself, *Whatever happens, she's had the dirty end of it. What a pity she's so plain! But what a good kid! And why do they always have to get the worst of it?*

Janet said with the quiet force of someone who has come to a firm decision after an inner struggle, "I want to be the one to take care of Jimmy and look after him. Doctor Lessing said there would have to be someone who could give him back his soul. I can do that. I can make him believe in himself again."

Suzy went over to Janet and sat down on the couch next her, signaling to Nick as she went. Nick caught it and, without a word, wandered from the room. Janet never saw him go. Her eyes were intent on Dr. Lessing, who sat down again at the head of the table and watched them both.

Suzy was very gentle. She said, "Janet—you love him, don't you?"

Janet looked at her with some surprise. She had thought everybody knew. "Of course."

"Does Jimmy love you?"

"I don't know. I don't think so. Does that matter?"

"Janet, dear," Suzy said, "have you thought this over carefully? Do you know what you would be taking on—the despair, the hatred of himself and everyone who reminded him of his ordeal, the black moods, the possible violence? Have you any idea of the extent to which they have broken him? Are you prepared to give up everything for him—your work, your freedom, your way of living, your whole future, perhaps?"

"Yes," Janet Goodpenny replied.

Dr. Lessing said, "Well, now—would you be so good and come over here and sit by me for a moment? What is your name?"

"Janet Goodpenny." She got up, went over, and sat down on a chair by his side very straight, looking astonishingly young and prim.

He studied her for a moment. "How old are you?"

"Twenty-seven."

"Hm. I took you for younger. Old enough to know your mind. How long have you loved this man?"

"From the moment I first laid eyes on him." She was shedding herself of all pretense. Only the truth could help her to prevail. Her instinct told her that here was a man to whom truth was everything, before whom she could dare to be herself.

"And when was that?"

"During the war—for just a moment."

The doctor held her with his searching eyes. "Has there been any—have you and he—"

"No. He kissed me once when we were out together, and again when he said good-by. He did not mean it either time."

Dr. Lessing exhaled a breath. "Ah," he said. "You do not delude yourself, do you, my dear? Are you also aware that even though you make this sacrifice for him, devote six months, a year, perhaps even two or three years of your life to him, he may leave you when he gets well?"

"Yes," Janet said once more.

Dr. Lessing folded his hands and leaned toward her, his eyes filled with warmth and understanding. "You do realize as well that the chances must be all against his learning or growing to love you, except through perhaps a miracle, because you will have seen him in his moment of greatest weakness, pitied him, cared for him, held out your hand to him, led him into the light out of the darkness, helped to give him his manhood back? And for that he must in the end betray you and abandon you because he is a man. Only a very great person could forgive a woman that."

Odd, Suzy thought to herself, *what does she remind me of, sitting there so straight, so upright, so intense, with the hair falling down on either side of her face, and those steadfast, unwavering eyes? Is it Victorian? No. I know now what it is. It is the pioneer women of New England. I have seen their pictures. Their strength is unbreakable, like a rock. They were unconquerable. And for this strength we Europeans must envy them.*

"Do you think that would stop me?" Janet asked. "Do you think that would keep me from helping him if I could?"

"Can she, Doctor Lessing?" Suzy cried. "Would you let her try? Do you think she would be able to help him in the manner you said? Would she be good for him?"

The doctor reflected a moment and then nodded his head gravely. "Oh, yes," he replied. "Yes, indeed. It is just some such devoted person that I had in mind and hoped could be found for his care. Yes, she would be very good for him. I am thinking only whether he would be good for her. I do not like to see a young life risk destruction."

But Janet had one more intensely-to-be-asked question. She cried fiercely, "Do you think I care what happens to *me?*"

Dr. Lessing rose. "In the end you must—for his sake. But we will discuss that later. Come to the hospital tomorrow morning at eleven and we will go in and visit him together for the first time and see if it can be worked out."

But to Suzy, as she accompanied him from the office to his car, he said, "There is hope there with that girl. She has courage and gallantry, but above all she is not afraid to face the truth. Her I may be able to help with the task she has taken on. I will teach her to value herself and perhaps in the end he will come to do so, also."

Alone in Nick's office, Janet gathered up her things, donned her leather jacket, and went out. She passed Suzy's room, opening off his, with the large mirror on the wall near her desk, and paused to take account of herself. There was the same Janet Goodpenny, the dark-brown eyes behind the horn-rimmed spectacles, short nose, and rounded chin and the straight, dark hair falling on either side of her face. Plain Jane. So she was, so she always would be. But she was surprised to find playing at the corners of her mouth something that looked extraordinarily like a smile of triumph.

In the country below Budapest a small boy was cruising through the meadow of a farm that descended in a gentle slope to the north bank of the Danube. He was twisting and doubling through the weeds and field flowers, playing at being a commando scout who had been dropped by parachute, and the foe was all about him. Every so often he would straighten up, shade his eyes with his hand in true scout-fashion, peer about him for any evidence of the enemy, and then continue his stalking.

But on one of his look-sees down toward the river, his attention became attracted by a strange object that appeared to be floating downstream close to the bank, bobbing, wallowing, and rolling just below the surface of the water and occasionally breaking to the top.

He forgot his game momentarily, owing to interest in this new development, and he stood there watching the object, trying to make out what it could be, but it was too far away from him to tell whether it was a log or something animal or human.

Then the current swirled the thing in toward the bank where it was caught suddenly by the outthrust branch of a dead tree that had fallen and lay half buried in the muddy water.

The boy now had a chance to satisfy his curiosity. His bare feet quickly found a path through the meadow and he ran down the hill, swiftly narrowing the distance of a hundred yards or so that lay between him and the bank.

But he had only proceeded halfway when the object, impelled by the current, freed itself again, turned over once, showing a flash of white that might or might not have been a face, and then continued its lazy rolling passage downstream.

The boy reached the shore and looked after it, standing on the trunk of the fallen tree. What an adventure, a real true one, instead of only play! With but a little imagination he could almost be sure that it had been the body of a man floating face down.

Then something caught his eye, something that had remained hanging on the very end of the branch and only just visible at the surface of the water where the object had paused. He crawled out carefully on the bole of the tree, reached down into the water, and retrieved it.

It proved to be only a sodden scarf of hideous color and design, a diamond pattern in red, yellow, and green, the colors of which had begun to run together.

But the small boy regarded it with considerable satisfaction. It was legitimate treasure trove and he had salvaged it all by himself.

He went back up the path through the field, dragging the wet garment behind him.